CAMBRIDGE CLASSICAL STUDIES

General Editors
M. F. BURNYEAT, M. K. HOPKINS, M. D. REEVE, A. M. SNODGRASS

LISTENING TO THE CICADAS
A Study of Plato's *Phaedrus*

'LISTENING TO THE CICADAS,
A Study of Plato's *Phaedrus*

G. R. F. FERRARI
Assistant Professor of Philosophy
Yale University

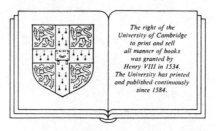

The right of the
University of Cambridge
to print and sell
all manner of books
was granted by
Henry VIII in 1534.
The University has printed
and published continuously
since 1584.

CAMBRIDGE UNIVERSITY PRESS
CAMBRIDGE
NEW YORK   NEW ROCHELLE   MELBOURNE   SYDNEY

Published by the Press Syndicate of the University of Cambridge
The Pitt Building, Trumpington Street, Cambridge CB2 1RP
32 East 57th Street, New York, NY 10022, USA
10 Stamford Road, Oakleigh, Melbourne 3166, Australia

First published 1987

Printed in Great Britain by
Redwood Burn Limited, Trowbridge, Wiltshire

British Library cataloguing in publication data
Ferrari, G. R. F.
Listening to the cicadas:
a study of Plato's Phaedrus. –
(Cambridge classical studies)
1. Plato. Phaedrus   2. Rhetoric, Ancient
3. Love
I. Title
184   B380

Library of Congress cataloguing in publication data
Ferrari, G. R. F. (Giovanni R. F.)
Listening to the cicadas.
(Cambridge classical studies)
Bibliography.
Includes index.
1. Plato. Phaedrus.   2. Love.
3. Rhetoric, Ancient.
I. Title.   II. Series.
B380.F47 1987   184   86–34334

ISBN 0 521 26778 1

For my mother
and in memory of
my father

GRÄFIN: Du Spiegelbild der verliebten Madeleine,
kannst du mir raten, kannst du mir helfen
den Schluß zu finden, den Schluß für ihre Oper?
Gibt es einen, der nicht trivial ist?

From *Capriccio* (libretto by Clemens Krauss)

CONTENTS

PREFACE

This is a book about Plato's *Phaedrus*, nothing more; but that is quite a lot. I shall dispense with a long preamble as to its contents. Rather, my way of orienting readers to Plato's concerns in this dialogue, and to my own in writing about it, will be to take them (in my opening chapter) for an extended tour of the dialogue's scenic beauties. Like all readers of this work, we shall learn something about love, and something about rhetoric, and will consider how the two are connected. In addition, I shall have much to say about Plato's use of myth, his writing of philosophic dialogues, and his mode of psychology – topics which the dialogue strikingly exemplifies.

However, I shall not – or not often – be concerned in this book to map the position of the *Phaedrus* against the landmarks provided by other dialogues, nor to consider its place in Plato's philosophic development. I am out to achieve something different: to live for a while within the environment of a single dialogue; and not just to survey its acres and mend its stiles, but to sit on the grass and breathe its special atmosphere. By this means I hope to gain a better understanding of the man's philosophy – a better feel for it – at least in so far as it shows through this dialogue; and so to bring back a souvenir for others that they may think worth keeping. But readers must judge this for themselves.

Despite the plan just stated, I will say this much in general about the dialogue's position in Plato's *oeuvre*: that although it is structurally and dramatically quite unusual, and although the life of philosophic lovers, which is the highpoint of its visionary sweep, is meant as an exceptional sort of life, even for philosophers, nevertheless this is not a deviancy that drains the dialogue of importance for the broader philosophic projects which we would want to attribute to Plato (and still less does it disconnect the piece from broader issues in later philosophy). If this dialogue stands out among its fellows like the tall plane-tree that Phaedrus descries against the horizon (but I am being partial), still it has its roots firmly planted in the common Platonic soil. But it is not my intention in this book to justify that claim, and I shall offer only occasional comparisons with other dialogues to indicate the path which such a justification might take.

I have attempted to make my account accessible, within the limits of its topic, to as wide a philosophic and literary audience as I can. I have translated almost all Greek, even in endnotes of a fairly technical sort, and have allowed it to appear in the body of the text only where it directly furthers the argument in progress. Greek script is transliterated throughout. This practice, admittedly more widespread among specialists in ancient philosophy than among classicists in general, I have found to be appreciated by those who approach Plato with philosophic or literary sophistication but little or no Greek, and I trust that classicists will not be unduly disturbed by it, especially since my quotations from the Greek are mostly brief. For similar reasons the details of scholarly controversy (as opposed to its substantive thrust) feature in the main text only when necessary to the exposition of my own interpretation, and are otherwise dealt with in endnotes. And in the bibliography the reader will find only those works to which I have appealed in order to make my case. I have not attempted to make this book a general bibliographic resource on Plato's *Phaedrus*.

I have been engaged with this work for some years now, and many people have helped me in this time. G. E. L. Owen bore the brunt of my first thoughts on the *Phaedrus* when I was his student at Cambridge. I shall not forget his intellectual example, his patience, and his kindness. It is a personal sadness to me that I shall never share with him the fruits of those thoughts. Geoffrey Lloyd has been a rock for me from first to last; I cannot imagine how this book would have come about but for his encouragement, his criticism when needed, the generosity with which he made himself available, and – not least – the benchmark he has set. Through Geoffrey Lloyd

I came to work at an early stage with Pierre Vidal-Naquet. My contact with him and with his colleagues at the Centre de Recherches Comparées sur les Sociétés Anciennes is a happy and stimulating memory for me. To the teaching and advice of Myles Burnyeat I owe a very great deal, and in particular to his comments and those of Alexander Nehamas on the rudimentary version of this work that saw light as my doctoral dissertation. I thank them for their encouragement, and for the inspiration that their work has been to me. Konrad Gaiser also read this version of my project, and wrote an exceptionally rich and helpful set of comments, for which I am most grateful.

Since coming to Yale, I have enjoyed the benefit of developing my ideas within a department in which an unusually broad range of philosophic interests is represented and encouraged – a particularly happy circumstance for my own project. If I thank my colleagues in the philosophy department collectively rather than singling out individuals, it is to reflect this fact. My work progressed appreciably during a year as a Mellon Fellow at the Whitney Humanities Center at Yale. I am grateful to Peter Brooks, its director, and to the Fellows of the Center in 1984–5, for having given me this opportunity, and for having made my time at the Center both stimulating and pleasant. I have twice had the benefit of teaching a course on the topic of this book to students at Yale, once when I was at a preliminary stage of writing and again when the book was almost whole. I would like to thank all my students in those seminars, but most especially those in the recent group, who not only helped me clear up many of my ideas at a crucial time, but, more importantly, combined to give that class a spirit I shall not forget, and will strive to recreate in future.

Anthony Long and Julius Moravcsik have helped my work through correspondence rather than personal contact; but their encouragement and example have been no less precious to me for that.

An earlier and considerably more exiguous version of what now appears as the final two sections of chapter six has been published in the journal *Ancient Philosophy* (Spring 1985). I take this opportunity to thank Harry Frankfurt for discussing that version with me.

Iris Hunter's perceptive copy-editing has rescued me from a number of infelicities.

Finally, my very special thanks to Mark Sacks and to Kate Toll. Not only did they read and comment on large stretches of the manuscript, but they talked me through the issues in this book, and sustained me with their affection. They have shown me how philosophy and friendship mix.

New Haven, Connecticut
July 1986   G.R.F.F.

ABBREVIATIONS

For the four commentaries on the *Phaedrus* to which I make frequent reference throughout this book I have adopted the following abbreviations:

H. Hackforth, R. 1952. *Plato's Phaedrus*. Cambridge.
R. Robin, L. 1961. *Platon, Phèdre*. Fifth Edition. Oeuvres Complètes IV, 3. Paris.
Th. Thompson, W. H. 1868. *The Phaedrus of Plato*. London.
de Vr. de Vries, G. J. 1969. *A Commentary on the Phaedrus of Plato*. Amsterdam.

I have in addition used the following standard abbreviations:

DK Diels, H. revised by Kranz, W. 1951–2. *Die Fragmente der Vorsokratiker*. Sixth Edition. Zürich.
LSJ Liddell, H. G. and Scott, R. revised by Jones, H. S. 1968. *A Greek–English Lexicon*. Ninth Edition with Supplement. Oxford.
OCT Oxford Classical Text.

CHAPTER ONE

ORIENTATION

Two questions

Socrates' conversation with Phaedrus is rich in references to its own setting. As the dialogue opens Phaedrus is about to take the air outside the city walls when he happens upon Socrates, who readily agrees to accompany him in return for an account of his morning's entertainment by the orator Lysias. Their conversation in these opening pages is peripatetic, and much of it is directly concerned with the landscape in which they walk and talk. Where they should sit for Phaedrus to deliver Lysias' speech; what landmarks they pass on the way; and (when they get there) whose shrine they have stumbled upon – such are the questions that exercise them as they stage-manage the speechmaking of the dialogue's first part. Their theatre even has a resident chorus: the 'chorus (*khoroī*) of cicadas' (230c3) whose summery treble Socrates takes note of on arrival.[1] The cicadas' song will be heard to greatest effect later in the dialogue, at the outset of the critique of rhetoric that makes up its second part. Before launching fully into their discussion of rhetoric, Socrates and Phaedrus will break off to consider their physical environment once again, when Socrates – arresting the action, as it were, to let the chorus have its moment – warns Phaedrus against the potentially mesmerising effect of the droning cicadas overhead and tells him a parable in which they are the main characters (see 258e6–259d8).

Why has Plato written into this conversation such elaborate references to its scene? And why, having brought his players to their rustic theatre at the outset of the dialogue, is he at pains to bring its set once more to our notice as his topic apparently shifts from love to rhetoric?

In response to the first question I will argue that by considering how Socrates and Phaedrus orient themselves in their physical environment, and by recognising what this reveals of their characters, the reader is oriented to the dialogue's major concerns; for in its opening pages Socrates and Phaedrus exhibit in their behaviour or allude to much of what is then explicitly analysed in the remainder of the dialogue, both in the speeches on love and in the critique of rhetoric. In response to the second I will argue that Plato redirects our attention to the conversational ambience at the crucial juncture between the two parts of the dialogue in order to guide our reading of its curious structure. The admonitions to which Socrates is prompted by the presence of the cicadas extend not only to Phaedrus but also to the reader. What is more, this mode of exposition – Plato's device of orienting his readers by narrating how his characters orient themselves in their landscape – is no literary toy, I will urge, but, given the concerns of this dialogue, has philosophic purpose.

So much by way of introduction to this chapter; let us turn now to appreciate the scenery.

Topic and topography

The first point to be established is how the manner of reference to the dramatic background in the *Phaedrus* differs from that of certain dialogues which have otherwise comparably vivid stage-sets. Often enough, of course, Plato furnishes his dialogues with only the sparest indications of time and place, sometimes none.[2] In a few cases, however, he embroiders the backcloth with as much care as in the *Phaedrus*. The strongest candidates for comparison are the *Protagoras* (think of the scholarly cacophony at the house of Callias), the *Phaedo* (with its descriptions of prison regime as prologue and epilogue), and the *Symposium* (which brings alive the dinner party at Agathon's). But in all three the scene is described by a narrator.[3] Through this expository device Plato formally distinguishes the voice describing the scene from the voices that conduct the conversation taking place within the scene described. The *Phaedrus*, by contrast, has no narrator; it is written as direct speech. Our only access to the background against which Socrates and Phaedrus walk and speak is through their comments on it.

When the narrator of a Platonic dialogue describes the background to the conversation of its characters (even if one of those characters is himself),[4] we conventionally read that description as a means of establishing the fictional world of the dialogue; but when those who describe the background are taking part directly in the dialogue's action, the same conventions of reading demand that we take their description as a spontaneous reaction to their fictional environment (rather than – as with a narrator – a premeditated manipulation of that environment). Of course, the effect need not be very different in practice. If the characters' reactions to their ambience are sufficiently casual and muted, they can map the coordinates of their fictional world almost as discreetly as any narrative voice could manage. But Plato has written the opening scene of the *Phaedrus* quite otherwise, exploiting the special possibilities of direct speech to full effect. Topography becomes the topic of conversation in a highly obtrusive manner. The diversion along the Ilissus prompts a discussion of the myth associated with the nearby shrine of Boreas (229b4–230a6), and Phaedrus' choice of shady arbour in which to sit spurs Socrates, on arrival, to such exaggerated transports of appreciation that Phaedrus cannot forbear commenting on how absurd he seems (230a6–d2). Later in the dialogue the local nymphs will emerge from the background to interfere directly with the action, causing Socrates to forget his intention simply to listen to a speech and inspiring him to deliver speeches himself, and speeches of unusual intensity at that (see 238c5–d7, 241e1–5); and as we have seen, when the speeches are over the action will be further prolonged by the obtrusive presence of the cicadas, whose surveillance Socrates cites as a stimulus to continued talk (258e6–259d8; and notice that he later adds the cicadas to his list of local divinities and sources of inspiration, at 262d2–6).

In short, what is particularly striking about this dialogue is that the background will not stay where it belongs. It becomes a prominent topic of discussion and a direct cause of the con-versational action rather than, as one would expect, at most an indirect influence on its course. This in turn should prompt us as readers to scrutinise it more closely than we might other-wise have done.

The impresario

Let us consider, then, how Socrates and Phaedrus interact with their landscape. Having secured Phaedrus' agreement to sit and read aloud the text of Lysias' speech, Socrates suggests that they cut off along the Ilissus, but leaves to Phaedrus the choice of a quiet spot in which to settle themselves (228e3–229a2). Phaedrus, his attention directed to the environment, begins to fuss over questions of fit and suitability. How 'appropriate' (*eis kairon*), he declares, that he came out bare-foot for his stroll (for they are to paddle along the river-bed); and how apt a plan this is for the time of year and day (229a5–6 – high summer and around noon respectively, as we learn from 230c2 and 242a4–5). He takes pains to select a suitable place for reading. A tall plane-tree nearby marks a zone of shelter from the sun, he judges, 'just the right breeze' (*pneuma metrion*), and soft grass to accommodate whichever posture they prefer, whether sitting or lying down (229a8–b2). On the way to this bower he speculates that they are pass-ing the very spot where according to story Boreas the wind-god snatched off the princess Oreithyia. What fuels his conjecture is, again, the recognition of fit: that the alluring purity of the water at this point makes it suitable (*epitēdeia*) for girls to play in (229b4–9). Furthermore, had Phaedrus not been struck at the outset of the dialogue by how especially 'appropriate' (*prosēkousa*) Lysias' speech on love would be for the notoriously 'erotic' Socrates to hear (227c3–5)[5] he would not now be applying to the environment this ability to recognise fit.

Phaedrus' careful matching of audience to performance and performance to environment shows him turning from the mere consumption of others' art[6] to the exercise of the art to

4

which he is peculiarly devoted. Having spent his morning in admiration of a master of the rhetorical art, he intends to spend his midday break as the obedient patient of a master of the medical art; for it is on the orders of doctor Acumenus that he takes his constitutional in the countryside rather than within the city limits (227a1–b1). As for the art that he himself practises – a short detour will prove instructive here.

When Socrates comes to his critique of rhetoric in the second part of the dialogue, he too evinces a combined appreciation of the rhetorical and medical arts (see 270b1–2 and cf. 268a–269c), and in the course of discussion Socrates and Phaedrus jointly stress the importance in the exercise of both disciplines of the ability to discern what is fitting or appropriate to each situation. No doctor worth the title knows only which drugs in his pharmacopoeia have which effects; he must also be able to recognise to which patients these drugs are suited, and when and in what dose their application is appropriate in each case (268a8–b8; notice that Acumenus' name reappears in conjunction with this point). Similarly, the truly competent orator would not simply know in the abstract which types of speech have what effect on which types of character, but would in addition be capable of recognising, as each situation confronts him, which items of knowledge from his technical storehouse are the appropriate ones to apply (271e2–272a8).[7]

This pattern could be readily generalised to less technical spheres of human behaviour, and is notably exhibited by Phaedrus as he recognises in his chance encounter with Socrates and in the particular features of the Ilissan landscape the opportunity to apply certain precepts – mostly the matter of common sense, of course, rather than of arcane art – about what audience and what venue is appropriate for what kind of performance.[8] His skill, to dignify it for convenience with a title, is that of intellectual 'impresario'. Phaedrus attaches himself to leading thinkers, spurs them to perform, and propagates the latest arguments and trends. Anachronistically put, he is literary journalist, publisher, and ubiquitous *salon* presence rolled together. In the course of the dialogue his talents are not only displayed but also explicitly brought to our attention more than once. When he prevails on Socrates not to leave after the débâcle of his first speech, Socrates declares himself awed by Phaedrus' ability to promote discourses, whether delivering them himself or milking them from others – an ability in which only Simmias of Thebes has the edge over him (242a7–b4); and his promise to compel Lysias to write a rejoinder to Socrates' second speech is capped by Socrates with the comment: 'That I believe, so long as you are who you are' (243e2). It is worth noting also that Phaedrus is the instigator and moderator of the round of speeches in the *Symposium*, as well as opening speaker in the series (*Smp.* 177a–178a; 194d).

Clearly, the craft of intellectual impresario is not a formal discipline on the order of medicine or rhetoric. Indeed, it might seem frivolous to make much of the parallel between Phaedrus' behaviour in the opening scene and the exercise of an established art. However, the comparison has a serious complexion in so far as it points to a serious danger for philosophy. Socrates' cross-reference to another of his conversational partners, Simmias (one of the interlocutors in the *Phaedo*), suggests that, even if the eliciting of intellectual talk is not a profession, it is a role to be reckoned with in Socratic dialogue. In fact, as we shall see (especially in the section 'What the cicadas sang' later in this chapter), it represents a capital danger endemic to the philosophic life: namely that the practice of philosophic argument over how to live the good life, together with the recognition that such argument is not just prefatory to but actually constitutive of the good life, should degenerate into the production of intellectual talk as an end in itself, a life of mere words. For this reason we must sharpen our awareness of Phaedrus' intellectual practice in order not to confuse it with true philosophy, a task made all the more imperative because the two are so close. After all, Socrates is only able to puncture Phaedrus' show of reluctance to retail Lysias' speech at the outset of the dialogue because he understands him like a second self ('If I don't know Phaedrus, I've forgotten who I am myself', 228a5–6);

and he touts himself as equally fanatical and sick with love of such discourse (228b6–c2; 230d5–e1).

Phaedrus loves to arrange talk. Even when he talks himself, it is as much for the excitement of provoking further talk as for the value of what he has to say. His enthusiasm for Lysias' speech is based no less on the claim that one could hardly say *more* on the topic than Lysias has said than on the claim that what he said was worth saying (234e3–4; 235b2–5); and no sooner has Socrates objected that he could add to Lysias' speech fresh points that would be 'no worse' (*mē kheirō*, 235c6) than Phaedrus has transferred his enthusiasm to the prospect of a further speech, picking up on Socrates' promise that what he says will be as much worth saying as was Lysias' speech but adding his own characteristic requirement that Socrates must not just add new points but say *more* overall than Lysias (235d6–7; 236b2).[9] Similarly, when Socrates subsequently disavows the content of both Lysias' and his own first speech and prepares to issue a rebuttal, Phaedrus expresses far less concern for the impugned worth of the speeches he had so recently espoused than an emphatic pleasure at the prospect of Socrates' delivering yet another speech in the series (243b8–9 – in contrast to the casual passivity with which he accedes to Socrates' disavowal: 242d8, 10; 243d2). It is notable too that when Socrates voices his amazement at Phaedrus' Simmias-like ability to induce intellectual talk, he mentions only the quantity and not the quality of that talk: no one has caused *more* speeches and talks to come about than Phaedrus (*pleious*, 242b1). Phaedrus, then, has a tendency to consider intellectual talk good just because it is intellectual talk, rather than because it is good talk. As a cultural impresario, he devotes himself to promoting the discourse of the mind as an end in itself, rather than evaluating it. Consequently, his recognition of the appropriate audience and site for a performance of Lysias' speech is predicated primarily on the disinterested pleasure such a performance will bring. Phaedrus himself derives pleasure from discovering a fellow enthusiast ('he was delighted to have a companion in Corybantism', 228b7); and he picks out the plane-tree pergola for its comfort, as Socrates' exaggerated praise of its sensual delights makes apparent (230b2–c5).[10]

But Phaedrus is not after pleasure at all costs. This becomes clear when, for example, he is affronted, after completing his performance of Lysias' speech, by Socrates' admission that what he enjoyed most about it was the spectacle of Phaedrus' beaming face as he read (234d1–7). Phaedrus' efforts as an impresario and performer can be successful only in so far as they pass unnoticed; for Socrates must take pleasure in Lysias' speech for its own sake: that is, for suitable and not just any reasons. If the physical arrangements for the performance become the focus of audience attention, those arrangements have failed in their purpose; and Phaedrus understands that his arrangements will give pleasure to the extent that they are appropriate, but must not be declared appropriate merely because they give pleasure. In this he has a fair grasp of his art as impresario. But he is far less secure in his understanding that the social appropriateness of his arrangements depends in turn on the goodness of what is arranged. It is not that he has no concern for how good or bad is the content of Lysias' speech; but his best shot at assessing its worth is the claim that it has said 'everything on the subject that is worth saying' (235b2–3). For Phaedrus, there are a certain number of appropriate topics in any field that ought to come to language. It is good that they should come to language; and if Socrates finds yet further suitable things to say, so much the better. However, Phaedrus gives every sign of not appreciating that these topics are not good because they are suitable, but suitable because they are good. In this he fails as a philosopher.

Indeed, he may even be thought to fail as an impresario. After all, if Socrates pays too much attention to Phaedrus' arrangements for their theatrical event, this is surely Phaedrus' fault, at least in part (it is also due in part to Socrates' own character: a topic I shall broach presently, in the section 'Professional and layman'). I have mentioned that when the pair arrive at the arbour which Phaedrus had designated Socrates launches into an encomium of its delights which leaves his companion nonplussed by its extravagance. But Phaedrus was not thinking carefully enough; he chose a spot that was just too perfect. If his mind were truly set on directing Socrates' attention to the merits of Lysias' speech, he should not have selected for the performance a pastoral bower of such dazzling rightness that Socrates could hardly help but be distracted towards the virtues of the performance itself, to the detriment of what was performed (as his subsequent comment on Phaedrus' beaming face duly attests).[11] We must ask, however, whether this is Phaedrus' personal failure as impresario, or if it is not rather an inadequacy in the very art of the impresario as such. For it is an art which focuses primarily on presentation, and only secondarily on the goodness of what is presented. Phaedrus had not intended to swamp Lysias' speech, but that is what he does; and this not so much because he is a bad impresario (although the result of his actions makes him seem one), as because, being a true impresario, he looks primarily to set up the perfect performance – of intellectual talk, in his case – and then leave the play of the intellect to take care of itself. He cannot conceive that the values of performance might actually prove a danger to the well-being of intellectual talk; cannot conceive, in other words, that he should aim to be a philosopher first, and an impresario only second.

In the course of the dialogue Phaedrus' inadequacy is a spring-board for exploration of how the talk of the true philosopher is indeed appropriate just to the extent that it is good. And our next step towards appreciating this difference must be to relate the philosopher's notion of the good to his notion of truth; we must be oriented and warmed to what truth means for Socrates. To this end I return to my scrutiny of Socrates' and Phaedrus' behaviour as they find their way along the Ilissus.

Boreas and his interpreters

So far I have shown how in the opening scene of the dialogue Phaedrus reveals his ability as cultural impresario, and I have suggested both the peculiar danger of this skill – that it passes itself off as philosophy – and its inadequacy – that its criterion is the fitting rather than the good.

Another episode in Socrates' and Phaedrus' progress towards the arbour points up a disparity, not between the fitting and the good, but between the fitting and the true. I have mentioned already how Phaedrus speculates that, since the delightfully pure waters of the Ilissus seem so apt for girlish play, he may be at the very spot from which Boreas snatched the unsuspecting Oreithyia (229b4–9). I did not mention that the speculation is false. Socrates gives the required correction: the actual site is two or three stades downstream, where it is marked by an altar to Boreas (229c1–3). A simple lesson is suggested: appropriateness is not a sufficient condition for truth. Immediately, however, the lesson is rendered less banal and more edifying by an elaboration to show that, in a certain sense of truth, truth is not what matters.

Since Socrates' confident location of the site of Oreithyia's rape by the wind-god implies that he believes it a fact, Phaedrus presses him: does he really think the myth is true (229c4–5)? In reply Socrates backs down from any commitment to topographic certainty, casually mentioning that an alternative story locates the incident on the Areopagus (229d1–2). Yet he is also cautious about adopting holus-bolus a sceptical attitude towards this and other myths. Given the fashion for demythologising the traditional tales that is current among 'intellectuals' (*hoi sophoi*, 229c6), he asserts, such scepticism on his part would not seem at all unusual or out of place.[12] He could safely strip the tale of its fantastic lumber and explain it away as having developed around a straightforward incident: say, that the daughter of Erechtheus was caught by a violent gust of wind while playing on the rocks by the river (229c6–d2). For such intellectuals, myth is a distorted record of what actually happened; its truth is historical truth. But Socrates has no time to waste on the enquiry into this sort of truth. Not that he is contemptuous of facts; after all, we have seen him quick to point out when Phaedrus has his topographic facts wrong. Rather, he is pain-

10

fully aware of the contingent limitations on our knowledge of historical truth, distorted as it must be by hearsay. He demonstrated these limitations when he admitted that some claim the Areopagus rather than the Ilissus as the spot where Boreas came to ground. In such circumstances, those intent on reducing the myths to their kernel of fact, not being themselves eyewitnesses to these facts, can at best issue what Socrates calls merely 'plausible' speculations (*kata to eikos*, 229e2).[13] Their ostensible search for the truth behind the tales will degenerate into speculation on the tales as hearsay. Mere antiquarians, for whom completeness is as or more important than enlightenment, they will laboriously add to their collection such exotic specimens as Centaurs, Gorgons, the Chimaera and Pegasus for no better reason than that their stories are bruited about (229d2–e4). But the truth of events is not what matters for Socrates; what does matter to him, he goes on to say, is the truth about himself (229e4–6).

It is the antiquarians' obsession with historical fact as an end in itself rather than their focus on myth as such that earns Socrates' disapproval; for though his curt insistence that he has no time to demythologise the corpus might seem a blanket dismissal of myth, it is important to see how he reinstates the value of myth in describing the truth that does matter to him. In taking not myth but himself as the object of study he hopes to discover whether he is a simple creature or 'a beast more complex and puffed up than Typhon' (230a3–5). That mythological monsters should continue to stalk Socrates' phraseology even after he has 'said goodbye' to myth (230a1–2) is not just a pleasant irony, but anticipates and exhibits a situation of epistemological significance. When Socrates, in the second of his speeches on love, offers his most sustained account of the human and especially the philosophic soul (that is, when he delivers the psychological analysis here promised), he finds himself incapable of describing it 'as it is', and compelled to resort to the simile of a chariot with winged horses and charioteer (246a3–7) – a simile which grows into a full mythical allegory as the chariot plies its way among the Olympian gods (246e4–249d3).[14] In turning eventually to the study here recommended, Socrates seems to return willy-nilly to considering the sort of composite mythical monster here rejected as unworthy of attention.

This ironic similarity of approach is only superficial, however, and serves rather to bring out a deep difference between Socrates and the antiquarians. For them, myth is the object of analysis; hence they are concerned only with the corpus already in existence. For Socrates, myth is a tool to be used in the analysis of himself as person and philosopher; hence he readily becomes a producer and re-creator of new myths – albeit within the existing tradition – rather than simply a commentator on the old. And this difference is connected with the different kinds of truth pursued by the two parties. It is because Socrates seeks general truths about his human nature rather than the truth of particular events that he finds myth an appropriate tool of expression.[15] We may compare Aristotle's well known statement in the *Poetics* that poetry is more philosophical than history because 'poetry tends to give general truths while history gives particular facts' (*Poetics*, 1451b).[16] And clearly, if such truths about his nature as a human are what Socrates seeks, he cannot properly conduct his search without concerning himself with what it is to live the good life. In this broad sense, the investigation of the true and of the good is one enterprise for him. But such answers as he arrives at will require delicate unravelling over the entire course of this book. At present, more needs to be said about the similarities and differences between Socrates and the intellectuals.

Professional and layman

What more there is to say emerges when Socrates breaks off his comments on the demythologisers to remark that he and Phaedrus have reached their destination, the plane-tree's shade (230a6–7). Phaedrus, we saw, had chosen the natural gazebo for its virtues as a background for high-brow talk, picking it out from the surrounding landscape precisely for its unobtrusiveness. To be sure, the plane-tree that he pointed out to Socrates is a distinctive marker (229a8); but what it marks off, according to Phaedrus' way of seeing it (229b1–2), is an area of green and breezy shade where two people can talk, as Socrates had requested, 'in peace' (229a2). Here, nature will not announce herself through the discomforts of bright sun, hard ground, or stifling air. In short, the place fits their purposes well precisely because they need not remark on how well it fits their purposes (and we have seen that as an 'impresario' Phaedrus would not want to have his manipulations upstage the performance). Yet remark on it Socrates proceeds to do. This we have seen to be partly Phaedrus' fault, but let us consider now how Socrates' distinctive personality is also a factor. What Phaedrus had concisely presented as simple virtues Socrates sauces with extravagant and detailed praise, noting every self-effacing trait as a distinct embellishment and a stimulus for the senses (230b2–c5). He concludes: 'So, my dear Phaedrus, you have been the stranger's perfect guide' (230c5). Phaedrus can only concur: 'Well, you, my amazing friend, strike me as the oddest of men (*atopōtatos tis*). Anyone would take you, as you say, for a stranger being shown the sights instead of a native. That's what comes of never leaving town to visit places over the border; I really believe you don't ever so much as set foot outside the walls' (230c5–d2).

This exchange is connected with Socrates' criticism of the demythologisers in an indirect but telling manner, which Plato marks by his careful positioning of the term *atopos*, 'strange', 'odd', or – paying more attention to etymology – 'out of place' (thus he does a little friendly guiding of his own for the reader). Socrates was confident that, were he to disencumber Boreas and Orcithyia of their fabulous mystique, he would not be thought at all 'odd' (*atopos*, 229c6); oddness here would rather be an attribute of the Chimaera and Gorgons whose claws the demythologiser is out to pull (called 'oddities', *atopiai*, at 229e1). But Socrates, we saw, had canvassed the idea that he might be psychologically akin to just such a mythical mongrel: Typhon (230a3–5); and now he seems to have provided evidence in favour of some such conclusion, for his outburst at the arbour provokes Phaedrus to declare him 'the oddest of men' (*atopōtatos tis*, 230c6). The nub of this strangeness is that Socrates is acting like a stranger even though he is a native Athenian (230c6–d2); for he refuses to allow Phaedrus to take for granted his skill in providing for the comfort and entertainment of his companion. The ultimate target of praise in his description of the arbour is less the physical features of the place than Phaedrus' achievement as tourist-guide in selecting them ('So, you've been the stranger's *perfect* guide', *hōste arista soi exenagetai*, 230c5). In this he confronts Phaedrus with what he would not normally notice: Phaedrus' quite ordinary ability (at least as Phaedrus himself sees it) to get successfully and appropriately oriented in his environment (a basic component of his more sophisticated skill as impresario).[17] By making a fuss over what Phaedrus designed to be a quiet background, Socrates brings into relief the basic skill that makes possible Phaedrus' design; a skill which would itself normally remain, as it were, in the background. Phaedrus was not thinking of himself as guide to strangers; but Socrates, through the very act of stressing this skill, has *made* him a guide to strangers; for he has made himself look strange. He is a 'stranger' (*atopos*) because he is alive to what it takes to be ordinary and native.

Surely, however, something similar could be said of the intellectuals who take it on themselves to historicise myth? In ritual and in the casual allusions of everyday talk these stories would be used unthinkingly, without special regard for the conditions under which they were generated as stories; so that these intellectuals, no less than Socrates, would be stirring up thought about what would normally pass unnoticed. Yet they are not, according to Socrates, considered 'odd' (*atopos*), while Socrates is (and Socrates holds that they ought indeed to be considered odd; for he calls their project 'absurd', *geloion*, 229e6). We must ask, then: why not? And the answer, I think, is this: that the intellectuals to whom Socrates refers puncture propriety as professionals, while Socrates does so as a private individual.

Burgeoning professionalism among sophists, rhetoricians,

and the like permits Socrates to label them simply (and with some irony) 'the wise' (*hoi sophoi*, 229c6) and expect to have his reference understood.[18] Moreover, Phaedrus had early brought the issue to our attention when he complained that as a 'layman' (*idiōtes*) he could not hope to retail Lysias' speech in a manner worthy of that 'most clever of present-day writers'; especially since Lysias had had time to compose the piece 'at his leisure' (*kata skholēn*) (227d6–228a3). Compare the 'leisure' (*skholēs*, 229e3) that Socrates says the demythologisers will need if they are to tackle the whole of the traditional bestiary, and contrast the 'leisure' he exhibited at the very outset of the dialogue when asked by Phaedrus if he had the time (*skholē* again, 227b8) to come and hear what Lysias had said. 'What?', he replies, 'Don't you think I'd make it, as Pindar says, something "above all business" to hear what happened with you and Lysias?' (227b9–11). Socrates is always free for a good talk; his 'leisure' is a constant improvisatory readiness to seize the moment and create free time even where there was none before. He has the flexible timetable of the layman. (Notice that while Phaedrus only happens to have come out barefoot today, Socrates is always without sandals – as Phaedrus remarks at 229a3–4. He is ready for anything.) Both Lysias and the demythologisers, by contrast, require the carefully budgeted scholastic 'leisure' (that is, time free from banausic cares) of the professional who works with his mind.[19] I am suggesting, then, that 'the wise' do not seem out of place in their rather intense speculation on everyday myths because the public actually expects them to exercise an unusually fine discernment on the web of social practice. This expectation is based in turn on their claim as professionals to have an expertise worth paying for, most especially in the art of public speaking but by extension in the analysis of all the varieties of discourse and story on which life in the society of the time depended.[20] Socrates' behaviour on arrival at the arbour, by contrast, exhibits for us how a philosopher differs from professionals in general and rhetoricians in particular. But let us look more closely at this display.

The philosopher as artist

I have argued that both Socrates and the demythologisers are unusually attentive to the ordinarily tacit conditions of everyday social practices; but that when Socrates brings Phaedrus alive to his previously unacknowledged and unremarkable ability to orient himself appropriately in his surroundings, he does so without a professional context to frame and make a place for his extraordinary attention to the ordinary; and that accordingly, this attention seems out of place (and Phaedrus, who found his way so easily along the Ilissus, has lost it in the conversation and can only comment on Socrates' oddness). I want now to show how Plato has pointed up the question of professionalism here by writing Socrates' outburst in such a way that it borrows from the technical wardrobe of those two professional disciplines that have figured prominently together in the dialogue's opening pages: rhetoric and medicine.

Already Hermias (apud 230b) noted how Socrates' description of the bower has the air of a formal rhetorical panegyric. Socrates' language is marked not only with elements of a generally sophisticated and elevated style,[21] but by those two typical features of rhetorical praise: exhaustiveness and exaggeration. Indeed, he gives the impression of systematically cataloguing the entire scene from the tip of the plane-tree to the grass beneath their feet, dividing the stimuli among the various senses and assigning to each its appropriate superlative.[22] Less obvious, perhaps, but equally striking once noticed (as it has not been by the commentators known to me), is the debt Socrates' enthusiasm here owes to medical techniques. In order to establish this point I must introduce a fairly lengthy quotation, the opening section of the Hippocratic treatise *Airs, Waters, Places*:

Whoever would study medicine aright must learn of the following subjects. First he must consider the effect of each of the seasons of the year and the differences between them. Secondly he must study the warm and the cold winds, both those which are common to every country and those peculiar to a particular locality. Lastly, the effect of water on the health must not be forgotten ... When, therefore, a physician comes to a district previously unknown to him, he should consider both its situation and its aspect to the winds ... Similarly, the nature of the water supply must be considered; is it marshy and soft, hard as it is when it flows from high and rocky ground, or salty with a hardness which is permanent? Then think of the soil, whether it be bare and waterless or thickly covered with vegetation and well-watered; whether in a hollow and stifling, or exposed and cold. Lastly consider the life of the inhabitants themselves; are they heavy drinkers and eaters and consequently unable to stand fatigue or, being fond of work and exercise, eat wisely but drink sparely? (trans. J. Chadwick and W. N. Mann)

Need I labour the parallel? On arrival at the shrine by the Ilissus Socrates gives every appearance of having come to a district previously unknown to him, as if he were a visiting foreigner; he examines the soil and finds it well watered (the spring) and thickly covered with vegetation (the lush grass, the plane- and agnus-trees); he checks the characteristics of the water supply (sweet and cool; and notice here the pedantically scientific 'as you can confirm with your toes', *hōste ge tōi podi tekmērasthai*, 230b7); he considers the winds (the pleasant breeze); and he concerns himself with the inhabitants of the place, detecting the presence of Achelous and the Nymphs and commenting on the musical activity of the cicadas – whose habits of spare eating and drinking and fondness for work he reserves, however, for later scrutiny (when he relates the myth of the cicadas, in which we learn that they 'sing continuously without food or drink until they die', 259c4–5).

I am not of course claiming that Socrates here manages to deliver a standard rhetorical panegyric and produce a proper Hippocratic analysis of the locality all at once; nor that Plato has directly calqued the quoted passage from *Airs, Waters, Places*. In Socrates' outburst at the arbour the techniques of rhetorician and doctor are not reliably reproduced but glimpsed as in a comic distorting mirror,[23] and in this parody Plato need appeal only to his audience's general knowledge of rhetorical and medical procedures rather than to an acquaintance with any actual panegyric or passage in the Hippocratic corpus. But the serious point of Plato's parody is this. By

17

comically assimilating Socrates' behaviour to that of various professionals, he displays Socrates' problematic status as philosopher: not a professional, yet a serious practitioner of a particular discipline; not just a layman, yet clinging to the layman's spontaneity.

Were a physician, for example, to scrutinise his new environment with an eye as sharp as Socrates' here, no one would 'think him strange'. The motivation for his behaviour would be clear: he would be gathering the data he needs to know if he is to achieve his professional goal of preventing disease and healing the sick. But there is no such professional motivation for Socrates' sensitivity to the scenery. Accordingly, his reaction on arrival seems spontaneous.[24] This does not mean, however, that his behaviour is not oriented towards a goal beyond the mere appraisal of local amenities and Phaedrus' skill as excursion leader. Rather, we should compare the behaviour of the philosophic lover as described for us by Socrates in his second speech. When struck by the sight and the prospect of a beautiful young partner in the philosophic life, this philosophic type is powerfully reminded of 'the beautiful itself', and in his enthusiasm neglects the common run of human concerns; with the result that most think him deviant and crazy (see 249c4–e4). The philosopher's wild reaction, though spontaneous, is ultimately determined by the memory of the beautiful itself, a memory which plays itself out through the living of a life oriented towards the good – for Plato, the philosophic life. And I suggest that Socrates on arrival at the pastoral oasis is overcome by an exemplary little bout of this philosophic madness; or at least, that his odd behaviour betrays a character susceptible to the full-blown experience of the philosophic lover.[25] He has what would normally be thought (and what Phaedrus marks as) a strange and excessive reaction to the beauty of the place and the excellence of Phaedrus' shepherding. Just as the philosophic lover cannot see the worldly beauty of his partner in a merely worldly fashion, so Socrates cannot accept the simple beauties of the bower and Phaedrus' competence as a guide in the unreflective manner of everyday.

Yet surely, it may be thought, I risk a mighty leap in comparing Socrates' momentary topographic enthusiasm to the noble heights of the philosophic lover's aspiration? And besides, if philosophic madness (however mild) is what Socrates exhibits here, why does an intellectual dilettante such as Phaedrus not appreciate it as such, rather than expressing the standard puzzlement of the majority?

The answers to these two objections are connected. To take the first. It is characteristic of the philosopher that while appreciating real differences of value between items on a scale he retains his interest in items at the lower end of the scale, because he is interested in the scale as a whole. The philosopher is excited by all beautiful things, a beautiful landscape as well as a beautiful person, because what bites him is the beautiful as such; and he will spare a moment for all arts, the art of guiding tourists as well as that of guiding souls (*psykhagōgia*, as rhetoric is later called, at 261a8), because he wants to know the general conditions of artistic competence. This point is explicitly stressed in those late dialogues that take up formally the dialectical technique of Collection and Division which is methodologically mooted in the second part of the *Phaedrus* (see 265d–266c). In the *Politicus* we learn that the dialectician will not hesitate to locate man and pig on the same level of his division, at least in that respect in which they are similar: 'lowly and exalted must receive equal consideration'. The same point is made about the relative dignity of bathman and physician at *Sophist* 227a7–b6. On the other hand, the dialectician is well aware of genuine differences of value within these similarities. He capitalises on these differences by using the humble as a more readily understood paradigm for the exalted. In the *Sophist* the unexceptional figure of the angler becomes a test case for the investigation of his fellow 'hunter', the enigmatic sophist (218d8 sq.; n.b. 221d8–13); in the *Politicus* the weaver serves the same function for the statesman (279a7 sq.). So too in the *Phaedrus* we are presented at the outset with an 'easy' – that is, casual and everyday – example of Socrates' philosophic strangeness before proceeding to the general account in Socrates' second speech of what full-blown philosophic madness is in its most exalted manifestation, the case of the philosophic lovers. Moreover, what marks Socrates as philosophically mad is precisely the equal enthusiasm with which he reacts to the high and the humble, seeing the one in the other (and Plato perhaps tests a similar enthusiasm in the reader by offering us the opportunity to see philosophic madness and philosophic significance even in this preliminary scene, rather than treating it as no more than colourful stage-business). Phaedrus' failure to appreciate this aspect of Socrates' outburst (and here I answer the second of the two objections and show its connection with the answer to the first) reveals him to be a mere philosophical impresario rather than a genuine philosopher. He cannot recognise as philosophy anything other than what bears the stylistically conventional features of philosophic discourse. For this reason, his is the life of mere words that I mentioned earlier: not a philosophic life, but a life styled after that of philosophers.

Bizarre as it is, Socrates' outburst (like the experience of the philosophic lover) is after all no passing whimsy but a typical piece of a life guided by an eye for the good in all its facets. To be sure, Socrates' remarks on arrival at the Ilissan shrine do not in themselves convey any substantial philosophic claim; rather they display his aptitude for philosophy. Only as the dialogue progresses does Socrates actually 'do' philosophy, as we like to say; but by writing the dialogue with this progression, Plato sharpens the distinction between philosophy and professional arts like medicine and rhetoric. Put baldly, the point is this: if there is a single best label for the art that philosophy is, it will be (for Plato) the art of living well. But in such an art the contrast between professional and private life can have no place. The doctor and rhetorician can take time off from their professional duties to enjoy the pleasures of the layman.[26] The philosopher, on the other hand, never seems more a philosopher than when immersed in the everyday (as is Socrates in the orientation along the Ilissus); for then it is most clear that his philosophic eye never sleeps, and keeps him from entering fully into the normal life of alternate work and play. Phaedrus, recall, left his sandals off by chance; but Socrates is always barefoot, and always 'at leisure' – a leisure that is his life's work. Because as a philosopher the whole of life is Socrates' artistic concern, and not just a professionalised piece of it, his response to the environment is presented as spontaneous, welling directly from ordinary life rather than set against it in the manner of professional analysis. Yet clearly the whole of life is *not* the concern, at least not the constant concern, of 'ordinary' people. The result is that the philosopher's position cannot be satisfactorily mapped onto the dichotomy between professional and lay, but is rather revealed through the inadequacy of any attempt at such mapping.[27]

Walking into the background

Now that I have oriented the reader this far, I am able to take account of an important metaphorical extension of the term 'background' that I have used up to this point without special comment. The Ilissan landscape in which Socrates and Phaedrus walk and talk is the background for their activity in the most literal, visual sense; but I have spoken also of how this background does not stay in the background, becoming instead an obtrusive topic of discussion (in the section 'Topic and topography'), and of how Socrates, in making much of Phaedrus' ability to orient himself appropriately against this background, brings out of the background what Phaedrus regards as a quite ordinary skill (in the section 'Professional and layman'). Of course, the countryside stretching off from the banks of the Ilissus remains the visual background even when Socrates and Phaedrus, by talking of it directly, pluck it from the conversational 'background'. This latter use of 'background' is a metaphor for the enabling conditions of their conversation and of their behaviour in general. Socrates and Phaedrus would not be able to walk and talk together in their environment if they did not bring to the task basic shared capacities to distinguish visual foreground from background, weigh what is perceptually salient, recognise appropriate paths and resting places, and so on; and these shared capacities make up the 'background' of their actual activity, which would normally remain unspoken and implicit in that activity.[28]

But we have seen that Socrates' demeanour does not remain normal. In the climax towards which Plato builds his opening scene Socrates scrutinises Phaedrus' 'background' capacity for appropriate orientation with the eye of a connoisseur, and awards him the fastidious praise one might expect for an achievement in the fine arts. From examining the environmental background along with Phaedrus he has now turned to consider and evaluate the very ability to examine that background, as exhibited by Phaedrus. Recall that Phaedrus, in exercising this ability (as a partial means towards his more specialised aims as impresario) conforms to the model for various more technical disciplines proposed in the second half of the dialogue. Thus, as the orator must not only know a body of explicit rules but also be able to recognise the appropriate circumstances for their implementation, so knowing a list of amenities featured in the arbour would have been useless to Phaedrus without the ability to recognise them as appropriate. Phaedrus in a sense *just saw* that the arbour *looked* right for their purposes. This recognition is not, of course, reducible to his knowing that where there are the three features he lists for Socrates – shade, breeze, and grass (229b1–2) – there we have a likely spot for high-flown chatter. These conditions are hardly sufficient in themselves (nor is any one of them strictly necessary); after all, they might well obtain on a football pitch with a match in progress. Phaedrus is communicating to Socrates what he has seen, as it were out of politeness and to check that Socrates sees things the same way. He is not transcribing his mental states but offering shorthand justifications after the event of recognition.

Plato brings this fact to our attention through Socrates' encomium of Phaedrus' skill; because for all Socrates' elaboration of Phaedrus' terse report of the arbour, he comes no closer to capturing the conditions of Phaedrus' competence but only provides an inappropriately baroque appreciation of its effects. The potential variation in any such explicit list of specifications and rules is vast; moreover, as is pointed out in the second part of the dialogue, however complete we make the list, competence in a skill is always also conditional on recognising where the rules are appropriate. And this is something the competent practitioner *just sees*, as Phaedrus just saw that the arbour looked right. This knowledge – knowing where the rules are appropriate – is not propositional; which is not to say that it is mysterious or inexpressible. It could be expressed, communicated, and learnt through suitable tables of explicit rules; only, what the practitioner knows is not co-extensive with the propositional content of those rules.

Now, we can readily see that the interaction between visual foreground and background makes a particularly happy metaphor for the way in which explicit knowledge and what we might call recognition or insight come together in the development of competence and understanding.[29] In one sense, Socrates and Phaedrus find the environmental backdrop fully accessible: you see that plane-tree in the distance? Let's go there. And they do. Yet in another sense, what could be less accessible than the background? They arrive at the arbour and find that it is now in the foreground. Any background can be foreground; only, you cannot walk into the background itself. It is always one step ahead. (Though again, once Socrates' surprise at the arbour has cooled, the place recedes into the role of immediate visual background against which to talk, as Phaedrus had planned. These saliencies are relative to the interest of the speakers.) Just so, Phaedrus can readily communicate – bring into the foreground – various conditions that he recognises as obtaining in the arbour; but let Socrates refine and add to these conditions as explicitly as he pleases, set in the foreground as many possible background criteria as he can think of, ultimately a background will always remain: the capacity in virtue of which Phaedrus recognises the criteria he is to follow.

The relation between knowledge and recognition is a theme that will run throughout this book. We will encounter it in

23

chapter three when we consider Socrates' critique of rhetoric – for the main count of his indictment is that in rhetoric as currently taught these two elements of understanding have, so to speak, come unstuck one from the other – and again in the fifth chapter when we consider why Socrates has recourse to the apparatus of myth and allegory in his investigation into the nature of soul. What I have to say now is preliminary to these developments. I want to claim that Plato's emphasis in these opening pages on how skilfully Phaedrus guides Socrates against the backcloth of the Ilissus gives us good reason to believe that the felicity of the metaphor of 'background' for what Plato wants to say about skills and arts in general is something that he recognises and consciously works with in this episode.

We have already seen how Socrates' reaction to his surroundings has the flavour of the philosophic madness scrutinised later in the dialogue. And now we can see that the action of the opening scene is paradigmatic in another way; for the ability of the characters to orient themselves in the landscape offers a simple paradigm for the interaction of knowledge and insight as that is later discussed in connection with more sophisticated skills. The landscape of the Ilissus becomes symbolically charged; and Socrates' and Phaedrus' walk into the background represents the beginnings of the search within the self that Socrates announces as his aim (229e5–230a1): a search in particular for the elusive background to the higher intellectual skills. But although, in finding their way to the arbour, Phaedrus and Socrates exercise a skill that itself functions in the manner that it emblematises (such is the way of paradigms), it is in itself a simple, almost 'biological' skill, which only the foolhardy would rank in point of sophistication with higher arts such as rhetoric or medicine. However, this only sharpens its interest as a paradigm. For while it is easy for us to accept the importance of the background in the exercise of biological capacities that become relatively automatic and in which explicit rules play little part, in the higher intellectual arts, by contrast, explicit rules based on a body of propositional knowledge can seem to be all there is to know; this, indeed, is what the writers of rhetorical manuals (criticised in the second part of the dialogue) capitalise upon.[30] All the more important, then, that the reader should not neglect the role of the background in these skills also, and should acknowledge what they share with the less remarkable capacities that engage attention in the dialogue's preliminary episode.

Of course, this is to review that episode with the hindsight available only to the close reader of the entire dialogue. On a first reading we are likely to be as intrigued by Plato's extra-ordinary play with the topography in general as Phaedrus is in particular by Socrates' extraordinary pastoral gushing. Our speculations will be guided by the hypothesis that, because this is literature and not life, Plato's unusually hot attention to the scenery is dictated not by fancy but by heavy purpose; with the result that Plato will have obliged us by literary arti-fice to take off our sandals and paddle – to train on life's sim-pler moments something like the philosophic eye for paradigms that an always unshod Socrates needs no such in-ducement to exert.

What the cicadas sang

In the opening section of this chapter I posed two questions: why does Plato build into the conversation between Socrates and Phaedrus so elaborate a consideration of its setting? And why, once he has sat his characters down in their pastoral theatre, does he again, and markedly, direct their interest towards the environment – allowing the cicadas' orchestral accompaniment its solo passage – at the crucial point where rhetoric ousts love from the spotlight of discussion? Up to this point I have explicated and defended my answer to the first question only. Now that I have adverted to the philosophical importance of the concept of 'background', I can turn to the second of my two questions. My anticipatory answer to this question was: Plato marks the transitional point between the two parts of the dialogue with renewed attention to its scene in order to orient our reading of its curious structure – the

25

brusque shift, that is, from celebration of love to cerebration over rhetoric. I have already shown how the characters' dealings with their dramatic ambience are paradigmatic of a larger pattern in the exercise of human skills and arts, and how Socrates' reactions in particular emblematise the distinctive quality of his philosophic art: that particular art which investigates (among other things) the conditions of art in general, including its own. But the *Phaedrus* is itself a product of this self-conscious philosophic art. Small wonder, then, that, as I will now argue, Plato steps up the emblematic charge of the dramatic action so that it empowers an interpretation of how the dialogue itself is to be read.

The chorus of cicadas takes centre-stage not immediately after Socrates has given the peroration of his great speech on love and the discussion veers, but when Socrates has reached agreement with Phaedrus (after a brief transitional passage, 257b7–258e5) that they need to investigate the criteria of good speaking and writing. Here he breaks off and alerts Phaedrus to the sound of the cicadas in the branches overhead. The cicadas are watching us, he insists. We should take care not to doze off in the noonday heat, but to keep our discussion alive; and if we put on a good show, they will grant us the reward that is theirs to give. Phaedrus has never heard of this prerogative of theirs, and asks Socrates to explain. Socrates replies with a short myth. The cicadas were men once, back in the time before the Muses were born; but the Muses came and brought song into the world and you would not believe the pleasure of it. Some people forgot their food and drink and sang themselves to death. The Muses turned them into the first cicadas so that they could sing all day without food or drink and at the end of their days appear before them with an account of who honoured which of them among men on earth. So if we want a good report to reach Calliope and Urania, the philosophic Muses, we had better not flag in the heat but push on with our fine talk (this in summary of 258e6–259d8).

Clearly, Socrates' pause to temper his and Phaedrus' resolve marks a new beginning. Moreover, the old beginning

26

resonates with Socrates' remark here that they have at any rate the 'leisure' (*skholē*, 258e6) to continue talking. Recall the prominent contrast in the dialogue's opening pages between the leisure of the professional and a layman's leisure. There Phaedrus asked Socrates if he had the time to come and hear Lysias' speech, and Socrates, the man 'sick for words' (228b6), assented with characteristic enthusiasm; but now that Socrates has captured the conversational initiative with the rhetorical *tour de force* of his speeches on love, it is he who asks Phaedrus whether they need to examine the criteria of good speaking and writing, and Phaedrus who eagerly concurs: 'You're asking if we need to do this? But why else would anyone bother even to live, you might say, if not for *this* sort of pleasure? Certainly not for that other sort, at any rate, where there must be a foregoing pain if there's to be any pleasure at all; something almost all bodily pleasures have. That is why they're rightly called "slavish" (*andrapodōdeis*)' (258e1–5). The unabashed delight in intellectual talk to which Phaedrus here gives vent is a philosophic trait; Socrates himself freely confesses and exhibits it. Yet it is at most a necessary, not a sufficient qualification for the life of philosophy. Indeed, as Socrates' admission that he is 'sick for words' suggests, such enthusiasm is double-edged; and Phaedrus is showing its dangerous side. We have seen how, as cultural 'impresario', he has a tendency to promote clever talk for its own sake, indiscriminately. I propose that through the myth of the cicadas Plato takes his stand against this tendency in such a way as to admonish readers that they too, at this delicate point in the action, must beware of careless discrimination among the breeds of intellectual discourse. (As Socrates warns, introducing the myth, 'no one who loves the Muses should be ignorant of such things', 259b5–6.)[31]

Just about all bodily pleasures are 'slavish', Phaedrus sweepingly declares; or rather, reports the declaration as an established philosophic dogma, to which he enthusiastically subscribes.[32] In response, Socrates indicates that even the pleasures of the mind promote their variety of slavishness; and furthermore, that this slavishness is of just the sort that

Phaedrus has displayed by citing authority in support of his personal predilections. If they allow themselves to be bewitched by the cicadas' drone, says Socrates, and doze off like sheep at siesta around the spring, the cicadas will rightly mock them as 'slavish types' (*andrapod' atta*, 259a4–5). Slavish with a bodily slavishness, we might think. Yet consider more closely the pleasures that the cicadas purvey. According to Socrates' figurative description, theirs is just that verbal virtuosity, in all its facets, which Phaedrus ranks most highly: they both 'sing and converse' (*aidontes kai allēlois dialegomenoi*, 258e7–259a1) in the foliage overhead; they are Sirens (259e7), whose seduction is in their voice; and it is the 'lazily relaxed mind' rather than body of the hearer (*di' argian tēs dianoias*, 259a3–4) that is sensible to the seductive pleasure of language stripped down to a mantra's hum. Moreover, none show better than the cicadas themselves the dangers of this pleasure. In Socrates' story they indulge indiscriminately in the gifts of the Muses, overwhelmed by the pleasure of song (see 259b8), and receive their just deserts: they become messengers, mere vehicles for conveying to all the Muses how others, but certainly not the cicadas themselves, discriminate between them in their devotion. The cicadas 'sing' and 'converse' at the same time (why make distinctions when glossolalia bites?), but Socrates has just switched, and abruptly so, from the 'singing' register of his poetic declamations on love[33] to the dialectical conversation with Phaedrus that makes up the second part of the dialogue. And whereas the cicadas run their errand for the entire band of Muses without distinction, Socrates does not hesitate to attribute to Calliope and Urania, Muses of philosophy, the 'fairest voice' (259d7) among them all. Not for him the cicadas' fate.

Phaedrus, on the other hand, is susceptible to their disease. Not only has he been temporarily overwhelmed by the beauty of Socrates' magnificent encomium of love (so that Socrates has had to correct his pendulum swing of sudden contempt for Lysias, 257b7–d7), but he is now all set to view the continuation of their subtle talk exclusively (and with an equally sudden shift of immediate perspective) as a prospect of further pleasure – albeit pleasure of the noblest rank. That is why the myth of the cicadas crops up not in the immediate after-shock of the poetic speechmaking but only when the decision has been taken to analyse rhetorical effectiveness in general; because it warns Phaedrus (and, indirectly, the reader) how *not* to take the transition between the overtly poetic and rhetorical speeches and the sober analysis of the art they exemplify.

For Phaedrus, analysis is desirable because it is more of the same, more highbrow talk; uppermost in his mind is not the truth it might reach but the pleasure it will bring just in getting itself said (typically, the snippet of philosophy he cites in encouragement at 258e3–4 – the dogma that his mind has retained – concerns not truth but pleasure). In this he ignores the implications of the very point they have just decided: that writing is not shameful as such (nor is Lysias the speechwriter to be condemned simply because he writes), but both writing and speaking are good and bad only in so far as what is said and written is properly or improperly said and written (258d1–7). The principle behind this claim would be that accidents of format are not a sound basis for judgments of value. Phaedrus agrees submissively enough (258d6), but in his subsequent outburst makes it clear that he considers all intellectual talk good for no more intrinsic reason than that it stimulates mental rather than visceral pleasure (a point not substantially affected by the fact that he recognises, as we saw, that the pleasure must be felt for the appropriate reasons; for he does not ask himself why those reasons are appropriate). For Socrates, by contrast, intellectual talk is pleasant because it is good – *if* it is good. He discriminates between good and bad within each mode of intellectual talk, and between better and worse modes overall. However, here we encounter a deep irony that makes of this scene not the somewhat smug put-down of Phaedrus' dilettantism that it might otherwise seem, but a revelation of Socratic modesty in Plato's teaching and a *vademecum* for the dialogue as a whole.

After all, on what is Socrates' discrimination to be

grounded? In giving philosophy the palm he mentions other Muses and their special provinces: Terpsichore and choral odes, Erato and love lyric (259c6–d3). Here, then, would be a ready basis for discrimination 'according to the form of honour paid each Muse' (259d2–3); for the choral dithyramb fits neither love lyric ... nor, one supposes, philosophy? But this will not do. To declare Calliope's voice the noblest for formal reasons – whether the form considered appropriate for philosophy be dialectical prose or the verse of an Empedocles – would be to fall back into Phaedrus' error of judging the good by externals. But might there not, after all, be some single most appropriate format for philosophy, just as in Plato's culture only metrical language can be properly called poetry? There might; but Plato's presentation of this scene indicates not only that philosophy is not to be accorded the highest place among the arts (if it deserves that place) on the strength of its format, but also that the aims of philosophy are ill-suited to the restrictions of a single format in any case, and can be most strikingly captured by the peculiar multiplicity of formats exhibited in the dialogue as a whole. For look again at the particular cast of Muses mentioned by Socrates: choral Terpsichore, Erato the erotic, the philosophic Calliope and Urania. Earlier, Socrates compared his first speech in emulation of Lysias to a choral dithyramb (228d2–3); and both of his speeches were erotic in theme. Is this a way for Plato to declare them unphilosophical, then? Yet of the supposedly philosophic Muses Urania's name recalls nothing so clearly as the metaphysical 'heaven' (*ouranos*) that enthralls us in the poetic myth of Socrates' second speech (see esp. 246e4; also 247b1 and 247c3), and Calliope, as de Vries points out (apud 259d6–7), 'is the Muse of poetry *par excellence*'.

Where, then, is the 'philosophy' in this dialogue? I am saying that it lies in *both* halves of the dialogue and, just as crucially, in the articulation between them.[34]

We have seen that through his characters' interest in the scenic background Plato offers an example and emblem of interaction between 'foreground' and 'background' of competence: between that aspect which is or can be made explicit, and that which is either contextually or, it may be, essentially tacit — which is shown rather than told. We can now see that the entire dialogue is jointed with such a dovetail of background and foreground. In its second part Socrates and Phaedrus attempt to describe and analyse the rhetorical competence that has been (only) displayed in the first. This much is made quite explicit; but the fact that the second part of the dialogue is heralded by the droning of the cicadas — for all the fleeting quality of this episode ('a relaxing intermezzo', says de Vries apud 258e6–7) — stands as a marker of what is less explicit but equally crucial for an understanding of the dialogue's structure. And here the casual manner in which the cicadas impinge upon the conversation is actually the clue to their importance. The place for a drone, after all, is in the background. Socrates and Phaedrus can remain alert to the cicadas only briefly. Once the real talk begins the sound recedes below the threshold of their (and our) attention, as it must; for background noise is not there to be talked about, it is there to be talked against or over.[35] Yet just this momentary passage into and out of earshot alerts the reader — at least, if the reader is the kind who worries at intermezzi — to the background, the constant pedal-note of the dialogue's second part: to what the dialectic in that second part is showing rather than to what it is saying. Its propositional content is an analysis of the rhetorical skills displayed in the earlier part of the dialogue; but what it in turn displays is, of course, that prime philosophic activity, the analysis of conditions of possibility (in this case of the rhetorical art). Rhetoric is first displayed then investigated; the investigation displays philosophic technique — this sequence should prompt in us the following question: what would it be for philosophy to turn from analysing the conditions of possibility of other arts to analysing its own conditions as an art? And we have only to look to the first part of the dialogue for one answer.[36] In the second part, rhetoric is examined and philosophy exhibited; in the first, conversely, rhetoric parades for the purpose of examining philosophy. For in Socrates' culminating speech Plato probes the conditions of possibility for the pursuit of philosophic love – the highest expression of philosophic art. The join between background and foreground in the two parts of this dialogue is thus truly a dovetail. One part thrusts out its arms where the other has drawn back; one is background to the other's foreground, foreground to the other's background.[37]

I am saying, then, that Plato chose to probe the conditions of philosophic art and the philosophic life in the first part of this dialogue in what is a confessedly poetic fashion. But why, we might ask, would he not rather turn his gaze on philosophy in the dialectical manner of the analysis of rhetoric? I have two replies to this question. First, to insist that only a dialectically styled account of philosophy can be properly philosophical would be to commit Phaedrus' and the cicadas' error of identifying a discipline with, and valuing it for, its (typical) bag of formal tricks. This would be an especially wry mistake in so far as the dialogue reveals in its investigation of verbal arts the inadequacy of all and any verbal means – whether mythical or dialectical – to capture what it is that the competent practitioner of those (and other) arts knows. Second, and more importantly, not only is myth a peculiarly appropriate recourse when philosophy probes itself, but also, and even though formal myth is not the only possible recourse for saying what needs to be said, these things cannot be any more clearly or explicitly said, I think, in a prose free from mythical and poetic marks.

To explain this second reply. A philosophic analysis of philosophy as an art is inevitably coloured by the special circumstance that philosophy is that art which examines all arts, all forms of knowledge, in order to discover what knowledge is, and what it is to be an art. Any such analysis must always to some extent show what it is trying to tell: not, however, as one might write rhetorically about rhetoric or couch a metrical primer in verse (for in these cases we have the option of composing in an unrhetorical style or in prose); rather, if philosophy is the art which analyses the general conditions of the diverse arts and forms of knowledge, and we wish to analyse the conditions of that art, we must ultimately attempt to analyse what makes possible such analysis of conditions of possibility (because just that will be what makes *philosophy* possible). But a successful attempt *must* therefore exhibit in the course of analysis the skill that it describes (there are no options in this case). In this sense, you already understand what you are discursively investigating – which is a common enough situation for the manual craftsman attempting to convey his competence in words. But for a philosopher the predicament is more exquisite. All competence, philosophy reveals, has a tacit as well as an explicit component; but only philosophy attempts to capture this phenomenon in explicit propositions. By its own conclusions, then, philosophic competence displays a tacit background even as it presses on with its propositional chase. But no sooner is *this* phenomenon described than it too becomes a proper object of explicit philosophic investigation. The philosopher longs for what his own verbal enquiries tell him is unattainable through verbal means, and cannot rest content with pat summaries of his longing of the type exemplified by the first limb of this sentence. To do so would be to settle after all for the Phaedran life of mere words. There is no such settlement for the Socrates we find in this dialogue: the man 'out of place', who cannot leave the background where it belongs; the man who listens to the cicadas.

(And we are beginning to see, I trust, that we shall hardly understand what Plato has to say about the philosophic life in this dialogue unless we get to know Phaedrus and Socrates: recognise who they are, what they are. To this end I have been peering at them in the mirror of their environment; for, after all, scenery is not important in itself, but only for the human reactions it bestirs. Or, to use Socrates' words at 230d4–5: 'landscapes and trees, you see, have nothing to teach me; only people in the city'.)

In the discussion of philosophic love in Socrates' great speech Plato expresses by means of a myth this sense in which the philosopher walks into a background that is always one step ahead: a myth which 'explains' the philosopher's prior understanding of what he investigates as a recollection of the

Forms (and which I will analyse – together with the need for those scare quotes – in chapters five and six). Platonic myth, being a verbal genre that confesses outright its inadequacy to convey truth (see 246a3–6), is a medium especially suited to this message. Nonetheless, it is not the only possible medium; I have here, after all, been trying to say the same thing in unmythical prose. Yet I have been compelled to take my distance from any pat formulation of the philosopher's predicament. That we have the ability to produce such formulations is in fact part of the predicament. Saying this in unmythical prose is not saying it better; only differently. And just this, I believe, is Plato's point in 'doing philosophy' in this dialogue through the two distinct and strikingly juxtaposed verbal paths of myth and dialectic. He allows neither path to reach a satisfactory goal; rather, one leads only to the other. If we want Plato's view on the philosophy displayed but not analysed in the dialogue's second part we must turn to the first; but there his view is presented only mythically; but if we turn back to the second part's philosophic account of the first in the hope of something more explicit, we find an analysis of its rhetorical style only, not of its substance ... And so, beginning from a due appreciation of the difference between the fervour of the speeches and the sobriety of the subsequent conversation (not allowing ourselves to be overwhelmed, as Phaedrus is), we are led to see that this contour of difference does not straightforwardly divide the poetry of the dialogue from its philosophy; all the more so because the conversation does indeed seem philosophic and the speeches poetic.[38] It is just the kinship in limitation of these otherwise very different paths of discourse, myth and argument – at least when the philosopher confronts his own art – that is of such philosophic interest.

Apologia pro capitulo suo

In this chapter, then, I have argued that Plato's extraordinary attention to topography in the *Phaedrus* is his means of orienting readers towards the dialogue's central philosophic concerns and guiding their reaction to its singular structure; and in order to expound this argument I have found myself using these topographic passages in a similar fashion, to introduce my interpretation of the dialogue to my own readers – who may have been troubled throughout the reading of this chapter by the following worry. Granting my interpretation, is it not perhaps frivolous of Plato to orient his readers by the literary device of reporting how his characters admonish and orient themselves in response to their ambience? Is this not an unnecessarily obscure mode of exposition, which indeed, so far from orienting readers, runs the risk of having them lose their way? And is my own exposition not culpable in a similar fashion?

My reply to these questions can be brief, because it appeals to the argument of the immediately preceding section. If, as I contend, Plato conducts in this dialogue a competent philosophic analysis of philosophic competence itself, he would naturally want his own product to conform to the general criteria it establishes. In particular, given the beliefs he expresses in the text, he would not want to pretend that philosophic competence can be learnt from the explicit statements contained in a text; we must in addition appreciate the competence that the text exhibits. This we shall not do if we are tempted to read 'through' the text for its immediate message; hence Plato's general need to draw the workings of the text to our attention, and his particular device (not, of course, the only possible device) of using Socrates' and Phaedrus' orientation to their environment to orient the reader to this text.[39] Our path through the woods will live in our minds the more vividly if we have to peer a little to see where the next tree-blaze has been painted.

Furthermore, interpreters who believe there is justice in Plato's attack on the pretensions of prosaic paraphrase to capture any better (rather than just differently) what he expresses through myth should feel themselves under a certain obligation. They should acknowledge that their own exegetical paraphrase of Plato's literary work, for which they are wont to claim the modest virtue that it speaks with greater explicitness than its object, cannot in this case (and it is, to be sure, a special case) give through language any more explicit an account of what Plato himself is silent over; it can only try a different way.

I make this acknowledgment, and have emulated Plato's own strategy in the *Phaedrus* for my opening chapter, not out of methodological self-absorption, but as the right beginning to the task of interpreting Plato's philosophic beliefs, most especially those he presents in the *Phaedrus*. Have I thereby risked disorienting my reader? I think not; less, certainly, than Plato himself did; for this is after all a work of philosophic exegesis rather than philosophic fiction. If anything, my extended tour through the literary landscape of the dialogue takes the risk of demanding a measure of trust from the philosophically-minded reader. But perhaps the reader can agree: it is a noble risk.

CHAPTER TWO

FROM ARGUMENT TO EXAMPLE

A change of course

In the pattern of my exegesis so far I have been guided by Plato's sense of drama. He begins both acts of the *Phaedrus* by fixing the reader's attention on the scenic background, and I have begun my interpretation with an analysis of this topographic ploy. But the time is ripe for emancipation from Plato's script.

I have shown, in a preliminary way, how important to the overall concerns of the dialogue is the effect of sudden downshift from the high rhetorical gear of the speeches on love to the comparatively sedate account of the rhetorical art they exemplify. However, an exegesis of this effect is not obliged to duplicate its jolt on the reader (for all that it cannot wholly escape the expository problems which, I have argued, that jolt brings alive: this we have just seen, in the final section of the previous chapter). Indeed, the order of understanding will be better served if at this point I reverse Plato's order of exposition, and tackle the account of rhetoric in the second part of the dialogue before the love-poetry of the first; for, to anticipate, a grasp of Plato's criticisms of the rhetorical art practised and taught in his society turns out to be an essential step towards our appreciating the following three crucial points about the actual samples of rhetorical art which precede those criticisms. The first concerns the very content of the speeches on love: it will turn out that the character and the message of the fictional speakers of each of those speeches are partly determined by the contrast between the rhetorical and the philosophic approach to the art of speaking. The second has to do with Plato's reasons for framing in poetic and mythical terms the content of Socrates' second speech in particular: we will find that in the critique of rhetoric Plato lays as much emphasis on what formal argument cannot achieve as on what it can. And the third concerns his reasons for structuring the dialogue around the fall from those heights: namely, that we ought first to get the general flavour of the philosophic life (according to Plato) which emerges from the action of the dialogue's second part, in order then to appreciate the special place in that life, the exceptional zest, of philosophic love.

In this chapter and the one that follows it, then, I propose to home in on Socrates' critique of rhetoric, although always with an eye for its links with the dialogue's first part. To some extent I will join in what has become the fairly general consensus among scholars that Socrates' shift of focus from the content of the speeches to a formal analysis of the rhetorical art they exhibit is only apparent. He argues, after all, that if rhetoric is to qualify as an art it must become philosophical, and re-interprets the traditional task of rhetoric – persuasion – in the light of its role in the task of teaching, which has as essential conditions a concern for the truth of one's beliefs and for genuine communication with one's audience. But such concern also marks the non-manipulative relationship between the philosophic lovers of Socrates' mythic hymn (although, of course, this is not *all* that they are concerned about in their relationship); so that the turn to style in the second part of the dialogue doubles back, at least in part, to the matter of the first.[1]

Where I will part company from the majority of commentators, however, is in my argument that Plato is in addition giving due recognition to an adjustment between philosophy and rhetoric that works in the opposite direction. That is, he holds that if rhetoric must become philosophical, then philosophy must acknowledge the extent to which it is rhetoric. Plato develops this thought by acknowledging that discursive argument alone cannot furnish Socrates with adequate means of persuading the adherents of rhetoric to become philosophical, but that he must in addition have recourse to the persuasive power of example. I say that 'Plato' rather than 'Socrates' develops this thought because it makes itself felt only when the interpreter listens both to the content of what Socrates says and to the cicadas singing behind him; attends, that is, to the verbal practice that Socrates displays in the course of his critique as well as the practice he explicitly discusses.

But before we consider what Plato thinks his arguments cannot do, we had better look at what he thinks they can. So I will first analyse the opening stretch of Socrates' argumentation, at 259e–262c, which culminates in the demonstration that the orator, despite his protests to the contrary, earns his claim to artistic competence only by virtue of a grasp of truth.[2]

Teaching and practice

Phaedrus, we have seen, is in danger of prizing intellectual talk only for the external goods it brings him: a sense of broaching 'deep' topics, and with it a feeling of superiority; membership of an attractive club; and the company of clever conversationalists. These goods are external because each could as well be achieved by ambition alone as by exertion of the intellect. They are not, however, merely contingent or accidental to the intellectual life; for philosophers too will enjoy the company of their fellows and the elation of pushing thoughts to their limit, and enjoy these as goods that belong to their way of life (only, they will not pursue them as ends in themselves).[3] That is why, to the extent that Phaedrus achieves such goods, he might pass for one who strives also for those internal goods that come only from the genuine exercise of the intellect, not its appearance; might pass for such, at least, in the company of conversationalists less sensitive and less concerned for him as a person than is Socrates. (But let me not seem too harsh on Phaedrus. I will stress again that he is represented as being *at risk* of trivialising the philosophic life, rather than as a hopeless case. He 'vacillates' (257b5) between the genuine and the spurious path. Indeed, the action of the dialogue is built around the possibility of his rescue – see 257b and 261a.)

Of course, it is easier to specify which goods are external, and why, than to give an account of the internal goods; and this is the problem that Socrates confronts in his critique of rhetoric. But it is equally the problem that contemporary rhetoricians capitalised upon. They were well aware that, since the goal of rhetoric is simply to bring the audience to a decision (as Aristotle puts it at *Rhetoric* II 1, 1377b21), external considerations can make a course of action attractive not only as effectively as internal ones but also far more readily; after all, we tend to know what we like, and what we want to believe, even when we don't know why we like or believe it. Hence the classic maxim of the rhetorical art: learn what the crowd will accept; never mind whether what they accept deserves acceptance.

Socrates' critique of rhetoric begins from this maxim. He has proposed to investigate the conditions of good speaking and writing (259e1–2); and his opening point is that it is surely a condition of proper speaking that we know the truth of what we are to speak about (259e3–6). Here Phaedrus introduces the rhetorical maxim on the orators' behalf. As he has heard it, the budding orator need not learn what is truly just or good or noble but rather what seems so to his audience; for persuasion only requires knowledge of the latter, not of truth (259e7–260a4). Socrates proposes to consider this challenge, and his first move is to gloss and develop it. Wouldn't such a precept (he begins) license the orator to praise, say, asses for horses? Suppose neither of us know what a horse is, but I do know that you think a horse is the tame animal that has the biggest ears. I could expatiate on the advantages of the 'horse' in warfare and persuade you to acquire one for that purpose, all within the parameters of the rhetorical maxim, while in reality propounding a ridiculous panegyric of the ass. Worse, orators do not generally speak of trivial matters, the truth of which is known to all, as with the difference between horse and ass, but rather of the difference between good and bad, the truth of which is both more difficult to ascertain and crucially important to us (this in paraphrase of 260b1–d2).

Socrates' development of the rhetorical slogan implies that orators are indifferent to morality and that this is a bad thing for a society in which ethical decisions are arrived at under their influence. But he quickly adds that this is a simplification, and one which might seem to miss the point entirely. It is a fact, after all, that when it comes to persuading others, being right is not enough; moreover (at least if success alone is our criterion, regardless of whether or not it is achieved by *art*), it is not even necessary; what *is* necessary is rather to be canny about the opinions of those others, whether right or wrong. To that extent, the task of persuasion is indifferent to truth. But this does not entail that those whose task it is to persuade need also be indifferent to truth. Thus Socrates imagines a personified Rhetoric replying as follows: for preference, the orator will indeed attempt to acquire knowledge rather than acquiesce in public opinion,[4] and by all means let him persuade from knowledge, where there is knowledge; but what the art of rhetoric contributes is something other than knowledge: namely, the power to persuade (260d3–9).[5]

Rhetoric has been stung here into revealing something very important about herself: the fact that she has two distinct voices. One is the voice she uses when practising her art; the other, the voice she employs to teach it.

I can best explain the point by comparison with a modern equivalent (taken from one branch of the persuasive art): the tension – still very much a live one – between the teaching of advocacy and its practice. The modern professor of law teaches students who will mostly become not academics but practising advocates. The students learn that the value of argument in a court of law depends primarily on its power to persuade, and only secondarily on its truth (that is, truth matters only because it tends to be persuasive); whereas the professional goal of the scholar who taught them this is truth first, persuasiveness second (in so far as it is required for communicating truth).[6] Of course, the rhetoricians with whom Plato is concerned themselves practised the skill that they taught (and forensic rhetoric was only one of their domains of expertise); and as a result they do not distinguish the two voices of rhetoric as neatly as the modern context allows.[7] Nevertheless, in her attempt at disarming Socrates' insinuations, Rhetoric does distinguish practitioners from practice. By all means let *practitioners* pursue truth, she declares, provided that they recognise that for the successful *practice* of persuasion a knowledge of truth is not sufficient. She herself, after all, speaking from the viewpoint of the teacher of rhetoric rather than the rhetorical performer, is not afraid to commit herself to the truth of this very advice, and of the maxim that began this dispute.[8] But she simply doesn't say, in her careful formulation of her position here, either whether it is essential or whether it is inessential for the orator *as performing advocate* to have a grasp of truth; she will only say: it is not sufficient for him to do so, whereas it is certainly essential that he know what is acceptable to the audience and will persuade them. In effect, her pious appeal to the pursuit of truth as a goal of the 'off-duty' orator (whether as teacher or just as citizen) has enabled her to fudge the issue of what the orator is committed to as orator. And the aim of the argument Socrates next brings to bear is to compel her to concentrate on the sound of her performing voice, as it were, and acknowledge its implications outright.

Socrates' argument is in fact designed to defend his original claim, now taking Rhetoric's riposte into account, that there can be no art of speaking without a grasp of truth (259e4–6; rephrased at 260e5–7). Let me first recount the course of the argument. What the speaker in court or in a political assembly needs is the ability to bring about in his audience whatever decision he, or his client, desires. But in these public fora, Socrates points out, speakers must contend with opponents who desire a different decision. Attempts to make a certain course of action seem beneficial or just to the citizenry or jury will be countered by depictions of that same course of action as pernicious or unjust; and rhetoric must supply the requirements of both sides. Rhetorical skill amounts, then, to the ability to assimilate and dissimilate at need (and as such it is not to be confined to the forensic or political sphere; we can compare, for example, the skill at arguing for opposite conclusions which Zeno demonstrated in philosophic discussion)[9] – this in summary of 261a7–e4. Now, Rhetoric has told the orator he needs to know what *seems* true to his audience, but not whether it *is* true or not; deception, after all, can be as persuasive as truth. But – Socrates takes up the point (261e6 sq.) – no one can deceive effectively with a claim that does not even *seem* true; for only by keeping to small divergences from that for which you pass the claim off will your ploy slip by undetected (261e6–262a3). So you will need the ability to gauge similarities and dissimilarities with some accuracy, at least if you intend to deceive without yourself being deceived (262a5–7). But such an ability presupposes knowledge of truth; else you cannot judge how far your deceit diverges from it (262a9–11). So, when an audience is deceived – made to take as true what isn't in fact true – the deception clearly comes about through similarities (that is, glossing Socrates' words, the passing off of one thing – seeming truth – for another – truth).[10] But we agreed that skilful manipulation of similarities is not possible without knowledge of truth (262b5–8). Therefore, the essential rhetorical skill of assimilating and dissimilating at need before an audience *requires* (and does not merely for preference presuppose) a grasp of truth (and not simply of what is taken for truth); and it would not otherwise qualify as an art (262c1–3; again, the parenthetic remarks are glosses).

The function of this argument is to sharpen our attention to what exactly Rhetoric claims when she claims to be, and to teach, an art (*tekhnē*). What is it that sets the professional orator apart from his lay audience? Socrates' way of putting it is that the orator is able to deceive his audience without himself being deceived. This is not an unnecessarily pejorative characterisation, but follows from the preceding claim that orators assimilate and dissimilate opposites at will; which does not entail that they *must* deceive, for perhaps the truth will serve to persuade; but it does entail that even in such a case the truth would not serve their purpose *as truth*, but only as a proposition the audience will accept – one which happens to be true. For it is by shirking the constraint of truth that the orator acquires his unparalleled ability to assimilate and dissimilate. He is in every case aware that what seems true to his

43

audience is, precisely, what only *seems* true to them, while in reality it may or may not be true. They, on the other hand, since they must be convinced and come to a decision on the basis of the conflicting arguments they hear, are asked to believe one or other side: that is, take one or other story to be true.[11] There is an asymmetry, then, between the manipulating orator and his manipulated audience. He takes an interest in the truth of what he is urging only to the extent that it furthers his intention to persuade (for him, truth is subordinate to persuasion); whereas they will be persuaded only of what they take to be true (persuasion is, for them, subordinate to truth).[12] However, even if the orator's interest in truth is subordinate to his goal of persuasion, it is an interest in truth nonetheless. But Rhetoric had remained non-committal as to whether the orator need take *any* interest in truth in order to persuade. Socrates' argument fixes on the case in which the orator seems most careless of truth, namely when his manipulations amount to deception, the knowing persuasion of untruth; and he shows how even in that case the orator cannot claim artistic superiority simply on the basis of an awareness, absent in his audience, that what he says is untrue, but must actively pursue the truth that he obfuscates. He must do so because of the asymmetry between himself and his audience. They are interested not just in being persuaded, but in being persuaded of truth; they actively pursue true beliefs. This, after all, is the reason why an orator who is out to deceive must take care to escape their detection (262a2–3). But he will be in a much better position to do so if he understands what they are looking for; so he must take an active interest in their interest; and their interest is truth. Accordingly, a grasp of true beliefs is no less a condition of the best rhetorical method than it is the goal of the rhetorical audience; Rhetoric cannot remain non-committal on this point.

We might be inclined to object that the orator, in taking an interest in the interest of his audience, is after all taking an interest only in what seems true to them, even if their interest is truth. But this would be a mistake. To be sure, the orator is not interested in truth *for the same reasons* as his audience;

but truth is what he is interested in, to the extent that he is interested in it; for on this depends his ability to account for and anticipate what his audience *takes* to be true (262b5–8). His attachment to truth is vicarious; but it is a genuine attachment nonetheless.

Socrates' argument seems to me to be sound, so far as it goes.[13] But it does not go very far. For consider: Socrates has argued that the practising orator cannot remain non-committal but must be actively concerned to grasp truth; but the orator could consistently accept this conclusion and yet seek truth only for the purpose of persuasion and not as the philosopher seeks truth: for its own sake. Socrates has shown that knowledge of truth must be a goal of rhetoric, but not that it must be rhetoric's primary goal. He has not, then, yet produced the argument that could demonstrate to Phaedrus, as he would wish, that unless he follows the philosophic path he will not master the art of speaking (261a3–5).

What the next development in the discussion reveals is that he does not indeed have any knock-down argument for that conclusion, nor does Plato think he *can* have any. But this is not to say that Socrates is bereft of the means to persuade Phaedrus that he should accept it.

Lysias lambasted

The development to which I refer is this: Socrates turns from formal argument to example. He proposes to Phaedrus that they see how the argument just made applies to the rhetorical speeches delivered that day, beginning with the speech of Lysias. Do the speeches qualify as products of rhetorical artistry, according to the criterion of art that has been established (262c5–7)?

The immediate dramatic motivation for this proposal would be Phaedrus' less than total conviction over the conclusion of Socrates' formal argument (262c4: 'so it would appear', *kindyneuei*); at any rate, Phaedrus welcomes the move on the grounds that 'we've been speaking rather abstractly, without adequate examples' (262c8–9). But for the reader of the dialogue the passage will have more than a merely illustrative function. Plato here explicitly brings the speeches of the first act of his drama into relation with the project of its second act; and we can therefore expect the passage to illuminate the overall interpretation of the dialogue. However, the account that Socrates proceeds to give of Lysias' speech bears irony on its face; indeed, Phaedrus finally complains that he is 'mocking' the piece (264e3). And perhaps this is the reason why commentators have in fact not generally looked to these pages for help in interpreting the structure of the dialogue as a whole, despite their formal relevance to the issue. For not only does Socrates' proposal to analyse the speech merely for its rhetorical features function rather to pose than to resolve the interpretive problem; but the obvious irony with which he laces his analysis seems only to complicate the problem further. Yet it seems to me, by contrast, that this irony, and, more generally, the apparent inadequacy of Socrates' criticisms – as flagged for the reader by Phaedrus' exasperation – is an important clue to Plato's purpose, and repays close attention.[14]

Consider Socrates' opening line of criticism. He has Phaedrus read out once more the first lines of Lysias' speech, in which the speaker announces to the boy who is the object of his desire that, now that he has made his seductive pass at the boy and has admitted that he is not 'in love' with him in any conventional sense, he is going to persuade him that this admission, however unorthodox, is no reason for his proposal to be rejected (262d8–e4). At this point Socrates interrupts Phaedrus' reading in order to criticise what he has heard. He begins by drawing the following distinction. There are some things about which we do not dispute, but immediately understand the reference of their names – silver or iron, for example; but about other things, notably the just and the good, we engage in constant dispute and cannot seem to reach agreement (agreement on such matters would, after all, bring about a society in full harmony over its goals – a utopian vision) (262e5–263b2). Clearly, then, if the orator is to influence our decisions he will do better to fasten on that class of matters about which we have not already reached a firm agreement and which we can therefore be more readily persuaded to decide in alternative directions; and any orator worth his salt ought accordingly to know the one class from the other and be able to recognise to which class his particular topic belongs (263b3–c6). Now, love evidently belongs to the class of disputables; witness the speeches of alternate blame and praise that were earlier devoted to it. But did Lysias in his erotic speech begin by defining love, and organise the rest of his speech around this starting-point, channelling his audience's understanding thereby towards the sense of the topic that he himself preferred (263c7–e2)? Socrates has Phaedrus re-read the opening lines of the speech, and declares absent in them the index that he seeks (263e2–264a8); and this is the first strike against Lysias.

Stripped of the saving irony with which it is presented, this criticism would surely border on the crass. In order to unearth direct evidence of whether Lysias is alive to the nature of disputables and the opportunities they afford the orator for manipulating his audience's understanding, Socrates looks to the actual words spoken in the voice of the fictional 'non-lover' to see whether *that* character is operating in the appropriate way. But why should he expect to find such evidence on the surface? Why should an example of Lysias' rhetorical practice directly reveal whether he is aware of the conditions of successful rhetorical practice? Of course, it *might* have; an overt definition of love, had there been one, could justifiably have been taken to suggest (if not to prove) awareness in the author of the need to limit the possibly conflicting associations that his audience might make, as Socrates indicates (263d7–e2). But the absence of a definition is not by any means the proof of *unawareness* on Lysias' part that Socrates seems to make of it; for of course Lysias is under no obligation to make the fictional non-lover express his author's rhetorical sensitivity (in the way in which, by ironic contrast, the fictional speaker of Socrates' first speech on love does indeed overtly express his author's philosophic sensitivity, at 237b7–d3), but can choose to channel the attention of his audience by more de-

47

vious means, using the non-lover not as a mouthpiece but genuinely as a fiction. The apparent crassness of Socrates' complaint lies, then, in this: he treats Lysias and Lysias' non-lover as one and the same person.[15]

But what could be the point of such an appearance of insensitivity on his part? As a first step towards unravelling its import, consider more closely his criticism that Lysias failed to compel his audience to think of love in a single sense that he had predetermined. Socrates cites as evidence the fact that Lysias' speech offers no formal definition of love, in contrast to his own first speech. But the comparison is clothed in very obvious irony:

SOCRATES: But tell me this – I was in such throes of inspiration at the time, you see (*egō gar toi dia to enthousiastikon*), that I can't remember at all – did I define love at the beginning of my speech?

PHAEDRUS: Heavens, yes! It was a definition-and-a-half (*Nē Dia amēkhanōs ge hōs sphodra*).

SOCRATES: Oh my, how much more skilful in speechmaking you make the Nymphs of Achelous and Pan son of Hermes out to be than Lysias son of Cephalus! (263d1–6)

It is Phaedrus, not Socrates, who is impressed by the emphatic formality of the definition of love, as propounded by the wily Socratic non-lover at 237b7–c4. And this should stir our suspicion, for we know that Phaedrus tends to be overawed by intellectual externals. Socrates' response clearly implies that the comparison needs closer scrutiny, and his reference to the amnesia caused by poetic inspiration gives the clue to what Phaedrus in turn is forgetting:[16] namely, that however elaborate its definition of love, the views set out in Socrates' first speech were subsequently challenged and controverted in his second, the mythic hymn – a speech which notably lacks a formal definition of its topic.[17] Moreover, the controversion depended precisely on the disputable nature of madness, of which love is one type and the poetic inspiration that Socrates here conveniently recalls for us another (243e9–245a8); for in the earlier speech Socrates' non-lover argued from his definition of love as an irrational desire to the conclusion that love is wholly bad; but this turned out to be only half of the story. Socrates' irony thus warns readers of a potentially Phaedran error they might make in comparing his rhetorical effort with that of Lysias, and directs us not to give it the palm for merely formalistic reasons.

But there is a deeper irony at work here; because despite the warning in his words, Socrates goes ahead and treats Lysias' speech – to all appearances – in much the superficial way that we and Phaedrus are admonished to avoid in the case of his own speeches. On hearing the opening lines of Lysias' speech read out yet again, Socrates declares that they do not have what he is looking for; rather, the speaker 'begins from the end', from the point at which a lover would have completed his address to the boy, and 'swims on his back, in reverse' along the speech (266a4–7). The speech begins with what for a conventional lover would be a peroration: the declaration that his suit has been made. But such a declaration leaves everything distinctive about the non-lover's proposal still to be said: the justification, that is, of his declared break with convention. Socrates' disappointment with these lines for not saying anything positive about love does indeed register a deep criticism of Lysias' ethical enterprise in the speech; for we shall see in chapter four that despite its appearance of iconoclasm the speech is in fact wholly parasitic on the conventional (and, Socrates feels, inadequate) conception of love. But on the surface it is oddly insensitive. Socrates is apparently faulting the speech for inverting the thematic order that a conventional suitor would follow. But what more natural order could there be for a speech that openly takes its stand against orthodoxy? Socrates seems simply to refuse to accept Lysias' achievement on its own terms.[18]

What is more, when we take into consideration the unorthodox message of Lysias' non-lover, it becomes clear that Lysias is in fact doing exactly what Socrates demanded of the skilful rhetorician: namely, predetermining the sense in which his topic will be understood by the audience; but he is doing so in a technically more subtle way than Socrates is prepared to countenance. At the outset of the dialogue we were told to think of Lysias' speech as a subtle and fancy piece of work (by

49

Phaedrus, that is, at 227c7). And part of its special subtlety, I propose, is that it employs the very absence of a definition (the facet of technique to which our attention is here drawn) as a means of channelling the audience's understanding; moreover, this is a means especially appropriate to its topic. But in order to explain this point I must briefly give the reader an anticipatory sense of the interpretation of Lysias' speech that I defend in chapter four. The next paragraph or two should accordingly be treated as a parenthetic window on subsequent material.

The seductive bait held out by the non-lover before the boy whose favours he solicits is the prospect of a trouble-free erotic liaison. The normal condition of such a liaison is for the seducer to be 'in love'; but love, as both the boy and the non-lover know (for it is the common knowledge of their culture), is an ambiguous and disputable thing, with its good and its bad sides. For this reason it makes ideal fuel for opposing rhetorical arguments, which would throw one side into relief while keeping the other in shadow – as we saw Socrates and Phaedrus point out (at 263b3–c9). But here Lysias' speech shows its unusual subtlety. Rather than simply accent the advantages or disadvantages of love, the non-lover touts the very fact that love lends itself to this alternative accentuation as its greatest disadvantage. His argument is on a second order. And his solution is to opt out of love entirely. A liaison with the non-lover would not belong to the disputable class, along with the just and the good, but would have the solidity of iron and silver, and the commercial value of a firm contract. This is the contrast envisaged in the opening lines that Phaedrus twice reads out: lovers will blow hot and cold; I will be stable.

Thus, if all a boy knows of the man who approaches him is that he wishes to fill the role of lover, he does not even know whether the approach is a good or bad thing. But the non-lover teases him with the promise of escape to a simpler environment, in which social roles determine value; a fairy-tale land where kings are good because they are kings, not kings because they are good.[19] The boy will get all the good *effects* of love (or at least, of the traditional homosexual relationship among Athenian aristocrats) – primarily a matter of social patronage – but will not need to ponder whether love is intrinsically good or bad; for he will have the effects without the love itself.

Lysias' non-lover, then, does not attempt to conceal the full ambivalence of his topic by pleading, in typical rhetorical fashion, only one side of the case; on the contrary, he makes that ambivalence the basis of his plea (which, to be sure, does not escape one-sidedness in its turn – just this is what Socrates discovers in his attempt to imitate Lysias' strategy in his own speeches). But this tactic of argument has a singular consequence. Because the non-lover is, so to speak, laying his rhetorical cards on the table, his words not only exhibit Lysias' skill, but also inform us of Lysias' own ethos.

The premiss of the genre to which this exhibition-piece belongs would, of course, normally dictate just the opposite: that we judge the arguments as a display of persuasion and not question whether the author believes them true. Their truth, as such, would not be what matters, but rather what the orator can make seem true, however counter-intuitive. But in this particular speech, the premiss of its genre also governs its fictional content. The non-lover fastens on the boy's unease – an unease supported by social convention – over whether he should allow himself to be seduced, and more generally, whether love is a good or bad thing. Rather than settle this unease, the non-lover exaggerates its very unsettlability, in order to offer in its place a specious security: the business-like attainment of those desirable effects traditionally associated with the partnership of lovers. But this is just the counterpart in an erotic context of what we have seen the orator offer in the political and forensic context. The orator takes advantage of society's acknowledged difficulty in settling what is good and what is just, and offers society the seductive promise of a decision. His talent is for making the audience settle. But the price to be paid for security is opting out of the search for truth. As the non-lover provides only the effects of love, not love itself, so the orator claims to provide only the desirable

51

effects of truth, not truth itself; decisions, not understanding. (We begin to see, then, why Socrates – as if instinctively – treats Lysias and his fictional non-lover as one and the same character; for in this particular case Lysias' professional code put him in a deep sense at one with the ethos of his non-lover, for all that he seems to be pleading the cause of non-love merely for argument's sake.)

With this interpretation in hand, let us look again at the absence of formal definition in Lysias' speech. We can now see that it makes good sense to take this not simply as a nicety of style, still less as straight ineptitude, but as a mode of introduction that furthers the message of the speech.[20] The non-lover does indeed want to direct the boy's attention to a single particular aspect of love: to wit, the fact that love is insidiously plural in its aspects. Its every good feature has a concomitant bad, and the question of whether it is good or bad overall cannot be settled as such (and *that* is bad). What more artistic – or at least artful – expression of this point than deliberately to avoid a single definition of this unsettlable phenomenon and launch immediately into a disparate catalogue of the many evils that cancel each of its conventional benefits?

Before considering just why Plato should allow his Socrates to miss the subtlety of Lysias' speech, let me add a final consideration to show that the reader is indeed being alerted here to a certain naïveté in Socrates. For this we must turn to the second of Socrates' criticisms (so far I have examined only the first), at 264b3–e3. Socrates claims that one point followed another in the speech in a rather haphazard fashion, as if the writer were writing things down just as they came into his head; whereas surely, he insists, any speech should be organically constructed, like a living creature, with its full complement of members, each disposed in its proper place (264b3–c5)? Nevertheless, he warns Phaedrus that this is the opinion of an 'ignoramus' in these matters (*hōs mēden eidoti*, 264b6). And the warning is apposite; for once again the charge that Socrates lays at Lysias' door lacks sophistication. He fails to consider the possibility that Lysias might have intentionally composed the piece in such a way as to produce an effect of haphazardness and spontaneity; yet this was a familiar item in the average speechwriter's box of tricks.[21] Thus what Socrates cites in order to demonstrate the absence of art could in fact be the index of its presence.

More importantly for the case I wish to make, Plato himself is using the very technique of writing that he has Socrates ignore; and he alerts us to this fact through the caveat with which Socrates prefaces his proposal to turn to the love-speeches as concrete examples of rhetorical achievement (at 262c10–d6). Says Socrates: it is 'by some chance, apparently' (*kata tykhēn ge tina, hōs eoiken*, 262c10), that the speeches furnish us with just the examples we require; and for his part, at least, he will lay no claim to artistry in speaking, but attributes any art his speeches might reveal to the influence either of the local gods (whom he credited at the time of performance, see 238c9–d3) or perhaps (now that he has explained their origin) of the musical cicadas. But this appeal to serendipity on the part of a character in the dialogue cannot but prompt us to see that his author has loaded the dice; has written into the dialogue at this point an effect of spontaneous rather than predetermined sequence.[22] Consider the irony: Plato has Socrates ignore a similar effect in Lysias' speech and judge its structure unfavourably against a standard of organic unity; but with those very words he makes him a mouthpiece for Lysias' technique and for a dialogue which, taken as a whole, is deliberately disunified in its structure – more exactly, attains organic unity only on a second order, by jarring its readers and urging them thereby to reconstitute the living creature from its scattered limbs.

So I come to my postponed question: why it is that Plato allows Socrates to skip over the subtler aspects of Lysias' speech, while nevertheless alerting the reader to their presence. I understand him to be representing in the peculiar inadequacy of Socrates' criticism a refusal on Socrates' part of what the non-lover's strategy and thesis reveals on a deeper level about Lysias' professional ethos; a refusal, that is, of

Lysias' way of life. And Plato takes this path because he has reached the limits of argument here, and wishes to demonstrate that fact.

Recall that Socrates' opening argument in his critique of rhetoric established that the orator *must* be concerned to grasp truth, but not that truth must be his *primary* concern. But just this is what separates Socrates from Lysias, as heard through the fictional spokesmen under reconsideration in the present passage. For on the one hand, Lysias indeed knows the truth about love and justice and his other favoured topics to the extent that he recognises their disputable status in society,[23] but his reaction to this truth is simply to opt out of any attempt to seek an explanation and possible resolution of this disputability, and rather to take it for granted and manipulate only its effects; thereby setting up as his primary goal the attainment of decision – the appearance of resolution – at whatever cost. On the other hand, the progression of Socrates' inspired speeches revealed a philosopher who begins from this same perception of disputability, but attempts to settle the dispute by investigating the effects of love with a view to uncovering their explanation: how it comes about that love is seen as both good and bad. What Lysias knows is true so far as it goes, but it does not go nearly far enough. And the reason he stops short is that for him – for the rhetorician – knowledge is just a resource, whereas for Socrates – for the philosopher – it is the primary goal. On what basis, then, is Socrates to persuade the rhetorician that the philosophic approach is the most choiceworthy? Not, as before, on the basis of what he needs to know in order to succeed. What is now in question is not the setting of conditions, but a restructuring of priorities among those conditions. And my proposal is that Plato here dramatises the fact that, in this case, no *argument* for such restructuring can even get off the ground; for a condition of its getting off the ground is that the restructuring for which it argues would have already taken place. Put another way: in the dialectical situation that Socrates' critique has now reached, the only way for him to go on is not through formal argument but through a certain courage, as it were, in his own crassness; and this is what Plato wishes to express for, and perhaps inspire in, his readers.[24]

For despite the fact that Socrates seems not to do justice to Lysias' speech, at the deeper level he is not being crass after all, but, within his own terms as a philosopher, is simply right. By refusing even to consider the super-subtlety of Lysias' technique he exhibits not so much insensitivity to style as whole-hearted rejection of Lysias' way of life. After all, the type of rhetorical subtlety that Socrates elides but which Plato allows to show through for the reader offers only a specious appearance of profundity. Its sparkling deviousness invites further thought and could generate pages of commentary, but only after the fashion of a complex maze which, when penetrated, discloses an empty centre. Socrates slashes through the thickets of this maze with the machete of his averred unprofessionalism.

In my opening chapter I indicated the strangeness of the figure cut by Socrates as philosopher: not a professional, but, in his exigent and methodical pursuit of truth, a serious practitioner of a particular art; yet clinging to the spontaneity of the layman by eschewing the external marks of guild-membership. In that sense, Socrates' art is one that rejects a show of artistry.[25] And this enables him simply to refuse to engage Lysias' speech in professional terms that Lysias himself could accept. Instead, he pierces its ethical heartlessness: reacts to its skirting the whole issue of what love really is (its 'beginning from the end'), and to the parasitism that permits its haphazard construction (for it is because the organising centre of the speech is an entirely conventional conception of love – a fact not acknowledged by Lysias – that the items of indictment can be simply appended to this central understanding, in no particular order). And he will not treat it simply as a rhetorical exercise, distinguishing Lysias' professional talent as stylist from the ethos expressed by his fictional non-lover. It is as if the bitter experience of his attempt to emulate Lysias in his own non-lover's speech (which, again, I will consider in detail in chapter four) has taught him that the distinction is indeed fictional; that Lysias the professional does after all espouse the ethos of his non-lover and is not to be treated separately.

Thus, in one sense Socrates is misreading Lysias' text and failing to do it justice; for he is not appreciating those facets of the piece which its author would have most wanted to see appreciated. In this sense, what happens to Lysias' text at Socrates' hands is a perfect example of the danger to which Socrates himself will later describe all written texts as being susceptible: namely, that they circulate too freely among readers who fail to appreciate them, so that they are not self-sufficient but would benefit from some defensive explanation from their 'father' or author (275d9–e5).[26] But in another and more important sense, we are to understand, justice is indeed being done to the speech. Lysias is getting the treatment he deserves, because his speech expresses and instantiates a rhetorical ethos against which this dialogue as a whole will take a firm stand; and to enter into the spirit of its stylistic achievement as an appreciative reader is to risk becoming complicit in that ethos.[27]

But it is not a stand that can be taken through formal argument alone. Indeed, Plato is not concerned here – as commentators generally take him to be concerned – to deliver straight criticism of Lysias' speech, using Socrates as a medium. Rather, he is dramatising the very elusiveness of the common argumentative ground between Socrates and Lysias upon which direct criticism could be built. The nub of the problem is that any attempt the two might make at direct criticism of one another must be made from within their respective ways of life; so that their exchange is set against two backgrounds which refuse to mesh. Moreover, because these are backgrounds to their way of speaking, nothing that they *say* – in particular, no argument they might make – can of itself compel a shift from one background to the other. For suppose that Lysias interprets the tenor of Socrates' criticisms – his attempt to reform Lysias' ethos in a philosophic direction (an intention Socrates voices at 257b2–3) – as being directed at him only as a private individual; the attempt will have already failed. But suppose Socrates were patiently to explain to him that this segregation of private from professional understanding is one of the very things he wants him to shun; that would not be an argument but a request: please make my background yours. And Lysias in response, if he did not simply think Socrates thick-headed for not seeing that he himself is neither approving nor disapproving of the non-lover's ethos but only showing that he can make out a case for it, could only look inside himself to find either acceptance or rejection; there could be no arguing the toss.[28]

This exchange over backgrounds itself lies in the background to the ironic misunderstanding dramatised in this passage; Plato does not make it explicit, as I just have, but displays its foreground effects. But we were warned at the outset to listen for the cicadas; for Socrates gave them the credit, we saw, for the happy artistry of his speeches (at 262d2–6) – a happiness which served to sharpen our attention to Plato's own artistry. And if any further warning were needed, Phaedrus' impatient response to Socrates' contortions of modesty provides it: 'Whatever you say [i.e. attribute your speeches to whomever you please]', he quickly agrees, 'only, explain what you mean [i.e. explain the substance of your critique]' (262d7).[29] Phaedrus is eager to turn to concrete examples of rhetoric (as he told us at 262c8–9), and the last thing he wants is for Socrates to get caught up again in the local background and the cicadas' hum. But he is too eager for his own good. Once before, as we know, the cicadas were used to admonish him, and indirectly the reader, to attend to the background as well as the foreground, verbal performance as well as verbal product, in order to discriminate between verbal arts on a more than merely superficial basis. So here, in his eagerness to get to examples, he neglects the philosophic example that Socrates is providing in his very critique of Lysias. Knowing Phaedrus as we do, we will not hasten to emulate him, but will learn from his mistakes.

Granted, however, that Plato draws our attention to the background in this passage, it remains to be asked why he nevertheless opts to leave his message in the background rather than present it more explicitly. A similar question arose at the conclusion of my opening chapter, and my reply here will follow the path to which I have already oriented the reader.

The message that I have extracted from the text, summarily put, is the following: Lysias and his fellow rhetoricians are wrong to think that the substantial truth of a message can be bracketed from its persuasive force without substantial and pernicious effects on the way of life of those who concur in such a belief; refusal to concur distinguishes the philosopher from the rhetorician; but there are no explicit knock-down arguments to support this refusal; not, however, that there are no supporting considerations at all, on the contrary; but that when they have all been said, conviction may, without inconsistency, still be lacking.[30] That is why it matters *how* they have been said, and why Plato accepts and acts upon rhetoric's insistence that truth is impotent without persuasion. Plato is out to dissuade us from one way of life – the rhetorical – and turn us to another – the philosophical; and he recognises that, because this suasion aims at the whole cloth of a life, background as well as foreground, any number of explicit considerations risks failure unless he can make us feel their force directly: through example. To be truly persuaded, we must in addition be presented with examples of those opposing lives, and simply find them attractive or unattractive. This, I take it, is what motivates the painstaking care with which Plato makes vivid for his readers the characters – the lives – of Socrates, of Phaedrus, of a Lysias reduced to his manuscript: so that we can know who we will be.[31] Notice that in the course of the dialogue Plato does not in the least spurn explicit considerations; but he adds to them a dramatic dimension. And this is no *mere* addition, but, ultimately, equally essential for conviction.[32]

As before, in making Plato's 'message' explicit I am not saying it better, only differently. More important, the explicit formulation is clearly lacking a dimension by comparison with Plato's mode of presentation; for the reader who is convinced by my interpretation of the text has nevertheless not been *convinced by the text*: hit by its persuasive force. But this is not, of course, to deny the value of exegesis. Not only would such a denial be self-defeating on my part, but it would be especially foolhardy (an additional spin to the already dizzy irony of this section) when the text under interpretation shows Socrates turning from his own creations to interpret the creations of others. Of course our business is to discuss Plato's philosophy, and others' discussions of his philosophy; only, this must not supplant entirely our encounter with his text.

The philosopher judges himself

In the preceding section I have let the cicadas sing loud and long, dwelling on the performative and dramatic aspects of Socrates' carping at Lysias. I have done so because Plato seems to me here to provide a philosophically important caveat on the limitations of the explicit argument in progress – a caveat ignored by most scholars. But we are not done with the cicadas yet. When Socrates subsequently turns from criticism of Lysias to discuss his own speeches as examples of rhetoric, what he exhibits through his verbal behaviour does not cease to contribute a significant commentary on what he actually says; for in looking back on his rhetorical efforts, he misremembers and rearranges their pattern and content to a remarkable degree. All commentators are struck by this; but differ in their assessment of its importance. I will argue that, by tinkering with Socrates' memory, Plato demonstrates that the leisurely perspective of analytic hindsight is just that: a perspective; and different from the perspective from which Socrates delivered the poetry he now misleadingly encapsulates. This directs the reader not to be misled by the apparent achievement of that encapsulation: namely, that it seems to synthesise at a higher level and in a definitive way the import of the poetry; rather, both perspectives are limited, in their different ways, and one must supplement the other. In the course of Socrates' self-examination, then, a seed sown by his critique of Lysias comes to fruit: we come to see how importantly the reappearance of the love-speeches as rhetorical examples bears on the interpretation of the overall structure of the dialogue (as promised at the outset of the previous section).

First, the catalogue of Socrates' lapses. He asserts that in his account of the four types of divine madness (that is, at the outset of his 'mythic hymn') he assigned each to the patronage of a divine authority (265b2–5); but in fact only one of the four authorities – the Muses – was actually mentioned at the time (at 245a1).[33] More importantly, he makes it seem that in his two speeches he considered the phenomenon of love under a single rubric: that of madness; and distinguished in his first speech a malignant type – the merely human madness of infatuation – and in his second a benign type – the 'divine' madness of philosophic love; and that the speeches gained their clarity by properly defining and unifying the domain within which to make that distinction (265a6–b1; 265d5–266b2). Yet his actual procedure was far more disorderly, not to say stressful, than this would suggest. In his formal definition of love in the first speech he assimilated it to irrational desire, which he castigated as wholly bad; and when in his second speech he fastened on the equation of love with madness made in the first (not, however, made in the formal definition but only casually towards the end, at 241a4), and out of this equation spins a tale of good madness to set against the bad (see 244a3–8), this is an achievement – a recognition, and one quite at odds with the view from the earlier speech.

With the complacency of hindsight, Socrates can give his non-lover credit for condemning the bad side of love 'very justly' (266a6); but while in the thick of rhetorical delivery, Socrates was still winning through to the gracious distance of this perspective – and having a hard time of it. As he brought his first speech to a close he became disgusted with himself, leaping to his feet and attempting to quit the scene (241de); and when finally persuaded to resume, opened his mythic hymn not in a spirit of compromise, as if with the non-lover's voice he had all along been hurling righteous invective at a target that richly deserved it, but in outright rejection of his earlier speech ('it is not true...' 244a3) for having been spoken from a crabbed and insensitive point of view.[34]

60

Socrates explains his rejection at 244a5–8: *if* madness were simply bad, then what was said would have been well said; *but* the greatest of our goods come through madness – divine madness, that is. The clear implication of these words is that, *pace* Socrates' retrospective opinion, what was said in his first speech was *not* well said. With hindsight, he sees how it might have been said, and soothes his outraged spirit by rearranging the past; but at the time, as we shall see in chapter four, he could not hide from himself how horribly well he had thought himself under the non-lover's skin. In short, Socrates did not, as he imagines himself to have done, first label the bottle and then analyse its ingredients; rather, labelling and analysis were achieved together.[35]

The combined effect of Socrates' misrememberings, then, is to make his procedure of discovery seem far smoother and more systematic than it actually was.[36] And this, I propose, is how Socrates' retrospective viewpoint shows its limitations: that is, in assessing how he scaled this peak, he suppresses awareness of how the climb affected him. But we might ask: why call that a *limitation*? Isn't Socrates leaving out only what is irrelevant to the method of discovery, at least as a method? On the contrary, he is leaving out – better, leaving in the background – the very thing that sets him apart as a philosopher from the rhetoricians. For if we take the procedure, praised by Socrates, of distinguishing types within a delimited domain (which is, of course, the method of 'Collection and Division' prominent in later dialogues such as the *Sophist* and *Politicus*), and consider it purely as a formal technique, it does not seem so very different from the skill of assimilation and dissimilation at which, as we saw Socrates determine, the orator must excel.[37] After all, Socrates had directly compared forensic and political oratory, in respect of this skill, to Zeno's philosophical dialectic (at 261d); and when he turned to the critique of the speeches on love declared that '*both* speeches' (that is, Lysias' speech and his own two considered as a single effort) were paradigms of how 'one who knows the truth might mislead his listeners' (262d1–2).[38]

Admittedly, Socrates emphasises, as contemporary rhetoricians did not, that the assimilations and dissimilations of the philosopher will be guided by a rule of cutting only along the 'natural joints' (265e1–2): that is, he intends to discover truths about the referent of those assimilations and dissimilations; whereas the rhetorician, as we have seen, is bound by such a rule only in his role as teacher and investigator (for Lysias will need to cut along the joints in cleaving disputed from undisputed terms; and in general he who knows the truth will best deceive), but is conspicuously free from its constraints once he mounts the rhetorical podium. However, it is one thing for Socrates to impose this restriction on the philosopher's collections and divisions, and quite another for him to capture in the quality of the formal operations that constitute the technique (the actual collecting and dividing) a specifiable mechanism that could direct the practitioner securely towards the 'natural' cleavages in the world. The difference between the positions of orator and of philosopher is the difference between knowing truth and seeking truth; between truth as intermediate and as primary goal. And this difference is not to be accounted for by the formal mechanism of collection and division, but by the structure of goals – the structure of life – within which the method is applied. For the advocate too could make use of entirely truthful assimilations and dissimilations, if this gave him the desired result in court; but then, he would indeed only be *using* the technique of dialectic. But what Socrates wants to say to him is: don't use it; live it. And this he cannot enjoin upon him through the formalities of method alone.[39] That is why it is so important not to forget how disturbing Socrates found his rhetorical adventure; for this reveals, in a way the formal account does not, an essential part of what makes him special as philosopher.

The feature of that episode which he first chooses to emphasise for Phaedrus is that his speeches contradicted one another (265a2–3). This, he says, is worth the attention of anyone interested in rhetoric (264e7–8). We recall that he had earlier stressed how orators both political and forensic spent their time arguing against each other towards opposite conclusions (at 261c4–d5). However, any orator on any one occasion is expected to argue for only one side of a case – unless, as with Antiphon's *Tetralogies*, he is displaying in a single performance that very ability to argue opposing sides of a case on different occasions. Socrates, by contrast, was moved to speak on both sides of his issue not as an exercise in moulding argument but because he saw the limitations of his first stab at the topic and was concerned about what this revealed of his person.[40] And as we have seen, no formal argument or specification of method is sufficient in itself to instil such concern; we must look also to Socrates' example.[41]

Plato slips in a strong enough reminder at this point of the example Socrates actually did set. Here is Phaedrus, responding to Socrates' emphasis on how his speeches contradicted one another: 'And most manfully so, too' (*kai mal'andrikōs*, 265a4); a comment Socrates reports mishearing in striking fashion: 'I thought you said "madly so" (*manikōs*), which would have been the truth. That was what I was looking for, you know. Didn't we say, after all, that love was a kind of madness?' (265a5–7). Now, clearly it is not compulsory for speeches equating love with madness to be themselves spoken madly. Why, then, is this what Socrates was looking for? Because, just as Lysias, despite himself, allowed his own ethos to show through the proposals of his non-lover, and so laid himself open to criticism, so the ethical backdrop to which Socrates' disturbed behaviour as orator gives us access is as important as, and (we are about to see) intrinsically connected with, the content of his rhetorical efforts.

Yet Plato makes this point only through an apparently casual mishearing, an eddy in the prevailing current of communication at this point; while what prevails, I have shown, is that Socrates smoothes over and minimises the troubled course of his advance towards the present reconciliation of his two speeches. Moreover, he goes so far as to assert that all aspects of those speeches other than their exemplification of the method of collection and division that marks dialectic seem to him 'really to have been played as a game' (*tōi onti paidiai pepaisthai*, 265c8–d1); and that even this aspect accrued to them 'by chance' (*ek tykhēs*, 265c9). If, as I have claimed, Plato thought it equally important for us to consider how Socrates felt about the content of his speeches as to extract a formal method from their structure, at least if we are correctly to assess what makes Socrates a 'dialectician' (266c1) rather than a rhetorician, why would he choose to express this thought through the devious means of suppressing it in Socrates? It would be too easy for me to reply that to suppress a thought in this way is an effective strategy for awakening it in the attentive reader. Not only would we still need to ask, granted the effectiveness of the strategy, why Plato should select *this* one among the many possible effective strategies at *this* juncture; but also, and more importantly, such a reply would oversimplify the point Plato is making about Socrates as dialectician. It would do so by throwing the weight of attention entirely behind the thought suppressed, at the expense of the thinking that has suppressed it. For let this be clear: I am not suggesting that Plato means the simple opposite of what he has Socrates say here – that, *pace* Socrates, the mythical hymn is the serious part of the dialogue, while the formalities of collection and division are just a game. Plato's point (I am saying) is this: that the mythical hymn (and Socrates' progress towards it) is an equally serious part of the dialogue, and equally important for what it reveals about Socrates as dialectician; but that, precisely because of this, because of what we learn about him as dialectician from the first part of the dialogue, we can understand why he now suppresses and devalues (why Plato makes him suppress and devalue) that earlier achievement.

To explain. Socrates' progress through his speeches has allowed us to appreciate the kind of person he is: one whose primary goal is truth. For this very reason he is also the kind of person to minimise in retrospect the personal details of his progress towards truth: because what matters *for him*, as a truth-lover, is that he recount the truth to which his speeches attained; and if that truth will be the more perspicuously presented by tidying up somewhat the account of its attainment, then so be it. Similarly, he is the kind of person who will hedge his bets as to whether the imaginative mythmaking in which he indulged himself in his second speech can attain truth at all: 'Perhaps we touched on some truth, but maybe too we wandered off in the wrong direction; at any rate, we concocted a not entirely unconvincing speech' (265b6–8). Notice the implication of these words: even when mythmaking, Socrates was actively seeking truth, not bracketing it as irrelevant; otherwise he would not describe failure to hit upon it as a move in the wrong direction. Only, his thought had reached limits where myth (or its equivalent) became indispensable.[42] And so he retrenches and insists rather on the seriousness of satisfying in a methodical way the urge to live a life with truth as its primary goal: an urge that the mythic hymn seriously exhibited in spirit, but, because of the nature of its topic, could not seriously satisfy.

However, in seeing why this is what matters for *Socrates*, we also see that it cannot be all that matters for *us*. We cannot, as Socrates does, bracket what we are learning about dialectic from what we have learnt about Socrates, personally, as dialectician; if only because we have understood him well enough to see why, as dialectician, he wants to bracket off his personality and imaginative flights. The formalities of the methodology to which Socrates retrenches distinguish him satisfactorily from the rhetorician only when considered against the background of Socrates' behaviour and sentiments in the speeches which he sees as its instantiation. And we must consider that background explicitly, and not simply speak *from* it as Socrates does; for we have set him up as the exemplar of a method and a life in which we are at most apprentices, if not disinterested observers (we would not otherwise need to read this dialogue). And so we reach the point where Socrates shows us as much about dialectic as he tells us – not only by his demeanour while an orator but equally by his current soft-pedalling of that demeanour – and shows us in particular that there is more to being a dialectician than simply sticking within the specifications he can explicitly describe.

With this recognition, we can more properly evaluate Socrates' revaluation of his mythic hymn. After all, if the content of his revaluation is a description of how dialecticians will proceed, the content of his mythic hymn amounts, in its own way, to nothing less – indeed, to rather more; at least in the sense that the philosophic lovers live an especially blessed and exemplary life even by comparison with other dialecticians. Plato plainly marks the connection between dialecticians and philosophic lovers in Socrates' final words on this topic:

'I am myself a lover (*erastēs*) of these divisions and collections, Phaedrus ... and if there is someone else whom I consider capable of looking into the one and the many in nature, I "pursue him, as if following in the footsteps of a god" [a Homericism]. And people with this ability I call – and god knows whether this is the right way to address them or not, but up till now I have been calling them "dialecticians".' (266b3–c1)

Socrates' dismissal of his mythic hymn as a game here coexists with a description of his approach to the serious business of dialectic, which nevertheless through its tone and terms links this approach directly with that of the philosophic lovers as described in the mythic hymn – where lovers pursue each other, lit up with the image of their god (252c3–253c6); an illumination that comes because they can see the one in the many, the many in the one (249b3–250c6); and where the narrator's language acknowledges its merely human limitations (246a3–6; 247c2–6).

Socrates' confession thus declares but does not analyse what his devaluation of the mythic hymn implies cannot be properly analysed: the love of proper analysis that is a background condition of the philosophic life. For this reason, his explicit analysis (in the description of Collection and Division) and labelling ('I call them "dialecticians"') of his very method of analysis and labelling is indeed a genuine and proper philosophic advance over the myth that it devalues; and yet – and this for the same reason – the myth is all of a piece with that explicit analysis. For the art of philosophy, as we saw in the previous chapter, has the peculiar quality of instantiating itself even as it examines its own conditions of possibility. Accordingly, when in his mythic hymn Socrates attempts to examine explicitly that part of the background to philosophy which philosophy itself rules beyond the domain of properly philosophical argument, what are we to make of his action? Is he doing philosophy? No: because his own philosophic canon rules this out. Yes: because to enquire generally into conditions of possibility, to attempt that extra step into the background, is the mark of the philosopher.

Looking again at Socrates' assertion that his mythic hymn was just a game, there seems to be nothing for it but to say – as Plato, by artfully framing that assertion,[43] also says – yes, the myth is serious, and yes, it is a game. For only by virtue of that love of truth that pushes up to and beyond the limits of argument – the love that led Socrates into myth, and to which only something as extreme as myth can testify – has Socrates earned the right to admonish himself as philosopher for overstepping those limits. Both ways – the bold leap, and the careful monitoring of the harmless fall – are necessary for the fullness of a philosophic life; and only together are they sufficient.

CHAPTER THREE

THE CRITIQUE OF PURE RHETORIC

Back to the orators

In the preceding chapter, I began considering Lysias' speech as a sample of rhetoric but ended by looking on Socrates' speeches as a swatch of philosophic rather than rhetorical method, and setting it against the whole cloth of the dialogue rather than of its critique of rhetoric alone. In this I followed in Socrates' footsteps. But this course strikes Phaedrus as beginning to drift. He agrees that Socrates has given a fair account of dialectical method; but is unsure of what has happened to the account of rhetorical method which they originally set out to provide (266c7–9). He is right, in a sense, to bring Socrates up short in this way; for Socrates has apparently digressed from examining the love-speeches purely for their rhetorical qualities in order to dwell on a dialectical technique that his own speeches exemplified, and even that only 'by chance' (265c9).[1]

But what Phaedrus misses is, as it were, the drift of Socrates' drifting; for Socrates has been illustrating the fact that whereas the rhetorician has two voices – that of teacher, and that of practitioner – the philosopher has only one. In other words: despite the stylistic disparity of his poetic speeches on love and their subsequent appearance as examples in his sober account of dialectical method, Socrates speaks on both occasions with a view to assessing what is important for the proper conduct of the philosophic life. His speeches and his analysis are not simply related as practice to theory (as would be the case with a rhetorician's analysis of his own speeches); rather, both are philosophic performances, marked by the same investigative intent. This is a consequence of the fact that to investigate philosophy is also to 'do' philosophy. But this fact has dangerous ramifications:

above all, the risk that within philosophy the question of its own status should become so dominant as to drain of their meaningfulness all other aspects of the philosophic life. Plato peers over the lip of this chasm when he has Socrates dismiss his speeches as a 'game' except to the extent that they illustrate dialectical method. But he does not linger at the brink; rather, he brings us back to safer territory by the expedient of Phaedrus' puzzlement. Phaedrus has not felt any philosophic giddiness at Socrates' move towards the edge; he simply thinks the discussion has lost direction. And so we return to his level for the second stretch of Socrates' argument against rhetoric.[2]

Before turning to that argument, however, let us take stock of the progress of Socrates' critique so far. He has already shown that orators are not entitled, as they suppose, to fudge about whether the practice of rhetoric (as well as the teaching of it) requires a grasp of truth, but must commit themselves, just as practising orators, to acquiring such a grasp. However, Socrates had as yet said nothing as to how they were to set about this task. In his subsequent analysis of the speeches on love, he has isolated the methodology by which he himself is 'able to speak and think' (266b4) – his own art of speaking; but at the same time limitations have emerged. His first argument cannot compel orators (on pain of inconsistency) to commit themselves to pursuing truth as their primary rather than intermediate goal, and for that reason even were Socrates to show – as he subsequently claims to do – that the best method for orators to use in reaching this goal (whatever its place in their structure of goals) is philosophic (dialectical) method, he will not have shown that they must share the structure of life characteristic of the philosopher, but only that they must use philosophy. In his second and final argument, now to be considered, Socrates works within this fundamental limitation, as Plato (I have argued) has acknowledged he must. He examines the content of what is currently taught as the art of speaking; argues that, given the condition that his previous argument imposed on any genuine art of speaking, current teaching is grossly inadequate to the art that should be taught; and proposes replacing that teaching with a theoretical approach clearly indebted to the ethos of dialectic. And his argument is now more general in its scope; it appeals for its effect to the necessary and sufficient conditions of any art, not simply of the art of speaking. So much by way of preface; let us look now at the steps by which Socrates makes out his case.

Wise words from Pericles

In response to Phaedrus' admonition that he has lost touch with their original topic, Socrates agrees to consider in more detail what rhetoricians actually tout before their students as the art of speaking. Phaedrus knows where to turn: to the contents of the handbooks of rhetoric written by the best-known practitioners of the art (266d5–6) – books which indeed bore their pretensions on their face, being known simply as 'Arts'.[3] (And in Phaedrus' refusal to neglect them we witness the success of their self-advertisement.) Socrates begins by listing the topics broached in these manuals by a broad array of writers (including several whom we know primarily as 'sophists' rather than 'rhetoricians': a fact discussed in my opening chapter). Their neologisms, on his lips, make a sardonic and dismissive music – as is generally felt by commentators on this passage.[4] Indeed, it may seem that he is unfairly dismissive; after all, his catalogue refers not only to stylistic tropes (such as Polus' 'Repetitive Mode', *diplasiologia*, 267c1) and the canonical sections of a speech (prologue, epilogue, narration, etc.) – matters which a Socrates might well consider to be of secondary importance[5] – but also (at 266e–267a) to types of (forensic) argument and proof which have a *prima facie* claim to serious philosophic attention.[6] But I need not confront the historical problem of whether or not Plato is giving the opposition a fair hearing; because his hostility here is directed not so much at the particular items, techniques of argument or otherwise, that Socrates ticks off, but at the very fact that Socrates is able to tick them off in this fashion. What he objects to is this: that since these rhetorical 'Arts' are no more

70

than collections of useful precepts and devices, a student could learn how they are useful without learning how to use them. And the point does not hang on the style of the actual manuals – whether they were in fact the kind of disconnected miscellany that Socrates' presentation here suggests – but simply on their nature as *books*: that is, their consisting of strings of explicit statements. It is time now to weigh this objection.

Indeed, we have in a sense been weighing it all along: judging Socrates' and Phaedrus' behaviour against various canons of art, of professionalism, of sensitivity – sniffing for the authentic. But only now, at 268a–269c, does artistic humbug become the explicit target of discussion. I have once already brought this passage to the fore, in my chapter of orientation; where it served as a template for Socrates' and Phaedrus' dealings with the environment. Socrates secures Phaedrus' ready agreement that practitioners of any art, to be competent, must know more than just recipes and rules. It is not enough for the doctor to know which drugs have which effects, nor for the tragedian to know what form of words will be the fuse for which dramatic firework. They must also recognise what is appropriate to the particular situation; and this recognition comes only if they have a sense of the whole – of the system which locates the particular situation and gives purpose to the rules and recipes. Similarly, what the budding orator finds in rhetorical handbooks are at most necessary but not sufficient conditions for competence in the art: 'necessary preliminaries' (269b7–8), tools for an art that he will not genuinely possess until he can build a whole speech with them and make it fly.

Having come back to give this part of the discussion a more careful hearing, I want first to cock a suspicious ear at the readiness and loquacity with which Phaedrus endorses Socrates' point. It is in fact Phaedrus who first makes the point, describing with boisterous confidence and at some length how lamentably the impostors whom Socrates proposes for his consideration – slaves to medical or poetic formula – would fall short of artistic competence (268a8–d5).[7]

The difference between the quacks and the professionals strikes him as obvious: 'What else could [real doctors] reply but ...' (268b6), he begins, as he springs to their defence and points out their distinctive sense of what is appropriate. And he becomes quite indignant when Socrates in response attributes to the impostor the claim that, although he himself does not possess this sense of the appropriate, his pupils will be able to pick it up of their own accord from studying the facts and precepts on offer. 'The man is mad' (268c2), Phaedrus imagines the doctors replying; and a Sophocles or Euripides he thinks would 'deride' (268d3) the corresponding fraud in the writing of tragedy.

At this point Socrates intervenes. Surely, he admonishes, such poets would not descend to blunt insult? They are cultured men, after all; and such people would rebuke even the most inartistic challenger in a gentle and measured way. So too, any really fine public speaker – Pericles, say – if he heard us lustily berating the rhetoricians for their tricks and tropes, would find cause to rebuke us in turn; not because our point is wrong, but because we are not making it in an appropriate manner (this in summary of 268d6–269c5). Socrates' corrective to the tone of Phaedrus' outburst is long and elaborate.[8] And I take it that Plato is thereby directing his readers to pay more than passing attention here to what might otherwise seem an unexceptionable but casual point: that artists – by that token, persons of culture – are likely to discuss their art, as they would discuss anything else, in an urbane manner.[9] For there is a significant lesson to be derived from Socrates' exchange with Phaedrus here. Although the point Phaedrus makes is correct and important (Socrates does not alter its substance in the reformulation that he puts in Pericles' mouth) it nevertheless approaches the truistic – at least, if one brandishes and bandies it about as Phaedrus does.

This, I propose, is Plato's reason for pressing the point through a person of Phaedrus' intellectual stature. There has to be a difference between the artist and the hack, and it has to be along these lines. If Phaedrus can give voice to this much, fine; but let him not get up on his high horse about it; not

WISE WORDS FROM PERICLES

because the achievement is paltry, but because he should want it to serve as a spur to, not a block on, further thinking. Indeed, to take the other approach is to join those who sparked his indignation in the first place. Phaedrus' appeal to the artist's sense of the appropriate shows every sign – this I take to be the nub of Socrates' admonishment – of ossifying into just that formulaic pose which he derides in the hack. Secure behind his slogans, Phaedrus sees no need to communicate his case to those who disagree, but dismisses them from rational discussion altogether.[10] Here he neglects an important feature of expressive arts such as poetry and rhetoric: that in so far as they are arts of communication, they should inspire in their practitioners an especial regard for communicating their art – teaching it. The point is informal in the case of poetry, since Socrates is hardly suggesting that the art of tragic poetry must be taught in iambics.[11] But its bite is more exact for rhetoric, which, considered simply as the art of persuasive speaking, must always be exhibited as well as spoken of by the successful teacher of the subject. Truth must be communicated if it is to be learnt; teaching is rhetoric too.[12] This an orator worth his salt will not forget, even when instructing the benighted.

But Phaedrus is not only ignoring this fact; he is closing his eyes to the implication of his own indignant claim that what the doctor or poet or artist in general knows is more than just a list of explicit rules: to wit, that if the artist is to communicate what he knows, he must, at least to some extent, teach by his own example. Accordingly, Pericles' suggestion to Socrates and Phaedrus that they moderate the tone of their rebuke is to be understood as stemming not solely from a habitual concern for the persuasive power of words but also from the awareness that such adaptability is itself a lesson in the art that lies beyond the 'necessary preliminaries'.[13] Setting an example in this way is not by any means the whole of teaching; but it is a crucial factor. What the pseudo-teachers have to *say* for themselves, after all – that if the apprentice will begin by learning explicit rules, the art will follow – is uncomfortably close to what a genuine master might *say*.

73

That is, the master too, if he is worthy of the title, will admit that he has no magic formula to transmute his students willy-nilly into accomplished practitioners (actually, he will also have more to say than the impostors in the way of explicit theory, as Socrates is about to indicate, at 270b1 sq.; nevertheless, the same reservation will apply even to this superior body of knowledge). But he would make this admission in a very different spirit: the spirit of a Pericles or 'mellifluous Adrastus' (269a5).

In other words, whereas the quacks, as Socrates presents them, cheerfully confess to lacking for themselves a sense of what is appropriate to each case, but insist that the student will pick this up, if he will only apply himself to conning his books (268b9–c1), the master knows that, although the art indeed has its beginning in the learning of explicit facts and formulas, it will not follow on from this just automatically; in particular, it will not follow if the learning is done in a spirit of imposture, but only if pursued (how else to say it?) appropriately: that is (at least in part), with the example of the master in mind. The quacks can see this much: that although there is more to an art than what can be made explicit in the form of rules, the art does get itself taught, somehow, through rules. Where they go wrong is in concluding that the something more can therefore be dismissed from consideration. True competence, by contrast, comes from never losing sight of the background: as well of what one's teachers cannot say, as of what they can.

Symptoms and causes

Suitably chastened, Phaedrus grants that Socrates' criticism of the current method of rhetorical instruction is justified, and asks how he would reform it (269c6–d1). In reply, Socrates prefaces his suggestions for reform with an interesting concession to contemporary rhetoric. To become an accomplished orator, he comfortingly begins, is 'like anything else' (269d3). It is reasonable to suppose that three things are required: 'natural talent' (*physis*), 'knowledge' (*epistēmē*), and 'practice' (*meletē*): lacking any one of which, you can hardly succeed (269d2–6). This trinity of requirements was in fact a commonplace among rhetoricians (as is indicated by the rather *blasé* manner in which Socrates introduces it).[14] But the concession is immediately followed by a challenge: 'However, in so far as it is a matter of art (*hoson de autou tekhnē*), the path that Lysias and Thrasymachus take does not seem to me to be the enlightened method' (269d6–8).

In turning to this 'matter of art', it is not as if Socrates simply accepts as obvious the need for 'talent' and 'practice' and proceeds to inject philosophy into rhetoric under the traditional head of 'knowledge' — although that is how his procedure is often interpreted.[15] Rather, what Socrates is objecting to is exactly this willingness on the part of contemporary rhetoricians to take for granted the requirements of talent and practice and to concentrate on those elements of style, presentation, and argumentative strategy that can most readily be formalised. And his objection is not simply that these formalities are jejune, but also that (as I am about to show) the rhetoricians have not appreciated how closely the explicit body of theory on which their activity is based must be integrated with the requirements of talent and practice — how the actual content of the theory should reflect the fact that knowledge of theory alone does not make an artist — if the activity is to qualify as a genuine art and not either a mere knack or a fraud. Socrates is about to propose a genuine integration of the trio of requirements, and not just pay lip-service to this as an ideal. That is why he makes free with the rhetorical commonplace: because his achievement will not be along the lines of making theoretically explicit what the orators through laziness or stolidity might have ignored; on the contrary, he gives fuller value than they — despite what they tout as their maxim — to what is not susceptible of explicit formulation, and as a result wins through to a more sophisticated formulation of what can indeed be made explicit. Thus he is, in a sense, saying the same thing as the orators; but in the sense in which we saw when considering Pericles' admonition that what the true artist can say might not be so different from what the impostors say. The orators say it, but Socrates says it and means it, and is about to show that he means it – to draw the consequences for theory.[16]

Those consequences can be summarised as follows. We have agreed (at 261a7) that rhetoric, being the art of persuasive speaking, targets its speeches on the hearts and minds of its audience; for it is there that persuasion takes effect (the backward reference is made explicit at 271c10). By analogy with the methods of the medical art (an analogy we have already pressed at 268a8–c4), practitioners of which target their drugs and remedies on the bodies of their patients (270b4–10), rhetoricians should determine, first, the nature of their target – the human soul – and analyse it into its parts, if it is complex rather than simple; second, not only should they examine it as a whole with its own parts, but they should also treat it as itself part of a larger whole or system, and ask how and what it affects and how and by what it is in turn affected (270c1–d8; 271a1–12) (this is my understanding of Socrates' insistence that the nature of the soul cannot be fully grasped 'without the nature of the whole', *aneu tēs tou holou physeōs*, 270c2; that is, I take 'the whole' here in the sense in which Phaedrus used it at 268d5 and Pericles at 269c3: that of 'overall system').[17] Moreover, just as the doctor must know his pharmacopoeia and its effects on the body, so there is a third requirement for the art of rhetoric: that the orator classify the kinds of speech and know which kinds have what effect on which type of soul (271b1–5). (This, however, is really an extension of the second requirement – that the orator know what the soul affects and is affected by – made specific to the effects of speech; for which reason, presumably, the corresponding requirement for medicine is not expressly mentioned in the general description of method at 270c10–d7. The core of the method is in its first two requirements.) Finally, we must realise that an orator can fulfil all three requirements and still fail to achieve rhetorical artistry if he cannot recognise the 'proper occasion' (*kairos*) for applying his store of knowledge in each particular case (271d7–272b4).

Now, all this might well strike the reader as easy enough for Socrates to say, but more like a pious statement of ideals than a compelling argument; and heavily dependent on an unsubstantiated analogy with medicine.[18] However, a little thought reveals that Plato has here a worthwhile argument (when the passage is taken in conjunction with the preceding rebuttal of the hacks, 268a–269c) to show that the only properly artistic method of rhetoric will be along the lines he indicates. And these are dialectical lines.

Socrates, we saw, rebutted the hacks by pointing out that a student could parrot their textbooks without understanding or being able to practise the art they claim to teach (see esp. 268e4–5); a fact implicitly recognised by the hacks when they agree that there is more to the art than book-learning, but insist that the student will pick this up for himself (268b9–c1; 269b7–c5). Socrates did not really answer this last point of theirs at the time; and we should ask now the following question. Given that Socrates acknowledges the crucial importance of recognising the appropriate occasion for applying even his dialectically reformed corpus of rhetorical knowledge, let alone the content of the traditional rhetorical manuals, how has he shown that the latter, when wielded by an orator with a sense of its appropriate application, will *not* result in art, and that only by applying the reformed corpus will the orator be a genuine artist? In other words, Socrates has shown why the standard manuals alone will not make an artist; but not why they are also inadequate – and must be replaced by dialectic – even when taken together with the ability to recognise their conditions of application.

But this, I submit, is what he shows in the passage presently under consideration. Let us take the analogy with medicine as our guide; for it is a useful one (although the point about rhetoric that it illuminates is valid independently of the analogy itself, and of any worries we might have about how far it can be pressed). Consider how the methods of the 'Hippocratic' physician described at 270b–d differ from those of the quack at 268a–c.[19] The quack knows only the effects or symptoms that his drugs will produce in patients: making them hot, or

cooling them, as he pleases; causing them to vomit, or evacu-
ate their bowels. But the Hippocratic physician enquires also
into the bodily causes of symptoms, and asks why these drugs
will replace these symptoms with these others. The equivalent
distinction in the domain of rhetoric is between the speaker
who knows only how to elicit various 'symptoms' in his audience – fear, hope, anger, pity, approval (cf. 267c7–d2) – and
one who understands the psychological explanation for the
success of his various routines – thus at 271b2 we read that
the genuine orator will 'go through all the reasons', *dieisi
pasas aitias*, why this speech has that effect on this type of soul
or character.[20] And now we can see why Plato insists that,
however skilful rhetoricians of the former type might become
at manipulating such symptoms, their skill is unworthy to be
designated an art. For, on the one hand, by their writing of
manuals and offers of formal instruction they claim to teach
something more than a mere knack (which could be picked up
by experience alone); they claim to disclose in explicit form
the secrets of an art. On the other hand, in the absence of a
proper theory of soul, what they deliver is a knowledge of the
overt symptoms of human behaviour, not of their hidden
causes; and we could reasonably expect that, since symptoms
are, by definition, wholly explicit, the 'art' which manipulates
them could also be made wholly a matter of explicit rules and
routines, encapsulated in and transmitted through a text-
book. Yet this is not the case, as even the hacks admit when
pressed (and as is acknowledged through the classic status of
the trio nature, knowledge, practice); rather, the student must
somehow acquire from his own resources the ability to manipulate the symptoms and effects that he learns about in a
manner appropriate to his purposes (268b9–c1; 269c2–5).
But then: this ability will be something that *just happens*. It
will not result from knowledge of symptoms, because these,
being superficial phenomena, can be fully known just in the
terms in which the textbooks presented them; alike, therefore,
by those who con their books but fail as orators (for lack of
that inner resource) as by those who go on to success. Accordingly, rather than *result from* knowledge of symptoms, it can

only be said to *supervene upon* that knowledge – as if by magic. The two components of rhetorical competence – knowledge (of symptoms and routines), and recognition, or the ability to exploit that knowledge – have, as it were, simply fallen apart. Hence the hacks' hand-waving as to how the student will learn to apply his encyclopedia, and their disingenuous refusal to worry about the matter.

The essence of Socrates' reformed methodology is to weld these two components into a working whole; which he does by so altering the type of knowledge to be provided in the rhetorical encyclopedia that it both takes account and gives an account of the second component of competence, the ability to apply that knowledge.[21] Where the contemporary orator is given knowledge of symptoms, the reformed orator will be taught about what those symptoms are symptoms *of*. Only so can we make sense of – not relinquish to 'blindness', to mere supervenience – the fact that knowledge of the encyclopedia must be supplemented by recognition: by the capacity to apply it to the particular case (270d9–e4). Only from such knowledge as the reformed orator has can recognition be truly said to result (and not just happen). Such knowledge is a determinant of recognition; for the simple reason that symptoms tell this orator something about something else: the soul; so he is always looking for what lies behind the symptoms, and his search is therefore open-ended, alike in his theoretical investigation as in rhetorical practice (since he will not encounter hidden causes independently of their symptoms) – as opposed to the mere list of symptoms and routines ingested by the traditional orator, which is in principle closed (although the point of closure may vary from manual to manual).

From such an open-ended, searching outlook it is natural and makes sense that recognition should follow. So at 271d7–e1 we read that the student must 'watch for' the contents of his theory 'occurring and being enacted in actual behaviour' (*theōmenon auta en tais praxesin onta te kai prattomena*). That is, since he has not just learned particular symptoms in isolation, but rather has related them to a typology of soul and of language (271d1–7), he does not approach actual human behaviour as a mere congeries of individual symptoms about which he already knows all there is to know, but as something particular to which he must adapt his general typology. That is why, even when he has seen that this particular case before him falls under this rule that he has learnt (271e2–272a3), recognition – in the sense of recognising what to do – is still a further step away. He must 'in addition' (*proslabonti*, 272a4) determine whether it is opportune to speak or hold off in this case, and how exactly he will phrase his appeal (272a3–7) – because what he has learnt is the typology of an entity postulated as real (hence distinct from the typology itself), and not a self-sufficient list of symptoms. Thus, even though he must understand to which type the case before him belongs, and recall the rule pertaining to the type, his action on this occasion is not completely determined by (although it does result from) this understanding and this recall; for what lies before him is not a type but a particular – a fact for which he was prepared by his theoretical training, and to which he is therefore ready to adapt as the 'occasion' (*kairous*, 272a3) demands.[22]

Of course, Socrates has in a sense not accounted for this ability to adapt to the occasion any more than did contemporary rhetoricians, if by 'accounting for' we mean subsuming under an explicit rule. But this would be impossible in the nature of the case; for such adaptability is precisely what escapes the straightforward implementation of rules. To subsume it under a rule would not, therefore, be to account for it, but to deny it. Nevertheless, through what we might call the 'realism' of his theory – the fact that the orator studies not just symptoms but that of which they are symptoms – Socrates has achieved two things: he has successfully accounted for the very unaccountability of this power of recognition; and, to the extent that recognition is (despite the first point) accountable, he has shown it to result from knowledge, and has thus fused knowledge and recognition into art. A Lysias or Thrasymachus (269d7–8), by contrast, offer on the one hand knowledge that can be attained merely by rote, and on the other hand an adaptability that, considered in isolation, can only be a knack.[23] In neither case do they offer what is worthy to be called art; and they are unable to make sense of how the two components mesh.

So Socrates has proved his case, limited though it is. If the rhetoricians are to justify their claim to practise and teach a genuine art of speaking, they must drop their current methods and adopt those of the dialectician (272a8–b4). Moreover, this conclusion holds regardless of whether the rhetorician aims at truth as his primary goal, as a philosopher would, or only as an intermediary on the way to persuasion; since, whatever place persuasion occupies in his structure of goals, to reach it through art he must follow the path that Socrates has blazed (cf. 277c5–6).[24] Of course, one would expect a rhetorician who submitted to the necessarily 'great effort' (273e5) and 'long circuit' (274a2) of Socrates' path to be at least somewhat influenced by the philosopher's ethic, even if this were not his original intention. But it is more likely that he would not even want to take the first step. Socrates' argument is not, indeed, primarily addressed to the die-hard rhetorician; it is addressed to Phaedrus – to those of us who vacillate.

Teisias at the bar

In his prospectus of reformed rhetoric Socrates has encapsulated the essence of his critique. Phaedrus' immediate reaction is to be concerned at how huge a task it would be to build on these bare girders (272b5–6). And this prompts Socrates to append a codicil to his argument. I shall bring this chapter to a close by examining it.

Socrates agrees that the task he has proposed for rhetoric is indeed arduous, and suggests that we should accordingly assure ourselves that the rhetoricians have no easier alternative to offer – at least, none that would be worthy (272b7–c2). To this end he returns to the rhetorical claim that Phaedrus introduced at the outset of the critique: namely, that the competent orator need have no understanding of what is truly just or good provided he knows what the audience will find plausible (272d2–e2, picking up 259e7–260a4); but now Socrates recounts a classic example from a rhetorical handbook, that of Teisias, designed to support this principle.[25] The example claims to show that in some circumstances the orator not only need not but must not present the true facts of the case to his audience – tell them 'what actually happened' (*auta ta prakhthenta*, 272e2) – if he intends to win the day. It runs as follows. A weak but plucky individual assaults and makes off with the cloak of a muscle-bound behemoth who, despite appearances, is cowardly. Goliath takes David to court. Because the truth in this case is so implausible, not even the plaintiff can appeal to it. He cannot expect a jury to believe it, and will in any case be anxious to conceal his cowardice. So he will entangle himself in a skein of lies, enabling David to repeat his victory in court and knock him dead with the unbeatably plausible claim: 'How could a man like me have assaulted a man like him?' (273a6–c5).

Socrates' riposte to Teisias' parry is dismissive. He showers irony upon it and its inventor – this example which illustrates 'what seems (*hōs eoike*) to be a wise and artistic discovery' (273b3), in which he 'seems (*eoiken*) to have uncovered the awesome secrets of a hidden art, this Teisias or whoever it was and however he got his name' (273c7–9).[26] (Notice the implication: the 'art' that overvalues mere seeming is itself only a seeming art.) But apart from this, Socrates simply refers back to his earlier principle that the plausible attains its plausibility by resemblance to the truth, and the argument he built upon it: that he best deceives who knows the truth. And he claims that this adequately disposes of Teisias' challenge, which has added nothing new to rebut (273d2–6).

Now, it seems undeniable that if Teisias' example were to become a reality, things would probably turn out as he predicts. But Socrates does not attempt to deny this. For in fact, Teisias' supposed counter-example to Socrates' principle of plausibility is nothing but the exception that proves the rule.

We have seen how the argument to which Socrates here looks back committed the orator vicariously to an interest in truth, parasitic on the interest of his audience; since only because the audience actively seeks to discover truth is it necessary to attempt to pass off as true what seems likely to them (that is, the plausible). Further, Plato's implicit assumption must be that the audience is largely successful (that most of the time what seems likely to them will in fact be the case); for otherwise it would make no sense to ascribe truth-seeking behaviour to them on the basis of what they find likely.[27] At any rate, it is clear that what is plausible, just because it is plausible rather than true, will not inevitably be the case; for naturally, implausible events do happen sometimes; and just such an implausible occurrence is what Teisias here exploits. In doing so, while he has indeed shown up the genuine predicament that such an implausibility would pose for the court, he has not in the least shown, as he claims, that the orator should as a general rule pursue the plausible, and never mind about the truth (272e4–5). To point out the exceptional case is not to undermine the rule; indeed, only by virtue of his vicarious interest in truth has Teisias hit upon an example of the proper implausibility to exploit in the first place. That is why Socrates is dismissive, and contents himself with indicating that Teisias' special case is not a genuine counterexample to the conclusion of his earlier argument.[28]

However, granting the validity of Socrates' rebuttal, we might well ask why Teisias' challenge, if it was indeed adequately thwarted by the earlier argument, did not crop up at that time in order to be duly rejected? Or if not then, at least when Socrates turned to consider the specific contents of the rhetorical handbooks, at 266c–267d – in the course of which Teisias did in fact receive a brief mention, but was 'left to sleep' (267a6)? Why did Plato bother to wake him again, and give his challenge such prominent billing, if – to judge from its treatment at Socrates' hands – he considers it so unworthy of serious or extended consideration?

As to the first question: the fact that Socrates does not turn to Teisias' challenge at the same time as he presents the argument that neutralises it seems adequately accounted for by Plato's not wanting to consider the actual contents of rhetori-

83

cal teaching at all until after he has made his general argument for a rhetorical interest in truth, and examined its limitations. But as to the second, why the challenge is not expounded along with the other contents of the handbooks: that is a subtler question; and I propose that Socrates' very dismissiveness provides an answer. Teisias' challenge is not important; but for that very reason it is an important example of rhetorical triviality: in particular, of how jejune the current rhetorical notion of truth could be. And since Socrates does not reveal the content and type of truth that he would have the competent orator investigate until the final stages of his critique, only now, and not when the handbooks were produced for inspection, does Teisias' thought show up by contrast in all its meagreness.

For consider: although at first blush Teisias would seem to confront directly the issue that a personified Rhetoric earlier bracketed, namely, what the actual content might be of the kind of truth that she claims the orator need not grasp, still, it is notable that his example does not in fact deal with what is truly just and good – the knowledge of which he insists (at 272d4–7) is dispensable to the orator – but makes a detour into historical truth. For his example is meant to illustrate that 'sometimes one should not even tell what actually happened (*auta ta prakhthenta*), unless it happened in a plausible way' (272e2–3). Socrates here phrases Teisias' claim in such a way as to suggest an *a fortiori* argument: that not even the actual facts of the case should necessarily enter into the rhetorical proceedings, let alone more nebulous truths about the just and the good. But not only does Teisias' claim about the role of truth fail as an argument; it also lionises in the process exactly the wrong sort of truth: merely historical truth. We have already witnessed Socrates' reaction to a similar error on the part of those other intellectuals who were too clever for their own good, the antiquarians who make it their task to distil the factual essence from the brew of traditional myth, but who end up – since the facts are of course lost to history – devising an elaborate cocktail of merely plausible speculation (*eikos*, 229e2).[29] Socrates proposed instead a creative use of myth to uncover general truths about his human nature; and here in the coda to his critique of rhetoric this approach is correlated with that of the rhetoricians. For a Teisias, what goes on in court is a matter of 'antiquarian' ingenuity. The jury is engaged in the game of merely plausible speculation about a historical truth to which they can have no direct access, and it is the advocate's job to exploit their inevitable distance from this truth and manipulate their speculations with the eye of a connoisseur. But just as the antiquarians sacrifice the psychological truth *in* myth to a historical truth independent of it, and land themselves as a result in a morass of conjecture, so Teisias, and rhetoric as taught by contemporaries, refuses to find in what the audience thinks a potential source of truth about human nature, nor does he require a serious appreciation of this sort of truth in order to transmit his 'art', but instead devalues it by comparison with his own jejune notion of truth, and is prompted thereby to reduce his project to a self-sufficient patchwork, however elaborate, of mere slogans and tropes and empirical guesses.

We see now why Plato has put Teisias' example in the spotlight: in order to *make* an example of it. Hence too Socrates concludes his dismissal of Teisias with a short homily on the different path towards truth that the philosopher will choose – the long and arduous path of pleasing the gods rather than one's fellow man – which sings a snatch of the exalted melody of his mythic hymn.[30] Soon we will attend to that erotic music in all its splendour and complexity. But in the next chapter we shall hear a preliminary chorus of voices raised in hostility against love.

CHAPTER FOUR

THE VOICE OF REASON?

From rhetoric to erotics

In my account of Socrates' critique of rhetoric, I have been at pains to show that the limitations of his arguments are as thematically important to the concerns of the dialogue as what can positively be claimed for them. We have seen – most especially in chapter two – that although Plato can argue the orators into formally adopting dialectical method in order to attain the grasp of truth required for their art, he cannot by discursive argument alone compel their commitment to that structure of goals, and that choice of life, which gives dialectical method its meaning for him. At some point, they must find it in themselves to either follow or reject the example that he sets. Not, however, that Plato is powerless to influence this impulse of attraction or disgust in those whom he would bend towards the philosophic life; rather, he must call upon resources other than those of formal argument, and paint a picture of the alternative choices of life from the full palette of colours at his imaginative disposal.

Now, I would be working against everything I have argued so far if, in turning from the critique of rhetoric to the speeches on love, I were to make it seem that I am about to forsake the black-and-white of philosophy for the technicolor of poetry. We have seen that the example Socrates sets by his procedure in the second part of the dialogue is as crucial (and imaginatively painted) a facet of the person that he is as anything to be found in the first; indeed, since a significant element of his procedure in the second part consists in his coming to terms with his own behaviour in the first, the portrait of the man is incomplete unless considered in the frame of the whole dialogue. Conversely, I have said before, and aim to substantiate in the chapters that follow, that the speeches on love, and most especially Socrates' mythic hymn, propound a serious argument in moral psychology. Nevertheless, the speeches on love are formally set off from the rest of the dialogue as rhetorical displays, and it is to these that Socrates refers us for examples of the contrast between the rhetorical and the philosophical approach to the art of speaking: which amounts, we have seen, to the contrast between the respective ways of life of orator and philosopher; for the dispute centres precisely around the issue of whether a true art of speaking should be kept in professonal quarantine from the moral and emotional life of its practitioner. It is here, then, that we can expect to find Plato's fullest embodiment of the values of display, and his most concerted appeal to our sensibility.

I have already had something to say (in my second chapter) about the form in which we find this appeal. Lysias and Socrates, I said, are made to display not just their rhetorical talents but themselves; although this emerges only gradually. Indeed, the first part of the dialogue is built around the drama with which it emerges, as Socrates finds it increasingly abhorrent and, finally, impossible to maintain the pose of delivering his first speech as a mere rhetorical exercise, and can allay his disgust only by delivering a hymn to love in which his whole person is invested. Here it is apparent that he is no longer elaborating a set theme, but moulding an ideal for himself and other philosophers; so that in the figure of the philosophic lover we naturally look to find traces of Socrates himself. And we can then return to the speech of Lysias that was the seed of this development, and discover with hindsight the ethos of the orator similarly laid bare through the declarations of his fictional non-lover. Philosopher and rhetorician, it turns out, are being portrayed in the characters they invent; the topic of the speeches is directly relevant to the issue that divides the speakers, and cannot – *pace* Lysias and his rhetorical ethos – be considered in professional detachment from it. That this should be so is appropriate enough, given that the speeches of philosopher and rhetorician alike have their home in the writing of one man, and him a philosopher.

I have shown how, in the course of the critique of rhetoric,

Plato exploits this correspondence between the characters who create the speeches, and the characters created in those speeches. I want now to consider more directly the created characters, and the substance of their claims, in order to judge the contrasting ethical voices with which Plato has endowed them. They will turn out to display contrasting aspects of but one voice: the voice of reason.

Lysias against love

In chapter two I drew attention to the special subtlety of Lysias' 'non-lover': how he does not, in typical rhetorical fashion, take advantage of love's ambivalence in driving home his attack and accentuate only its bad side; but rather condemns love on a second order for its very ambivalence, and promises in its stead a relationship without harmful side-effects. As I tune in now on the voice of the non-lover, I will begin by substantiating this interpretive claim.

It does not, indeed, require any great acumen to see that Lysias' non-lover makes no attempt to deny to the boy whom he would seduce that a more conventional erotic relationship would bring him *some* good. Indeed, his major argument against love depends on admitting as much (and that this is indeed his major argument can be seen from the summary of his points at 233e5–234b1); for his claim is not that love will bring *no* good, but that the good it brings is only temporary and will lead to a counterbalancing bad.

It is the claim with which he opens his speech: that the good-will which the lover bears towards the object of his affections lasts only as long as his desire (*epithymia*, 231a3); and desire is a passing thing. When it is gone, the lover will regard the favours that his good-will has prompted him to bestow on his beloved as so much effort expended in a cause he no longer considers worthy, and will deem himself acquitted of all obligation; so that the beloved can expect no friendship from him in the future (231a2–3, a6–b2; the non-lover comes back to this point more than once in the course of the speech: see 232e5–6, and 234a1–2, 5–7). What is worse, the boy can expect actual enmity from his ex-lover, and that for two reasons. One is that lovers are naturally inclined to be partisan. They will praise and favour their beloved not for his deserts but simply because he is the beloved, and disregard any harm they do to others in pursuing this end. Accordingly, when the beloved is no longer loved, he can expect treatment similar to that meted out to those who were previously 'others' (231b7–c7; cf. 233a5–7, b6–7). The second reason is that the lover may actively resent the problems and general neglect that his past infatuation will have brought about in his family and financial affairs, and indulge this resentment against the object of that infatuation (231b2–5; 234a7–8).

This counterbalancing of good with bad in the standard erotic liaison, the non-lover urges, is itself a bad thing, and an unreasonable course for the beloved to enter upon (231c7–d6); and he offers in its place a relationship which he sums up as having only benefits for both parties, with no harmful aspects at all (234c3–4). It would thus be unmarked by love's ambivalence.

In effect, the non-lover is only sharpening a traditional complaint with which the boy would be familiar. He makes this fact explicit at one point: 'And how can it be appropriate to lavish what is so precious [i.e. one's sexual favours] on someone suffering from an affliction so grave that no one who has any experience of it would even attempt a cure? Why, they themselves admit that they are not sane, but sick (*nosein mallon ē sōphronein*)' (231c7–d3). Lovers have no need to hide that their love is a kind of madness, for this is indeed the common cultural understanding of their feelings and behaviour. Socrates himself appeals to a rich tradition of such portrayals of the phenomenon of love when he invokes the names of Sappho and Anacreon as rival authors on the topic (235b6–c4). Society accepts that lovers will not act sensibly or within the regular bounds of decorum; that is why the non-lover is able to generalise so freely and pejoratively about what the boy can expect from his lover, and qualify his generalisations as 'likely' (*eikos*, 231e4; *eikotōs*, 232c2: the same term that we have seen Teisias use to label the social commonplaces and plausibilities that he required the orator to know and manipulate). And this same term appears in the challenge that I have just quoted, where I translated it as 'appropriate' (*eikos*, 231c7 – a sense the word often bears: see LSJ sub voc. II). The non-lover's challenge, then, consists in this: he presents the boy with a projection which fits with what he knows him to expect of love, and asks, how *can* this 'fit' with expectations? How can it be deemed fitting at all? Why, indeed, should such behaviour be tolerated? In love, society finds a place where the unfitting can fit; where behaviour that exceeds what would normally be found acceptable – the lover's boastful indiscretion (232a2–4), his extreme sensitivity (232c3–4), his importunacy (233d5–7) – can be, if not accepted without qualms, at least condoned.[1] And the non-lover's strategy is simply to bring those qualms to the fore by presenting them with the voice of reason; to acknowledge that society does not expect a lover to be reasonable, and then ask what reason society can have for such tolerance, when a better alternative exists.

In order to appreciate why the non-lover might expect this strategy to result in success, we must recall the well-known asymmetry in the conventional Athenian homoerotic relationship which is its context.[2] Only the older partner was expected (whatever the reality may have been) to enjoy sexual arousal, and therefore to be susceptible to the infatuation that might accompany it. What the boy conventionally derived from the relationship was not sexual pleasure but social advancement and the friendship of an adult mentor (an especially important consideration in the upper strata of society, with which our sources are primarily concerned). The non-lover might well expect the boy to listen to reason, then, rather than look starry-eyed upon the failings of lovers; for indeed, to the boy's ears it is rather the voice of reason than the urging of passion that counsels his entry even upon a conventional erotic relationship in the first place (which is not to say that the boy was expected to be cold and self-interested, but only that the affection which the older man sought to arouse in him was the controlled affection of friendship rather than a potentially disorienting crush).[3]

Let us consider more closely now why the non-lover thinks his the better alternative for the boy. The essence of his proposal is that he has discovered a way of attaining the desirable effects of the conventional erotic relationship without the undesirable effects that stem from the lover's being in love. The boy will get what he wants from love, which is friendship and patronage, and it will be a friendship that lasts rather than foundering on the fickleness of infatuation (234a1–b1); and the non-lover in his turn will get what he wants from the boy, namely his sexual favours – which he will enjoy unhampered by problems of jealousy and possessiveness (232b2–5, d4–e2).[4]

The crucial point to notice about this proposal – for it is this point that Socrates will develop and eventually react against – is that the voice of reason in the non-lover reasons only about means to ends, not about the ends themselves. Indeed, he does not in the least question whether the respective goals of lover and beloved in the traditional relationship are proper goals for them to have; rather, he claims that the emotional effects of such a relationship on the lover actually prevent the couple from attaining their goals in the most efficient manner, and touts his new brand of liaison for its effectiveness in smoothing the path towards those goals. When the non-lover waxes indignant about the boy's tolerance for so damaging a relationship, he is not, despite the unconventionality of his scheme, suggesting to the youth any radical rethinking of ethical purpose, but only that he be more prudent in calculating the steps toward the objective that custom has determined.

Let us check this interpretation against some details of the text. Twice the non-lover stresses that, if the boy grants his favours to him rather than to a lover, he will have a 'much better expectation' (*poly pleiōn elpis*, 231d8–e1; 232d7–e1) of finding the 'friendship' (*philia*) that he seeks from love; for in the first place there are far more non-lovers than lovers, so

91

that the boy can pick and choose from a wider field, and secondly the non-lover whom he eventually selects will be less possessive and resentful of his friendship with others. The boy is simply being advised to maximise his chances.[5] On a similar but more negative note, he is also urged to hedge his bets. The non-lover openly appeals to the boy's fear: his fear of being shamed by public gossip if he consents to sex (231e3–4), and his fear of the instability of friendships developed through sexual partnership, and the possibility of dangerous quarrels arising from it (232b5–c3). In both cases, the non-lover points out that there is less reason to fear such an outcome from a liaison with him than with a lover. And thus the boy will get maximum return from his investment, by yielding not to the one who asks for the most by way of favours, but to the one who is most able to give favours in return (233e5–7). Small wonder that when Socrates comes to recall the voice of the non-lover at the close of his mythic hymn he condemns it for its 'penny-pinching' tone (*pheidōla oikonomousa*, 256e5–6).[6]

It has to be said, however, that there is a certain magnificent audacity in the non-lover's suggestion – a provocativeness that has Phaedrus beaming as he reads, but which Socrates, who sees deeper, can appreciate only with qualms, and vicariously (227c5–7; 234c6–235a8). After all, one of the functions served by conventional erotic behaviour was to mark off sexual relationships between aristocratic peers from those commercially procured from social inferiors – male and female courtesans and prostitutes. The elaborate emotional antics and rituals of courtship expected from the lover, extending even to stylised limitations on the sexual act itself,[7] were in effect a badge of rank for both partners. Accordingly, the outrageous twist in the arguments of the non-lover is that by pooh-poohing the traditional agonies he comes close to using the boy as his whore. He is buying sex from him. Not with coin, of course; but with the value-for-money of a trouble-free friendship. And the rhetorical challenge he dares to face is to deck out this proposal in the finery of rational concern for their mutual welfare.[8]

The non-lover presents himself, then, as the boy's very best bet of winning the very biggest jackpot of friendship; the best bet of getting hold of some in the first place, and of hanging onto it for the longest time once he has got it. However, almost nothing is said – a most significant touch – about friendship (*philia*) itself: what sort of a goal it is, and why one should desire it; for as we have seen, the non-lover's proposition leaves the traditional goals of the erotic partnership in place, and is indeed wholly parasitic upon them. His only remark about friendship as such comes in an aside (and that it should come only in an aside is telling in itself). Speaking of his tolerance towards allowing the boy to converse with other men, he claims to realise that it is only natural for people to want to talk together 'through friendship or for some other pleasure' (*dia philian ... e di' allēn tina hēdonēn*, 232b4–5). This gives a hedonistic cast to the ethical coloration of the speech, since he suggests (by the very casualness of his allusion) that the only reason for the boy or anyone else to pursue friendship is that it is a pleasure; and we are prevented thereby from reading too much into his high-sounding claim that he will put the boy's 'future benefit' (*ōphelia*) before 'immediate pleasure' (233b6–c1). The operative contrast here, when the phrase is viewed in the context of the speech as a whole, is rather between the immediate present and the long-term future than between pleasure and benefit as such. The benefits the non-lover has to offer are those which derive from a hedonistic calculus.

For the rest, the non-lover (as his label would suggest) has nothing but negation to add to the traditional mix. He intends not to reform love, but to opt out of it (whereas Socrates will eventually work around to a new conception of love in his mythic hymn). Indeed, so little does he attempt to alter tradition that his description of the likely behaviour of the lover who has fallen out of love can be seen to encapsulate his own position. The ex-lover, he claims, will scrutinise the dissolved relationship with a now coolly commercial eye, putting in the opposite pan of the scales for the first time all those favours and sufferings which he previously considered it a privilege to confer and undergo for the sake of his beloved, and reckoning that they cancel out the benefits which he derived from his love (231a6–b2). But just such an assessment is what persuades the non-lover to avoid love in the first place; that is, he judges its sweets to be offset by countervailing evils. He differs from the lover not in his ambitions but in thinking that he has hit on a way of fulfilling them without suffering for it.

The question that the non-lover's strategy raises is similar (and not fortuitously so) to that raised throughout the dialogue by Phaedrus' eagerness as an impresario. We have seen how Phaedrus is at risk of pursuing intellectual life for its extrinsic goods alone (the company of clever people, the thrill of swimming in deep waters), but I also pointed out that these goods, extrinsic in the sense that they could be won by mere ambition, without exercise of the intellect, were not simply contingent to the intellectual life, but would also be prized by genuine philosophers, and prized as belonging to their chosen way of life (but not prized as ends in themselves). So too with the non-lover's challenge. By arguing that the sweets of love can be enjoyed without the exercise of love, he forces us to question the status of those goods. Are they then merely incidental to love, if they can as well be attained without it? Have we been misled by social conventions? What Socrates will eventually claim is that, just as there are goods of the intellectual life which must be rated extrinsic to it if pursued as ends in themselves but the enjoyment of which nevertheless belongs to the intellectual life when properly pursued, so these goods of love are not to be pursued for their own sake, since they could then be sought without love (just this is what gave the arguments of the non-lover their point of entry); but it is not simply irrelevant that they are attached to the phenomenon of passionate love. Genuine love has a different goal: neither friendship as such, nor (still less) sexual gratification, but (to put it properly but as yet uninformatively) the common good of the lovers. But both friendship and, if not the gratification, at least the passion that attends sexual arousal, *belong* to the loving relationship, and never so truly to any other. Of course, Socrates' counter-proposal entails something of an upheaval of the traditional conception of

94

love; but just as Phaedrus' bad example shows us that the life of mere words is not the philosophic life, yet comes perilously close to passing for it, so the non-lover's attack obligingly reveals to us that what we generally take for love can be similarly spurious in relation to the genuine article. And because the non-lover seems to be attacking the spurious kind of love to which Socrates too will prove hostile (although in reality the non-lover's horizon is no less spurious), he can give voice to apparently exalted ethical sentiments of the sort that Socrates might be expected to approve (see e.g. 231a5; 232d4–5; 233b6–c1); and it is this deceptive resemblance that allows Socrates to become so deeply engaged in his own emulation of Lysias' speech, for all that he embarks upon it as a rhetorical exercise. Let us pass on, then, to the analysis of that emulative effort.

Socrates to compete

Socrates is persuaded to rival Lysias with a new speech on the same theme only after much cajoling on Phaedrus' part. He had made the mistake of refusing to accept Phaedrus' opinion that Lysias had said all that there was to be said on the topic (235b1–c1) – an open invitation for so eager a fan of fine discourse as Phaedrus to badger him into substantiating his refusal by producing the goods (235d4–236e7). That Socrates delivers his version of the non-lover's speech only under duress will prove important. It will help us to locate the voice of Socrates' non-lover in the moral development expressed through the three love-speeches taken as a series; and I shall return to it presently. But first I want to consider directly the content of his non-lover's overture, in order to assess how it differs from that of Lysias' non-lover.

I will begin by focusing on the very different psychological picture that Socrates' non-lover sketches.[9] We have seen how Lysias' man took for granted his and the boy's objectives in love, and concentrated on arguing that his was the most prudent path towards securing them. Socrates' character, in contrast, begins by discussing not means but ends, and stresses that ends can come into conflict. He takes us, for the first

95

time, *within* the soul, and finds there a scene of struggle. It is true that in Lysias' speech the non-lover talks of fostering future benefit rather than immediate pleasure, and doing so because he is in control of himself and has not succumbed to erotic passion (233b6–c2); but we saw that his ethical ticket, to the extent that he can be pinned down to one, is hedonistic, and that he is not opposing pleasure to benefit as such, but the temporary pleasures of erotic association with the secure and long-term pleasures of erotic (but not passionate) friendship. He does not give the impression of aiming at something entirely different from the lover, but rather of setting his sights on the same target with a cooler eye.

In Socrates' speech, by contrast, the seducer makes a point of explicitly opposing pleasure as a whole to his notion of the *good*, and assigning them as two potentially conflicting goals to two different principles in the soul: one, our natural desire (*epithymia*), which aims at pleasure, and the other an acquired judgment (*doxa*), which aims at what is best (237d6–e2). And throughout the speech he contrasts the selfish pleasure sought by the lover with a list of goods which the boy has the sense to pursue, but of which the lover's selfishness will deprive him. These goods are not presented as themselves pleasures (albeit more lasting pleasures) that the boy seeks in turn; rather, they are tagged with such epithets as 'good' (*agathos*), 'upright' (*orthos*), 'divine' (*theios*), 'most dear' (*philtatos*), 'valuable' (*timios*), and invariably contrasted with what the lover finds 'sweet' or 'pleasurable' (*hēdys*) (see 238b7–c1; 239b4–8; 239c4–5; 239e3–240a2; 241c4–6). In other words, the non-lover styles these goods – which range from physical fitness and a life in the open air, through social and financial standing and a good relationship with one's family, to the training and development of character and understanding (*psykhēs paideusin*, 241c5) – as choiceworthy in themselves, rather than for the pleasure they bring; and the lover's pursuit of sexual pleasure he therefore sees as a victory of that in him which seeks pleasure over that which seeks the good – a victory that leaves no room in his soul for any concern for the welfare of the beloved, since that goal has been exclusively assigned to the defeated principle (238a1–c4).

It is for this reason that the argument which bulked so prominently in Lysias' speech – the appeal to the fleeting and fickle nature of love – is relegated to the rearguard in the arguments marshalled by Socrates' man. He devotes his speech to listing the harm that a lover would do the boy while yet in love, and only at the end (240e7–241c1) turns to the additional point that, when he falls out of love, the boy can expect still more trouble from him. Lysias' non-lover takes a prudential approach, and so puts the appeal to instability in the van of his attack; for he has no desire to deny that a lover would bring the boy profit, but only that, through fickleness, he would not maximise such profit as he brings (in addition to incurring debts while in love). Socrates' non-lover reverses this emphasis. Because he has directly opposed the pursuit of pleasure to the pursuit of good, he is unwilling to see the lover as bringing *any* good to the relationship; and for him the expectation of fickleness comes simply as the last straw in a long catalogue of evils (240e8–9). He makes no attempt to integrate pleasure with the good; rather, he gives it the function of disguising and tempting us into what is not in our best interests, as when we fall for a charming flatterer, or succumb to the allure of a courtesan (240a9–b5) – although, he insists, the boy will not even get pleasure from the conventional type of liaison, let alone good; the pleasure will be all on the lover's side (240b6–c2). The non-lover's attitude to pleasure here is thus one of outright hostility. Moreover, he combines this with a measure of puzzlement. 'Some spirit has mixed' pleasure in with what is bad for us, he declares (*tis daimōn emeixe*, 240a9). He cannot understand why this should be so, and does not attempt to; pleasure is a curse to be confronted, not understood.

It is a severe and paternal voice, then, this voice that Socrates has adopted. There is none of the zestful audacity that we found in Lysias' non-lover, nor his potentially refreshing straightforwardness. And here it is important to bear in mind that Socrates' character is in reality no less a lover than any other of the boy's suitors (237b3–6). He yearns for the boy, with passion; and the whole speech is therefore an exercise in suppressing his deepest feelings. It is no exaggeration, indeed, to see it as a speech of self-hate. Considering that, according to the scenario Socrates has adopted from Lysias, his non-lover will expect the boy's sexual favours in return for his protection of the boy's best interests, it is quite remarkable to find him describing vividly, elaborately, and at length the horrors of submitting to the sexual pestering of an older man (240c1–e7). Doubtless he means to suggest that the boy can expect less pestering from him than from a lover (though he does not make this explicit); still, he declares the very act of sex with one who has lost his youth (never mind whether constantly solicited) to be an unpleasant chore (240c1–6, d6–e2) – a point which would seem to work against his own suit also.

Yet this makes good psychological sense when we take into account the passionate love that he is attempting to conceal. Precisely because he does not want merely to use the boy for sex, but is really in love, he is sufficiently concerned for the feelings of the other to imagine how things seem from his standpoint, and in particular to appreciate vividly how his own weathered and alarmingly mature physique must look to one still fresh of limb. These are the anxieties of passionate involvement; and the theme is notable for its total absence from Lysias' speech (indeed, Lysias' persona gives no sign of any empathetic appreciation of the boy's feelings). But anxiety has here turned passion in against itself. Gripped by powerful feelings that he is uncertain of satisfying, Socrates' non-lover turns hostile against the very pleasure that he longs to taste; and as a result those longings become shameful, neither to be confessed nor understood ('some spirit' has mixed pleasure in with sex); and if satisfied at all, then by cunning and devious means.

There is none of this in Lysias' man. The shamefulness of sex he recognises only as a matter of 'current custom' (*ton nomon ton kathestēkota*, 231e3) and a possible source of fear in the boy, which he must work to allay. He himself makes no bones about wanting sex from the lad; and in general gives a no-nonsense impression of breezy, clear-headed confidence (sec esp. 230c7–231a2; 234c4–5) where the Socratic persona is gothic and gloomy, and at times almost maudlin (see esp. 240a6; 241c2–6).

Nevertheless, it seems clear that Plato means Socrates' non-lover to come across as having the higher moral tone.[10] His explicit distinction between pleasure and what is best, his talk of ethical rather than merely prudential conflict between these goals, his high valuation of 'educating the soul' (241c5) and of what he calls 'divine philosophy' (*hē theia philosophia*, 239b4) – whatever his intentions, he boasts a distinctively moral superiority to the type of lover whom he would supplant. Lysias' man, by contrast, claims greater worthiness than the lover only on the strength of his having more sense. Yet from Socrates' subsequent disgust with what his adoption of the non-lover's mask has prompted him to say, together with his more sanguine criticisms in the second part of the dialogue (which we have already considered), it is equally clear that we are to think of this speech as still far from adequate in its ethical stance.

Notice the implication. We have heard in Socrates' non-lover the voice of puritanism: by which I mean an automatic hostility towards pleasure as such, and an inability to integrate pleasure in an honest fashion with the pursuit of the good. And in the popular and encyclopedic conception of the history of Western philosophy, this is of course often thought of as Plato's own voice. That this is a mishearing is quite clear even from so classic a work as the *Republic*, in which we read, for example at IX 586d4–587a2, that all parts of the soul and classes in the state have their appropriate pleasures, and that one of the results of pursuing the good is that each element can enjoy its pleasure without infringing on the pleasure of the others.[11] But the *Phaedrus* does represent perhaps his most concerted reaction against puritanism. Of course, Plato too never fails to oppose the goal of pleasure to the goal of what is best. But he is not hostile to pleasure as such; rather, he holds that the true philosopher, precisely because he does not pursue the philosophic life primarily for the pleasure that it brings, will get to enjoy not only the pleasure appropriate to

99

the philosophic life as such but also, and in due proportion, the pleasures of more commonplace practices. Pleasure, then, would be like a mislaid key: you only find it when you stop looking for it. So in the mythic hymn we will see Socrates transcend the simple opposition of pleasure and the good, and find a place for love, and its attendant delights, in the pursuit of what is best.

But let us consider more closely the simplifications in the psychological picture that Socrates' non-lover paints. If we turn to his definition of love – the definition from which we have seen Plato spin such irony in the later critique of rhetoric – the limitations under which he works become apparent. It is obvious, he begins, that love is a kind of desire (*epithymia*, 237d3); but it is a fact that 'even those who are not in love desire what is beautiful' (237d4–5): so we need to understand more precisely what desire is, and what its species are. Robin rightly compares the quoted phrase with Diotima's speech in the *Symposium* (see R. lxix–lxx), especially *Smp.* 205b–d, in which she re-describes erotic passion as one among many kinds of desire for happiness, thereby laying the foundations of her account of the development of philosophic love, directed towards the beautiful as such, out of erotic beginnings. But this comparison only serves to display the opportunity that the non-lover has muffed. 'Desire for the beautiful' is ambivalent between the goals of pleasure and of the good; but in his subsequent definition he makes it clear that he thinks of desire as striving exclusively for pleasure, at the expense of what is best, and that by the desires of those who are not in love he meant the whole range of self-indulgent appetites among which erotic passion is to be ranked, such as gluttony and drunkenness (237d6–238c4). He shows no inkling, then, that 'desire for the beautiful' could be thought of as proper to the aims of that other principle in the soul: its better judgment.[12] That would be the path along which one could hope to integrate the desires of the whole soul; but Socrates' non-lover has instead paved the way for constant struggle.[13]

Nevertheless, even in Socrates' mythic hymn, as we shall see, it is only through struggle that integration is achieved.

Thus it is no accident that in this speech we hear for the first time of the ideal of 'divine philosophy' (239b4) and witness a concern for clear definitions and rules of enquiry (237b7–d3),[14] since by positing a struggle in the soul the non-lover has at least made an opening for a philosophically mature approach to the ethical issues raised by his suit, and a genuine advance on the thesis of Lysias' persona;[15] so that for all the limitations of his definition of love, its redirection of the focus of discussion to within the soul has had a salutary effect. Hence too, even if Plato accords it only ironic praise in the course of Socrates' retrospective critique, this is to be thought of not as wholesale subversion but rather as a necessary qualification of praise that it has gone some way towards meriting.

Many scholars recognise in the simplifications of Socrates' non-lover the ethical stance and non-technical vocabulary of the average person, such as Socrates also confronts in the *Protagoras* (352d sq.), where he claims that most people view their ethical life in terms of a conflict between acknowledging what is best and wanting what is pleasant.[16] This I think is right; except that the Socratic persona's high-minded allusions to the 'training of the soul' and to 'divine philosophy' seem to put him on a rather more exalted level than the average, although still lacking in philosophic sophistication. We might compare the portrait of the honour-loving 'timocratic' man of the *Republic* (VIII 548b sq.), who is second only to the philosopher in ethical character. The honour-loving person prizes what is best – in the sense of what will redound to his credit among his peers – above the mere satisfaction of his appetite for pleasure; but because he lacks a truly philosophic education, he has not reasoned himself into this course but is following tradition: obeying the voice of the father. Not really understanding *why* he should keep his appetite for pleasure in check, he simply represses it; with the result we might expect. The repressed appetite, as Plato imagines it, is disavowed in public but burns bright within the secret recesses of his soul; and he will sate it in private lovenests financed by clandestine wealth (for that too must not be openly amassed), in which he can thumb his nose at the paternal command with impunity: 'running away from the law as boys from a father' (548b6–7). And this private indulgence in what he feels is unworthy makes him the more hostile in public towards all that he regards as inferior: slaves, for example; to whom he is actively harsh rather than simply indifferent, 'as a sufficiently educated man would be' (549a2). These traits we have seen in Socrates' non-lover also: the hypocritical refusal to acknowledge the passion he longs to indulge; the repression of pleasure without proper understanding of why it should be repressed, or of what its proper place might be; and a consequent hostility and harshness towards it in his public stance.[17]

In terms of the simile that Socrates will fashion for the soul in the properly complex account that he gives of it in his mythic hymn, Lysias' non-lover speaks with the voice of the lustful black horse, for whom there can be no ethical conflict but at most a prudential deferral of the immediate satisfaction of pleasure for the sake of its future maximisation; Socrates' man adds to this drama the voice of the white horse, who seeks honour with the same unreflective determination that his black yoke-mate applies to the pursuit of pleasure, and so can do nothing but bluntly resist the other's aims when they come into conflict with its own;[18] and although both characters claim to speak with the voice of reason, what we have yet to hear is reason's true voice: that of the charioteer, who cannot achieve his own ends without learning from and harmonising *all* voices in the soul.[19]

I will examine that fuller orchestration in the next two chapters; but, granting the limitations of the Socratic non-lover's perspective, we have yet to consider why Plato has Socrates give vent to so inadequate a conception of love in the first place. To understand this we must turn to the dramatic context of the speech, and most especially to the fact which I mentioned at the outset of this section and left in abeyance: that Socrates delivers it under duress.

A manipulative affair

Within the drama of the dialogue, the reason why Socrates comes up with an inadequate psychological account of love in his first speech is clear enough. He has promised Phaedrus to emulate the very same theme that Lysias propounded: that is, to argue the benefits of association with a non-lover rather than a lover; and for this task, he insists, certain commonplaces cannot be dispensed with, such as praise for the non-lover's sobriety and good sense, and the corresponding condemnation of its absence in the lover (235e2–236a3). Before he even begins, then, Socrates has ruled out of court the type of argument required for an adequate phenomenology of love: praise of what is positive in the lover's 'madness'. By allowing himself to be pushed into taking up the issue in the spirit of a rhetorical exercise, in which the speaker's achievement is gauged as much by how he re-styles existing commonplaces as by what new arguments he finds (236a3–6), Socrates has accepted an unnecessarily restrictive set of blinkers on his philosophic vision.

This 'internal' explanation for the inadequacy of Socrates' speech is satisfactory at its own level; but we still need to ask why Plato chose to script the drama in this particular way. I propose that he does so in order to indicate that to pursue such a discussion in the spirit of a rhetorical exercise is no harmless game, but genuinely damaging to the spirit of enquiry;[20] and to show, moreover, that the psychological damage in question – the result, in a word, of manipulativeness – is akin to that described in the very account of love that is supposedly an arena only for rhetorical sport. Let us test this claim.

I have mentioned already that when Socrates refused to accept that Lysias had said all there was to be said on his topic, it was as if he were flicking his cape before the bull; and Phaedrus duly charges. With the prospect of a fresh speech before him, he first tries bribery, promising Socrates nothing less than a golden statue of himself at Delphi if he will make good his criticism and compete with Lysias (235d4–e1) – an

103

offer he then raises, in the face of Socrates' reluctance, to that of a statue by the side of Zeus at Olympia (236b3–4, with the note in de Vr.). From bribery he proceeds to the threat of force (236c8–d3), to no greater avail. Socrates, pleading his status as a layman, refuses to be drawn into competition with a professional like Lysias (236d4–5). But Phaedrus finally comes up with an offer that Socrates can't refuse: he swears a solemn oath that he will never again perform or even report to Socrates any speeches or discussions that he hears in the future, unless Socrates gives him what he wants (236d6–e3). Here at last Socrates' defences crumble, and he declares himself too much a 'word-lover' (*andri philologōi*) to resist Phaedrus' prospective 'feast' (*thoinēs*) (236e4–8). But he is not happy about what he has agreed to do. He covers his head before beginning to speak, claiming that he must veil himself from Phaedrus' sight so as to get through the speech with the greatest possible dispatch and not be distracted by catching Phaedrus' eye, which would shame him into drying up (237a4–5).

Socrates is right to be unhappy. What he has agreed to do, in effect, is to deliver a speech for no better reason than to buy more speeches with it. He is surrendering to his passion for words, unable to resist the banquet Phaedrus spreads before him. But surely this smacks of unsavoury greed? Or does Socrates have a worthier end in view, and is he therefore just playing along with Phaedrus here? The point is this. Socrates may indeed be playing along with Phaedrus – joining in the game he loves to arrange as impresario – for worthy reasons: not because he shares Phaedrus' tendency to value intellectual discussion for its external goods, but because he wants at all costs not to close off the opportunity for further philosophic discussion. But it is a very dangerous game to play nonetheless.

To explain. We have once more come up against those goods of the intellectual life – including friendly association with conversational partners – which, while external to that life, are not merely contingent to it (in the sense recalled earlier in this chapter). Socrates does not pursue intellectual discourse as an end in itself, but in order to discover truth (hence his contempt for the demythologising antiquarians). However, because philosophic conversation is his chosen path towards that goal, he is always ready to talk (this man without sandals, who sits in the agora), at least when he feels there is a hope of leading the conversation in a genuinely philosophic direction; and he is unwilling to let even an unsatisfactory conversation die.[21] But this means that he must constantly struggle to prevent the life of philosophic talk degenerating through its participants into the life of mere words — a danger we have seen abundantly illustrated already, and one which is especially difficult to avoid with a conversational partner such as Phaedrus, who can disarm even an argument designed expressly to win him over to the philosophic life, simply by taking it as just more talk (as the cicadas warned).

Here Socrates has allowed himself, against his better judgment, to be manipulated by Phaedrus; and it is small consolation for him if he is in turn manipulating Phaedrus into providing him a future opportunity for something more genuinely philosophic; for he would prefer not to have to play this conversation as a game of manipulation at all. The tit for tat by which Phaedrus compels Socrates' assent (notice especially the phrasing of 236b9–c6) treats intellectual talk as a commodity which is less important for what it is than for its effects: the system of exchange that it creates. Talk engenders more talk, and Phaedrus' trump is to wager the very existence of the market against Socrates' participation. And Socrates cannot refuse; for he too is in the market, even if he objects to its values.

Those values we have seen, of course, in the rhetorician, who makes a commodity of words in far more than the merely literal sense that he earns his living through speeches.[22] All his professional speeches — not only the display-pieces — are so many rhetorical exercises, since (as he readily admits when teaching) they are valuable not for what they say, but only for the effects of what they say (their effectiveness in persuasion). And we have seen these values too in Lysias' non-lover, who makes a point of caring only for the effects of love, not love itself. It should not surprise us, then, that in his approach to

105

Phaedrus' commerce of words Socrates takes the more shame-faced attitude of his own non-lover. His eagerness for the 'feast' could indeed be mistaken for the cheerful profiteering of Lysias' man; but his subsequent retreat to the veil shows that he cannot indulge in such commercialism without the pious misgivings that lent a sour taste, I showed, to the hypo-critical proposals of his own persona. Phaedrus is impelling Socrates towards hypocrisy: not in the sense that he is about to urge what he does not believe (as we have seen, he later recognises the validity of his non-lover's account, provided it is taken as applying only to an inferior kind of love), but in the sense that he is having to act the rhetorician, and – however eloquently he speaks – he is, in the deepest sense, no rhetori-cian.[23] And Plato marks the parallel with the shiftiness of the non-lover in order to prepare the ground for the final sym-biosis of topic and speaker in Socrates' mythic hymn, in which love of discussion and love for one's discussant are swept up in a single remarkable conception.

Because hostility to love has been *forced* upon Socrates by rhetorical convention – just as his speaker, who is really in love, adopts a hostile tone towards love for strategic reasons only, at least initially – it turns sour inside him, and leads him to indulge *mere* hostility, as opposed to the sober criticism that we have seen him extract from this speech in retrospect – as, by repressing his passion, the non-lover embitters himself against it and in his vivid description of the horrors of mis-matched sex comes to flagellate his own back. Through the mask of his non-lover, Socrates evokes a love that is simply sick: in which lovers, apparently intent on thwarting them-selves, work to render the object of their desire less desirable in order to ensure that it remain in their possession (much as Socrates himself agrees to participate in what he knows to be an unworthy type of intellectual exchange with Phaedrus just in order to ensure Phaedrus' continued cooperation in future conversations). For this kind of lover, domination of the be-loved has become an end in itself. He will do all he can to pre-vent the boy leading a healthy and athletic life, keep him from his family, and from the proper management of his financial affairs, work against his ethical and intellectual development – in short, deprive him of every opportunity of attaining to what his culture agrees is fine and worthy in a person – simply in order to ensure that the boy is not poached by rivals, nor strong enough in character to free himself of his own accord from his lover's control (see esp. 239b4–8; 239e5–240a4). Socrates in effect enlarges the picture of what goes on between the two parts of the lover's soul – in which judgment becomes the outright slave of desire – into an equally one-sided picture of the relationship between lover and beloved, in which the beloved is indentured to the lover and beholden to him in all things (that this is Socrates' procedure he makes explicit at 238e2–4; and cf. its converse at 241a2–b5).

We have already seen the limitations of this conception of the psychology of love by comparison with what Socrates is about to produce in his mythic hymn; but notice that it is a one-sided conception even by comparison with the more standard psychology of love from which it takes its disparaging force. This, indeed, we should expect; for we have seen that, and why, Socrates' non-lover refused to acknowledge any of the traditional benefits of love, which Lysias' more sanguine persona cheerfully recognises. The lover of whom we read in Socrates' speech would utterly crush the boy he pursues; but in the kind of love-poetry to which Socrates refers as his source (he mentions Sappho and Anacreon as its emblems, at 235c3), and from which he has taken such traditional themes as dominance, pursuit, and manipulation, the roles of master and slave are more ambivalently distributed between the partners. To follow after the beloved may indeed be to hunt him aggressively; but it is also to submit to having one's path mapped out by the whim of the elusive prey. Thus, although the love-poets frequently characterise the lover as an aggressor, they view the beloved as a conqueror in his turn; for he subdues lovers with his beauty, and holds the power to grant their desires or not, as he pleases.[24] The lover is said to be sick, and the beloved holds the drug that would cure him;[25] and for all that the lover intends to 'ride' the beloved, the power vested in the beloved to refuse the ride leaves him 'holding the reins'.[26] In all this the exchange of roles between lover and boy does not occur, as Socrates' non-lover would have it, simply when the lover has fallen out of love, and the boy, anxious to claim the rewards of love, is compelled to pursue his former pursuer (241a2–c1), but rather in the course of the erotic liaison itself, in which both partners are allowed their measure of manipulation.

However, the ambivalence that Socrates' non-lover suppresses in his account of love is very evident in the power-broking that Socrates and Phaedrus transact over the speech itself. Here it is Phaedrus, identifying himself as the younger partner in the discussion (236d1), who puts his charms on show – not, of course, his sexuality, but what for a man like Socrates is more fatally attractive: his treasure-house of words – and bargains with this plenty in order to compel Socrates to substantiate his claim (which Phaedrus calls a 'promise', 235d7) to be able to emulate Lysias. And unlike the boy whom Socrates' non-lover pictures running after his faithless seducer, berating him for welching on his promises (241ab), Phaedrus puts his complaints and threats to effective use; for he had not first given away the prize that Socrates seeks, before making his trade.

But for all that this transaction displays a more even distribution of power between its partners, it is nevertheless wholly manipulative (as also is the case – or rather, slips too easily into being the case – with the conventional erotic relationship that it mirrors; just this, indeed, is what prompts the non-lover to cynicism about love and offers him the opportunity to simplify). Phaedrus is determined that Socrates will speak, and pressures him into satisfying this determination regardless of Socrates' own interests – notice that he refuses to acknowledge Socrates' obvious discomfort when he covers his head: 'So long as you speak, I don't mind what else you do' (237a6). And he has, as it were, bought the rights to this pressure by an earlier loss of his own, when Socrates refused to grant Phaedrus what he most wanted, which was to extemporise his own version of Lysias' speech, and insisted that he read instead from Lysias' own text (228c5–d5; of which scene

Phaedrus reminds us here, at 236b9–c6). Phaedrus can understand Socrates' reluctance only as the false bashfulness that he
himself showed (236d6), and an invitation to extract a tit for
tat (236c3).

What is missing from all this is the pursuit of a conjoint interest, common to both partners – as opposed to the mutual
compromise of individual interest.[27] Neither erotic love, nor
discourse among friends, should be a market; and in his
mythic hymn Socrates will transcend the manipulative strategy that has marked both relationships so far by considering
them together, under the single category of loving friendship;
with the result that, from that larger perspective, we will see it
as no accident that Socrates' blinkered account of erotic love
was prompted by manipulative pressure from his conversational partner. For just as Socrates will find a way to reconcile the philosopher's erotic impulse with his intellectual
aspirations, so here, conversely, a souring of intellectual
friendship has a like effect on the attitude taken to erotic
love.[28]

One last consideration will bear out my understanding of
this scene: to wit, Socrates' awkwardness with the poetry of
his own speech. Remember that Phaedrus has forced this
speech on Socrates. Although it is true that Socrates had
claimed without prompting to have something inside himself
on the topic of love which, if it found expression, would be no
worse than Lysias' speech, nevertheless he had represented
this as inchoate, a fullness of heart that he could not properly
understand, and of which he felt unworthy (235c1–d3). But
Phaedrus had immediately trivialised Socrates' feelings by
pressing them into service for rhetorical display and emulation – the kind of practice which would be familiar to him
from his acquaintance with the orators. This Socrates sees
and resents. He knows he is being asked to produce something even more 'sparkling' (*poikilōteron*, 236b7–8) than
Lysias' piece, and grumpily attributes Phaedrus' insistence to
a desire on his part to make his friend Lysias shine the brighter
by comparison (237a9–b1).[29] He duly rises to the challenge,
however, producing in his definition of love (237d6–238c4) a

passage resonant with rhetorical noise – as marked by elaborate systems of synonyms (of which let one example among several suffice: the various verbs of domination at 237d7, e2; 238b2, b5, c3), liberal use of polyptoton (238a4–5, a7, b4, c2) and isocolon (237e2–238a2), not to mention the tortuous syntax of the six-line definition proper (238b7–c4).

Given that this voice has been imposed upon him, it is not to be wondered at that Socrates should react to it as something alien. Having uttered his definition, he breaks off to remark with some astonishment that what he has said comes close to the dithyramb – in Plato's day an archaic form and a by-word for bombast. Some god has affected him; the place must indeed be full of spirits; who knows what might yet happen? And for all this, Phaedrus is responsible (238c5–d7). What happens, we know, is that Socrates proceeds to impersonate an especially inverted and self-castigating character, who becomes quite carried away with hostility towards his own pleasure; and this excess is marked for us in the culminating line of the speech, a motto framed almost in the rhythm of an epic hexameter (241d1). At this point Socrates again breaks off, and this time he professes to be so anxious at the alien poetry falling from his lips – not just dithyrambs now, but epic verse, the loftiest form of all – that he will not risk going on; indeed, he will not continue the discussion in any form, but announces summarily that he is going home (241d2–242a2). And now his resentment of Phaedrus' manipulation comes out in full recriminatory force: not only is Phaedrus responsible for this, but he did it all with malice aforethought (241e4).

Socrates, then, is unable to integrate poetry into his speech for the same reason that he is unable within that speech to integrate pleasure, especially the pleasure of erotic love, into the best kind of life: because of the restrictions that he has wrongly allowed a manipulative Phaedrus to impose on him. As he veiled himself from Phaedrus, in token of resistance against his imposition, and later blames him for what has happened, so he resisted the poetry in his speech as it cropped up, breaking off to put distance between himself and his words; and later makes their metricality an excuse for running away. But it is silly to blame on dithyrambs and epics what is more deeply, psychologically wrong with the speech. This Socrates will implicitly acknowledge, when in his mythic hymn he successfully combines a high poetic tone with a philosophically sophisticated account of love, and distinguishes in the process the truly inspired from the merely technical poet (at 245a1–8). It is the merely technical poet who would fixate on metrical form; and when Socrates comes at last to do justice to the inchoate poetic inspiration he had earlier confessed, it is not poetry as such, any more than it is madness as such, that he condemns, but only poetry improperly – competitively, manipulatively – employed.

Certainly, Socrates continues in his mythic hymn to attribute his inspiration to others – to Stesichorus, since it is a palinode (244a2–3); and he even continues to account Phaedrus responsible for its 'rather poetic vocabulary' (257a5–6). This is only to be expected; after all, we saw in chapter two that, as a philosopher, Socrates is naturally wary of the capacity of poetry to hinder as well as help his pursuit of truth. He does not just *use* poetry, he also thematises it – ponders over the resort to poetic and mythical means to which philosophic speculation has driven him. These means must always remain somewhat alien; for did he not regard them as such, he would not travel in thought to the limits at which they become necessary. And the same can be said, we shall see, of his attitude towards erotic love. To say that Socrates integrates the philosopher's erotic feelings with his intellectual aspirations is not to say that he countenances the indulgence of those feelings between philosophic lovers; he does not (see 256a7–e2). It is rather to say that his philosophic lover does not simply run away from his erotic feelings, as Socrates here would run away from his poetry, but thematises and learns from them. Hence Socrates' appeal to poetic sources and influences in his mythic hymn does not disrupt or distract from the course of his speech but is more fully a part of the hymn itself (the crediting of Stesichorus is delivered in character, witness the address to the boy at 243e9;

and the mention of Phaedrus' influence comes in an *envoi* to Eros – see 257a3).[30]

Let me not, however, appear too acquiescent towards Socrates' own excuses, and place all the blame for the excesses of his non-lover's speech on the restrictions imported by Phaedrus. After all, as I have abundantly acknowledged, Socrates does not in retrospect disavow the content of the speech, but only its lack of integration into a larger perspective. There is indeed something of his non-lover in Socrates. He never ceases to regard the flesh with suspicion – as a contingent casing for the soul (246c2–4) – even when he is learning rather than running from it, and there is but a short step between suspicion and puritanical fear. That is why he is so shaken by how things have developed; for he has felt how susceptible he is to this poisonous drug (see 242d11–e1, and cf. 230d5–e1).[31] What he must overcome, then, is not simply a procedural restriction on Phaedrus' part, but a real fear within himself; and only the sudden shock of seeing what it could do to him proves strong enough to make him confront, in its full complexity, the task of soothing and conquering that fear.

To this task we must now turn; but let us pause, and face up to it in a fresh chapter.

CHAPTER FIVE

MYTH AND UNDERSTANDING

Socrates' preamble

The first thing I wish to note about Socrates' mythic hymn is that it does not begin mythically.[1] Rather, Socrates opens with a catalogue of the benefits historically attributed to madness, in order to controvert a premiss on which the non-lover's argument crucially depends: that madness is simply bad (244a5–8). Socrates, by contrast, has now seen that in certain circumstances madness can achieve beneficial results that would be beyond the reach of sobriety. In particular, he will contend that a philosophic life can best bloom when rooted in what he calls the 'divine' madness of love, as opposed to a merely 'mortal' self-control (256e3–5). It is to support this contention that he will call upon the resources of myth; but first he enumerates three established examples, in domains other than the erotic, of what he means: the prophetic madness of the Delphic Pythia and the priestesses at Dodona, among others, by whose inspired counsel all Hellas has often regulated its decisions for the better (a madness to be contrasted with the sober interpretation of bird-flight and other signs taken as portents of the future) (244a8–d5); the 'telestic' madness of those officiants who, we are told, ritually purified great families in the past of their ancestral crimes and 'diseases': what we might call 'faith-healing' (244d5–245a1);[2] and the poetic madness of those who are seized by the Muses and truly inspired to glorify the deeds of past heroes – as contrasted with the uninspired hack who thinks technique alone will make a poet of him (245a1–8).

We have met before with the contrast that Socrates here presents as holding between the intoxicated and the sober pursuit of various arts: namely, when Socrates assessed with some theoretical abstractness, at the culmination of his critique of rhetoric, what it is that separates the true practitioner of an art from the merely mechanical technician (268a sq.). The difference between the inspired raving of the Pythia and the reading of signs and omens is related – as that metaphor of 'reading' would suggest – to those dangers of the textbook which bulk so large in the second part of the dialogue. For the patterns of bird-flight can be codified, and so offer access to imitative and slavish humbug; but one cannot produce a Pythian oracle by following rules; the only way to do it is to become the Pythia – which is to say, become mad.

What I want to stress is the historical presentation that the issue receives here at the outset of Socrates' speech. Whereas in his critique of rhetoric, as befits a theoretical account which aims to legislate current rhetorical practice, he invokes the most modern strain of medicine (the Hippocratic) and contemporary poets (Sophocles and Euripides), in his mythic hymn he adduces rather those ancient rites of healing which Hippocratic physicians in his day were casting in the un-favourable light of superstition;[3] and he names no contem-porary poets, but rather emphasises how trūe poetry adorns the 'achievements of the ancients' (*tōn palaiōn erga*, 245a4 – as it is 'ancient pollution' in the great families, *palaiōn ek mēnimatōn*, 244d6, that he claims was cleansed by the rites of healing). His star example, however, is the art of prophecy; and here too he highlights past rather than current achieve-ment – and this even though the Delphic oracle, for one, was still active in his time. Thus the mere mention of the Pythia, the Sibyl, and others is sufficient to invoke a rich tradition of involvement in the grand events of Greek history, which Socrates can pass over as well known to all (244a8–b5); and the heyday of the prophetic art he situates in the ancestral past, when the ancients (*palaiōn*, again, 244b6) appreciated prophetic madness for what it was, and distinguished it from the reading of portents. This he supports with some extrava-gant etymology: the 'mantic' art was originally the 'manic', showing clearly its connection with madness, and the 'oion-istic' art of reading bird-flight (*oiōnos*, 'a bird of omen') would derive its name, by contrast, from a cocktail of words denoting 'sequential thought' (*oiēsis*, 'thinking'; *nous*, 'mind'; and *historia*, 'enquiry', 'account'). But the finer points of these etymologies, no less, he implies, than of the arts they name, are lost on the present generation (244c1–d5).

As he prepared to deliver his speech, Socrates had compared it to the *Palinode* of Stesichorus, in which the poet atoned for his blasphemy against Helen by a public recantation, and cured himself, in the process, of the blindness which that blasphemy had incurred. So too, Socrates will abjure his earlier blasphemy against the god of Love, adopting what he calls this 'ancient spell of purification' (*katharmos arkhaios*, 243a4). So we should not be surprised at the fact that he begins his hymn with praise for all that is archaic, and a measure of contempt for the new. By the same token, however, it is not surprising that in his critique of rhetoric, when he comes to adduce contemporary arts for comparison, prophecy is not even mentioned; for the role of what in his hymn he calls 'the finest art, by which the future is judged (*hēi to mellon krinetai*)' (244c1) had been largely usurped in his society by rhetoric itself. Key speakers in political assemblies could now be regarded as having the kind of power over social planning for the future that was once a prerogative of oracles (cf. 260c6–d1) – and which Plato dreamed of committing to the hands of philosophers.

Now, we need not doubt the sincerity of the praise for a bygone age that Plato puts on Socrates' lips. One target of Socrates' invocation of the past is the risk which attends the practice of any art as it acquires a history and a set of traditions: that it should become burdened with mere procedure, elaborated for its own sake. That is surely one of the points made by the fancy etymologies. In the present day, it is suggested, we ignore the important distinction between prophetic madness and the reading of portents, but are very careful to mind our p's and q's in the names we assign to practices that we no longer fully appreciate – rather, our omegas and omikrons, for the moderns insist on spelling the 'oionistic' art with that new-fangled long 'o' (244c5–d1), camouflaging their ignorance of what matters with a fastidious attention to

115

externals.[4] And a similar ignorance is seen in the merely technical poet, who believes that he need only learn what can be codified, and he will be able to produce good poetry (as the moderns do not appreciate the distinction between a skill like reading bird-flight, which can be passably practised by learning a fixed code, and the prophetic ability of the Pythia, in which codification has no part).[5] The whole tenor of Socrates' subsequent critique of rhetoric, as we have seen, is to show the extent to which contemporary rhetoric has fallen into this trap – the excessive emphasis on textbook codification and on externals – and to elaborate a means of avoiding it.

Nevertheless, if Socrates' appeal to the past sets out a genuine danger for the present, it does not suggest that the way to eliminate it would be simply to turn back the clock. Notice that, when he came to the decision to deliver a palinode, Socrates declared himself 'a prophet, though not an entirely serious one (*mantis men, ou pany de spoudaios*) . . . but good enough for my own purposes' (242c4–5); for he had realised what future course he must take in order to correct his error (242c5–d2). I take this as a due qualification on the seriousness of his appeal to an earlier age: namely, that if philosophy is to take over from inspired prophecy as the practice which governs the course of our lives, it must not simply repeat its method – or rather, lack of method. Socrates hedges over his prophetic power – just as he cannot espouse myth wholeheartedly, but only as a necessary resource from which he must maintain a careful distance (this we have seen already, and will examine further in what follows) – for his 'daemonic sign', in obedience to which he stays to make his palinode (242b8–c3), acts only to restrain him from an improper course of action (cf. *Apology* 31c7–d4), but does not tell him what he must do. Unlike the Pythia, who acts purely as a medium for the god's voice, and issues positive commands or messages in his name, Socrates' daemonic sign remains in the background – maps out, indeed, the background limits to his life, what he *cannot* find it in himself to do, and therefore, what he can – and leaves to philosophy all the positive work of understanding what is proper (in addition to shrinking

116

from what is felt as improper), of winning that understanding through methodical discussion, and so justifying the decisions taken at the prompting of the daemonic voice.[6] Thus Socrates will not rest with his ancient spell of purification, but will proceed to modern-minded theorising in his critique of rhetoric; and as we have seen, it is by appreciating the limitations of both that he comes to terms with his own art, and sees what the rhetoricians and sophists ignore at their peril.

This is another point made by Socrates' use of etymology. That he must trace the ancient wisdom by rifling the debris of the dictionary indicates that those for whom prophetic madness truly meant something spoke a language that we no longer speak.[7] As the sober scrutineers of bird-flight rely on external signs alone for their judgments, and do not hear an inner voice, so when it comes to the ancient seers Socrates must look to signs in order to evaluate what once was. It is not in this art that his aspirations can take wing; that he can become bird rather than – better, as well as – bird-watcher (the philosopher in the throes of love and recollection of the Forms is compared to a bird later in the speech, at 249d5– e1).[8] Yet he does at least recognise what the contemporary thematisation of the technical component of art, with its emphasis on handbooks and treatises, stands at risk of losing; he reads the signs of what can go wrong when the reading of signs is overvalued.[9]

This interpretation of the historical strain in Socrates' preamble, I submit, is confirmed by, and gives good sense to, a later passage in the mythic hymn which has proved a puzzle and source of contention among commentators. In the course of his myth, Socrates first describes the activity of our disembodied souls, and then their fall to earth and embodiment in a particular type of human life. These types of life he disposes in a descending hierarchy of nine ranks, and invokes a cosmic law which assigns each soul to one of these ranks on the basis of how full a vision it has enjoyed of the realm of Forms. King of the castle, of course, is the philosopher (248d3–4); but only fifth and sixth in line, after the monarch, the statesman, and the physician, and at the cusp before the clearly inferior types of life of the manual craftsman, the sophist, and the tyrant, come the prophet and the poet respectively (248d4–e2). Now, this would appear to jar with what Socrates had said in his preamble; for there he had portrayed the inspired prophet and poet in a favourable light, as affected by kinds of madness different from but quite on a par, it seemed, with the erotic madness which he was about to consider in the philosopher.

One proposal for reconciling the two passages is that the prophets and poets who occupy these low ranks are the merely technical, uninspired practitioners with whom Socrates contrasts the god-maddened Pythia and the true poet.[10] But it founders on the following difficulty: if this were Plato's intention, why would he simply refer to the low-ranking practitioners as 'prophets' and 'poets', without any saving restriction of the sort that he had previously specified?[11]

A better understanding of the apparent inconsistency becomes available if we bear in mind the two points which I have been stressing: that in his preamble Socrates adopts a historical perspective, and that he does not turn to myth until coming to his account of the erotic madness of the philosopher – to which the nine-fold hierarchy belongs. Inspired love, although a further kind of god-given madness (245b7–c1), requires a different approach from that taken to the three previous kinds. Socrates does not recount its historical achievements but begins a 'demonstration' (*apodeixis*) of its potential benefits (245b1–c4).[12] And this demonstration engages him in a myth that radically revises the moral psychology of love. We can therefore see why it is that Socrates turns from history to myth at this point: he has no choice. There is no widely acknowledged historical precedent for the benefits of philosophic love; for the philosophic way of life is a new way, which does not simply establish itself alongside the more ancient paths of inspiration, but – as we saw when considering Socrates' emphasis on the archaic nature of those paths – partly usurps their function.

Thus, when he comes to establish the new order by means

of myth, Socrates puts the present-day prophet and poet firmly in their place, and wreathes the philosopher in a complex array of titles: 'a seeker after wisdom or beauty, a follower of the Muses and a lover' (248d3–4). The philosopher, it is suggested, must be the 'compleat' artist: as counsellor, as poet, as healer of souls (since this, we shall see, is the role that lovers bear to one another); for the world has grown up, and has left the more traditional arts behind – at least in their earlier role as guides for how to live one's life. In short: for all that Socrates' hymn appeals to timeless standards (the Forms), it is infused with historical awareness – the awareness that appreciation of those standards has been developing over time; and in this light it seems natural that what Socrates sets out in his myth should not match the historical viewpoint of his preamble.

However, I do not wish to minimise the fact that Plato has written the mismatch with no explanation or dampening of its effect, so that it will jar on any attentive reader. This strikes me as all of a piece with the jarring effect that governs the dialogue as a whole, in its bruque transition from poetry to analysis. He wants us to see, I take it, that the development of philosophy out of other arts is not smooth or clean; that a certain reserve, even awkwardness towards its parents is characteristic of this art that examines the conditions of all arts.[13]

Coping with contingency

I have said that Socrates has no choice but to shift from the historical to the mythical register when he comes to establish the benefits of philosophic love, since there was no historical precedent for this new kind of divine madness. This consideration, however, shows only why Socrates cannot in this case appeal to history; not why he must therefore turn to myth (as opposed to straight argumentation, of the type exemplified in the previous speeches). The immediate cause of his recourse to myth is that, in order properly to assess the value of the loving relationship among philosophic types, he deems it necessary

119

to give an account of the nature of the soul (245c2–4) – thus in a sense following the advice he later gives the orators to establish their relation with the audience on the strength of psychological understanding (at 270b–271c). But to render such an account directly, to describe the soul 'as it is' (*hoion men esti*), would, he insists, be 'in every way a matter of utterly divine and lengthy discourse'; whereas to state 'what it resembles' (*hōi de eoiken*) – which will in fact amount to a full-blown mythical allegory – is discourse of a 'human and shorter' kind, and the path that he will therefore take (246a4–6).

Now, it is difficult to gauge whether Plato means to dismiss any attempt to describe the soul 'as it is', on the grounds that this would be to aim for an outright impossibility; and if so, what bearing such a dismissal would have on Socrates' subsequent recommendation to the orators that they analyse the nature of the soul. The phrasing here seems deliberately to shun hard and fast categorisation. When Socrates calls a task 'divine' he is not necessarily putting it beyond philosophic reach – at least if we bear in mind that he will go on to describe the philosophic lover as moulding himself and his beloved in the image of his god. And are we to think of 'lengthy' (*makras*) as a litotes for that which transcends considerations of length, or understand it rather in terms of the 'long circuit' (*makra periodos*, 274a2) that Socrates recommends to Teisias, and which refers to the pattern of a human (not divine) life lived out with a 'cosmic' perspective; with a sense that the soul is not ultimately constrained by the temporal limits of that life?[14]

It seems that Plato avoids giving a straightforward reply to the question whether an account of the soul 'as it is' is an attainable ideal. But one thing is clear: that when Socrates comes to describe the soul, he declares himself somehow *constrained* to the indirect approach of allegory; and I want now to consider why this should be so. And my answer will also illuminate Plato's caginess over the attainability of the direct account. I have had something to say already in this book, especially in my opening two chapters, on why Socrates is made to resort to myth, and why a non-mythical paraphrase leaves us no better off: briefly, because to attempt to capture the conditions of the philosophic life, as Socrates does, is already to engage in philosophy, and therefore, inevitably, to show what one is telling; and that myth, which for Plato has become a verbal medium that confesses its own inadequacy, is an ideal medium to convey the non-verbal background to philosophic verbalising – the sense in which philosophers learn their art by learning *about* their art (that is, the sense in which that particular kind of philosophic 'saying' is also a philosophic 'doing'). Put that way, however, there is a danger that the point might seem merely technical: not a true plumbing of philosophic depths, but simply the familiar effect of vertigo that meta-philosophic considerations readily induce. This danger is averted, I believe, and the point made more meaningful, if we bear in mind that Plato equates the practice of philosophy with the right way to live. Thus, the sense in which philosophers, just by seeking the conditions of philosophy, already have some understanding of what they seek to understand fully (which is what requires an appeal to the 'background' of understanding), is to be interpreted not just as a curious epistemological feature of philosophic practice, but rather with an ethical force: as the way in which the search for the good life can be said to be partly constitutive of the good life itself. By setting up the soul as the target of his myth, Socrates gives this ethical turn to his walk into the background. I will establish that thesis only gradually, by examining the mythic hymn as it unfolds; indeed, since the point I have just made about the good life, taken by itself, is something of a chestnut, the psychological detail with which it emerges is rather what must hold our attention. But I will state the nub of what I have to say now, as a preliminary guide.

A special characteristic of any investigation into the nature of the soul is this: that the understanding gained about the soul in general has the potential to change the soul of the investigator in particular. By looking into your soul as one among others, you can make it truly yours: mould your character, fashion a life for yourself. In this sense, to *learn about* the soul can also be – will also be, if approached in the right spirit – to *learn* a way of life (as I said the philosopher learns philosophy partly by learning about it). In accordance with this phenomenon, Socrates in his mythic hymn examines not only the nature of the soul but also the nature of the phenomenon itself: what happens to philosophers when they look into the soul; for he wants to stress the subjective effects of the investigation on the investigators, as well as its objective results. And he does so by analysing, not the philosopher's examination of himself, but how he both teaches and learns from that second self, his beloved. But, given that this is Socrates' purpose, it would not do for him to pretend that an objective and impersonal analysis of the soul is the whole of what the philosopher should aim at, although it will certainly be *part* of his goal; rather, he must in addition be aware of what he is doing to his own soul (and to the soul of his beloved) by adopting the impersonal perspective.

And here mythic allegory takes up its proper place. Consider: we are looking at the soul in general as a way of looking into our own souls; so that from the outset we are concerned not only to understand the soul impersonally but also to understand what meaning our discoveries have in the context of our own lives. Hence, as we discover truths about the soul as such, we bring about a change in the object of investigation that we call our selves. Now, an allegory does not present the soul as it is, but says what it is like. It is a way – not the only way, perhaps, but an excellent way – of both acknowledging and putting into effect the twofold perspective of our enquiry: how we are looking into the soul in general, and our own (and our lovers') souls in particular; and how we are thus not only scrutinising our target from a distance, but changing its nature, creating it anew.[15] So too Socrates' mythic allegory, for all that it is inspired by contemplation of an object that exists independently of himself, bears on its face the fact that it is his *creation*; and this is crucial to his kind of self-scrutiny. For in order to change his soul, and the souls of his audience (or beloved), it would not be sufficient to describe the soul as it is, even if he were capable of doing so; he must in addition paint a picture – say what the soul is like – in which he and his audience can *recognise* themselves: only so can the enquiry be meaningful for them.[16] And yet he devalues the allegorical task, despite its necessity, in relation to the impersonal description: *that*, he says, would be the divine achievement. Indeed; for he regards the need for myth as unfortunate, a result of the sad contingency of our embodied state. The mythical tale that he tells – like the idealisations that lovers construct of one another – is a way of both expressing and coping with this fact of contingency; and it is a major feature of Plato's world-view that he sees contingency as something to be coped with, rather than glorified.[17]

Myth as explanation: the self-moving soul

I will begin to put some flesh on the bones of my interpretation by considering why it is that, even after Socrates has announced his shift from a historical roll-call of the benefits of various kinds of madness to a demonstration of the advantages of love-madness in particular, he does not in fact immediately have recourse to allegory, but prefaces his myth with a brief argument to prove the immortality of the soul – an argument based on the bare capacity of the soul to change itself, and presented in a thoroughly abstract and rigorous style (245c5–246a2).

I shall not tarry over the question of its soundness, which has been adequately discussed by others.[18] As an argument that begins with a definition and ends with an eternal existent, it is no less stimulating than it is dubious. But what I do wish to stress is that the shift from rigorous argument to mythical allegory confronts us with just that interplay between the impersonal and the individualised view of the soul which was summarised in the previous section. Even if we were to consider the argument sound, the 'self-moving soul' whose immortality it establishes is presented in what we might call a cosmic guise, as no more than a motor for inanimate matter (245c7–9; 245e4–6), rather than as the quiddity of the individual – a point which holds regardless of whether Plato felt that his argument nevertheless supported a belief in personal immortality. Scholarly debate on this latter question begins from the ambiguity of the declaration with which he opens the argument. Are the words *'psykhē pasa athanatos'* (245c5) to be understood as saying *'all* soul is immortal', or that *'every* soul is immortal'? A decision in favour of the former alternative would suggest that something like the 'world-soul' of the *Timaeus* is primarily before Plato's mind, whereas one in favour of the latter, although presumably no one would deny the cosmic viewpoint of the argument, would stem from a belief that Plato wishes to enlist this viewpoint in the cause of personal immortality. Scholars have been unable to find conclusive reasons for a decision either way, and some have been prompted thereby to assert that the distinction is not here in Plato's thoughts.[19] I wish to suggest, on the contrary (and the plausibility of this suggestion must rest on how well it fits with my interpretation of the speech as a whole) that the distinction is very much in his thoughts; that the ambiguity of 'all soul/every soul' is an intended ambiguity if ever there was one. For it is emblematic of the insufficiency of the impersonal view of the soul fully to capture what Socrates demands of psychological enquiry.

To explain this point. Socrates' argument treats the soul as cosmic 'soul-stuff': the general principle and source of change for the universe (245d1–e2). But whether or not he believes that his conclusions apply also to that portion of soul-stuff which we each possess as individuals, it remains the case that when he comes to describe the soul he must have recourse to myth – to a story – because only in a story can we recognise ourselves (that is, dramatically identify ourselves) as human agents, and only so can our enquiry *change* us as individuals – at least, only so can it change us in ways of which we are aware; and thus enable us to gain self-knowledge. Hence the argument for immortality is intentionally ambivalent as to its range of application; for even if it applies to the individual, it cannot alone affect the individual.

However, it is surely significant that the peculiar quality of psychological enquiry derives from the very same principle as that from which Socrates argues the immortality of the soul. By thinking about the soul, I noted, we can change our souls – in other words, the soul is able to change itself by virtue of its own proper activity, thought – and this change will have consequences for the furniture of the world we inhabit, and which we like to rearrange. What is this but a particular application to the philosophic enquirer of Socrates' impersonal account of the soul as that which alone can change itself, and affects things other than itself by virtue of that power?[20] Plato's point would be this: if we look on the soul from an impersonal standpoint, we see that its capacity to provide its own source of change is essential to it; but for that very reason the impersonal view is insufficient for the enquiry into the soul, even according to its own parameters: for, if we claim that the soul, seen impersonally, can personally change itself by its own activity, we must, as a direct consequence of our impersonal explanation, also acknowledge the personal effect on the soul of adopting this impersonal view – an effect which cannot be conveyed purely in impersonal terms, even though it can be seen as resulting from their adoption.

On this interpretation, Plato would be recognising the importance of the contingent aspect of the philosophic life (and of myth as a tool for coping with it), an importance which springs from the very fact that philosophers attempt to render themselves so far as possible independent of human contingency.

Myth as explanation: gods and men

Let us pursue this train of thought by considering a well-known crux that presents itself at the outset of the mythical allegory. Socrates likens the immortal souls of both men and gods to a winged assemblage of two horses and a charioteer. In divine souls, both horses are good; whereas the team in a human soul is unmatched, one horse being good, the other bad (246a6–b4). Thus, he apparently holds that the disembodied soul is a composite entity. But this is difficult to square

125

with views propounded elsewhere in the dialogues. In the *Phaedo* the immortal soul is described as incomposite in its true nature, indeed immortal just to the extent that it is incomposite (78b–81a); *Republic* X tells a similar story (611d–612a), and this despite the tripartition of the soul in Book IV; while in the *Timaeus* immortality is granted only the controlling, 'divine' part of the soul, with the other two parts being described as mortal, and relegated to separate zones of the body (69c–72d). In *Laws* X, however, we find a view more like that in the *Phaedrus*: the 'motions' attributed to the immortal soul cover the whole range of human psychological states (897ab). The reactions of commentators are also tripartite. There are those who give full value to the details of the Phaedran allegory, and argue a development in Plato's psychology;[21] those who suggest that such details are not to be pressed, and hold that Plato's view here is fundamentally the same as that of *Republic* X and the *Timaeus*;[22] and those who believe that Plato simply vacillated on the issue throughout his life.[23]

I side with the first camp, at least in so far as I accept the argument that so important and pervasive a detail of the myth cannot be passed over as a narrative convenience (I am less sure of how radical a development in Plato's psychology this would represent);[24] and my explanation of why Plato should stress that even the divine soul has a composite nature is the following.[25] All soul, says Socrates, 'cares for' (*epimeleitai*) the inanimate; but whereas when the soul is 'perfect' (*telea*) it governs the cosmos as a whole, if it should lose its wings it falls to earth and becomes the motive force for only a single, mortal body (246b6–c6). Thus it is not only the human soul which changes other things – such as the human body – by virtue of its power to change itself (see 246c4); this activity is equally characteristic of the divine soul, albeit at a more cosmic level (compare how Zeus is later said to 'order and care for' – *epimeloumenos* – 'everything', 246e5–6). Here I find Plato's motive for stressing the complexity of the soul at all levels. When Socrates comes to examine in detail (at 253c7–255a1) the behaviour of the charioteer in the philosopher's soul – his naturally controlling part – we shall see that the charioteer's own special goal is to ensure that the special goals of all three actors in the soul, his own and those of the two horses, find their proper fulfilment (where by 'proper' is meant, of course, what the charioteer deems proper). His goal is thus distinct from theirs, but distinct precisely in that it fulfils itself *through* his concern for the proper fulfilment of their goals. So too with divine purpose: the gods, no less than any disembodied soul (and, in the mythical hierarchy, rather more), are concerned for all parts of the cosmos, not just for their place in it; hence also for inanimate matter. And this concern for the material, I suggest, Plato thinks of as the divine equivalent of embodied human appetites, and models in the matched horses: the 'sensuous' side, as it were, of the gods' nature. Being a distinct element in the make-up of the gods, the horses require their own special food: not the vision of the Forms on which the charioteer 'feasts' (247e3), but the more traditional mythic fare of nectar and ambrosia (247e4– 6) – since, although the highest activity of these traditionally named gods is a most untraditional philosophic contemplation, their concern for earthly goings-on links them still with the Homeric originals.

That Plato sees fit to set the divine horses at a separate manger is a good indication that he thinks the distinction between the parts of divine soul worth marking in itself, rather than simply for the sake of a tidy correspondence with the human soul-chariot, on which he subsequently focuses. But it may be thought that I have not yet made out the independent need for such a distinction. If it is characteristic of the charioteer to be concerned for the whole soul, and thus for the relation of the soul to its environment, why cannot the gods' concern for the cosmos stem purely from this rational desire for overall well-being? Why would Plato choose to model this involvement, as I claim, by complexifying the divine soul, when it seems that he could have achieved the same result with a soul that was, as it were, all charioteer? I reply: because he wants to show that his gods, no less than mythmaking mortals, must cope with contingency.

127

The charioteer, as I have mentioned, represents the 'naturally' governing part of the soul (a characteristic which I will consider more explicitly and theoretically in the next chapter), and thus has *par excellence* that power which in the argument for the immortality of the soul is attributed to the soul in general: the power to change other things by virtue of its capacity for self-change. The charioteer is thus indeed the source of the soul's concern to order and control 'the inanimate' (*tou apsykhou*, 246b6). However, a concern for the inanimate – that which is not soul – is not equivalent to a concern for the material environment which, *as it happens*, constitutes the inanimate. For Plato, the nature of the material realm which is ordered by the disembodied soul under the guidance of its charioteer is quite accidental to the nature of the Forms, the vision of which the charioteer alone enjoys (247c7–8).[26] The charioteer's own desire is to order the whole soul, hence to bring it into harmonious relation with its environment. But, so far as the charioteer is concerned, it is the activity of ordering that counts, not the contents of the environment; his concern for the environment is, one might say, a concern for *whatever else there is*, and not for the material realm as such. That larger concern is represented as resulting from the charioteer's vision of the Forms; and it is merely contingent that the administrative activity which that vision sustains has as its object our material cosmos. Yet, once given this ultimate contingency, the soul's desire to administer the stuff of things will nevertheless stem from its essential nature.

The reader will recognise here the recurrence, albeit in mythical terms, of a feature of the philosophic life upon which I have already had more than one occasion to remark: the curious status of those goods which, although external to the philosophic life, nevertheless belong to it more than just accidentally; goods such as intellectual friendship and the thrill of discovery; all those goods, in short, which result from the realisation of the philosophic impulse in our actual lives – and which, of course, are goods that philosophic lovers bring to one another. Now, the status of these goods is illuminated

128

for us by Plato's mythical projection onto the cosmic screen of questions arising from the philosophic life – a screen where philosophic contemplation of the Forms is seen to be the sustaining condition (the 'food'; see 247a8) of the gods' concern for a cosmos the sensible element of which is alien to them; and where these gods represent the highest model to which the human soul can aspire (248a1–4). For we thus see that such cosmic projection is not a mere indulgence of mythical fancy, but an example of what philosophers *must* do if they are to approach these peculiar goods of the philosophic life with the appropriate attitude. In other words, it is just by taking a 'cosmic' view of, say, friendship – seeing it as an ultimately contingent function of the paraphernalia in the playground in which their philosophic impulse has been left to roam – that philosophers can keep it from becoming an end in itself, and so losing its benefits; and yet can enjoy those benefits as especially proper to the philosophic character, just because, again, their impulse is to take the cosmic view of them. That is, they genuinely care for friendship – and do not simply use it as a means to some higher goal – just to the extent that they recognise that it is, ultimately, only accidental that they care for *friendship* (and not some other thing), yet also recognise that that recognition is intrinsic to their way of life.[27]

I submit, then, that Plato invents his cosmic myth in order to illuminate – make us recognise – what happens when philosophers cope with contingency by attempting to gain the cosmic or impersonal perspective while maintaining their personal sense of who they are and why they are making the attempt – an example of which is furnished by the myth itself. And this also explains why the gods have horses. They are not needed to model the possibility of moral conflict (to which only human souls, with their unbalanced team, are inherently susceptible) but in order to capture, first, how the gods' concern for the material cosmos as such is only contingent to their concern for the whole, on which it depends; but second, how, precisely because of this contingency (because, as it were, they find the material cosmos thrust upon them) the

129

gods nevertheless really *are* concerned for the material cosmos *as such*, and not simply as a means to satisfy their concern for the whole (the desire of the charioteer). For that supposed concern for the whole would not be genuine, nor genuinely satisfied, if the gods were just to *use* the cosmos in this fashion. But the charioteer's care nevertheless is not, and cannot be, directed towards the material *as such* (cf. 247d1–2); hence this care must be lodged in a separate centre of desire: the horses.[28] Let the unchanging Forms be independent of what lies outside them; but not the active gods.

To understand the divine model is not, of course, to succeed in thinking oneself into the psychology of the god. But the importance of the model, as I have explained, stems rather from its power to illuminate how, and in what circumstances, the human soul attempts that feat of imagination, and why the attempt is worthwhile. These gods are not beyond our imagination; the difference between the divine and the human soul is one of degree rather than kind. For what distinguishes the divine soul is not the simple unity of pure reason but the perfect harmony of its parts, resulting from complete understanding (the vision of the Forms); but human souls too can attain understanding and induce concord between the parts; only less, and with great effort – for our parts are not inherently harmonious (246b4; 248a1–5).[29] The gods are perfect because they perfectly understand how to cope with contingency, and evade its potentially disruptive psychological effects.

Before leaving this issue, I will briefly show how two further details of the myth – details which are somewhat disconcerting at first glance – fit well with my interpretation. First, it is notable that, when Socrates distinguishes the divine from the human soul (246a–d), and when he describes the gods' vision of the Forms (247c–e), he likens each god to the whole assemblage of charioteer and horses; but when, in between these passages (at 246e–247c), he pictures the progress of 'Zeus, the mighty leader in heaven, who drives his winged chariot' in company with the traditional pantheon (246e4–5), he is clearly equating each god with the charioteer alone.

Were Zeus to step down from his chariot, he would still be Zeus; allegory proper alternates with full-scale myth. The point, I take it, is that the charioteer does indeed represent the essential nature of the god, in the sense that only by virtue of the charioteer's successful vision of the Forms is he in need of horses; only by virtue of the activity of the part of the soul which reflects on the proper activity for the whole soul (that is, for the soul in relation to its environment) does the god have that concern for the cosmos which cannot be equated with the activity of its reflective part alone (as just shown).

Second, it is striking that these gods are not represented as engaged in eternal contemplation of the Forms, but 'feast' on that vision only periodically, and for the span of a fixed revolution of the heavens (247c1–2, d5, e2–4). Their proper home is in the heavens (246d7; 247e4); but the Forms belong elsewhere, in a 'place beyond the heavens' (*hyperouranion topon*, 247c3) which the gods must travel to reach – for all that their journey is no effort to them. We do not explicitly hear of this place in any other of Plato's myths; and indeed his depiction of the gods here makes something of a contrast with that of, say, the *Symposium* (esp. 202c sq.) or the *Republic* (esp. II 380e sq.), according to which the gods are models of perfect and unchanging wisdom, who lack nothing that is good. The two portrayals are not by any means incompatible, since neither do the Phaedran gods lack for anything. Their periodic journey is effortless and imposes no felt constraint. Yet in those other dialogues the gods enjoy an existence free from the periodicity and sense of journeying that give shape – and travail – to a human life; so that here in the *Phaedrus* it is strange to find divine perfection mythically expressed through just those motifs. Hackforth suggests that Plato was responding only to the exigencies of mythical topography: 'We are not to infer that the gods' contemplation of [the Forms] is only occasional, and limited on each occasion to the definite time occupied by the revolution... The gods' movements are merely consequent upon the conception of a supracelestial region' (H. 80). I find this too swift a leap from the literal to the purely literary. We can readily grant that Plato is not concerned to impose time-constraints on divine contemplation, without therefore assuming that those constraints are written in simply for dramatic verisimilitude. Rather, we should at least consider whether they are not part and parcel of the philosophic preoccupation which led Plato here to locate the Forms in a special 'supra-celestial region' in the first place.

In Plato's various descriptions of the gods we surely find different aspects of the ideal by which human beings are to regulate their lives (albeit by recognising the extent to which the ideal is unrealisable in a human life); and the variety of those descriptions is best accounted for by relating each to the particular philosophic concerns of the dialogue in which it is embedded. In the *Symposium* he enlists the psychological effects of love primarily in the cause of emancipating the philosopher from contingency, and accordingly, in his description of the gods, he emphasises their freedom from the very structure of human concerns, and assigns to Eros the status of intermediary 'daemon' (*Smp.* 202de); in the *Phaedrus*, by contrast, he is more directly concerned with how such ideas and feelings as those examined in the *Symposium* get themselves communicated (hence too with what philosophy owes to rhetoric), and focuses on the human quality of the relationship between philosophic lovers:[30] on how they can justifiably shape their lives around one another even while recognising the ultimate contingency of their friendship; how they can reconcile their common goal in coming together, the attainment of the impersonal perspective, with their personal concern for one another. And so it is the ease with which the gods reconcile their contemplation of the Forms with their activity as administrators of the contingent – an idealised version of the structure of human activity rather than a quite different structure – that he chooses to emphasise, while reserving that quite other dimension for the Forms; and with the gods brought thus closer to earth, the status of Eros can now be assessed more casually as that of 'a god or something divine' (*theos ē ti theion*, 242e2).[31]

132

Myth as explanation: choice and chance

It is becoming clear, I trust, that Plato's mythical account of the adventures of the disembodied soul does two jobs at once: it both describes the place of contingency in the philosophic life, and in so doing *makes* a place for it; makes bearable the contingency of the contingent. The myth is a weapon in the struggle for understanding that it describes. I will select one final element of its rich eschatology in order to bring this point to a sharp focus.

In the opening section of this chapter, we saw that the outcome of the soul's struggle to glimpse the region beyond the heavens dictated the kind of life it would lead after falling to earth and taking up its place in one of the nine ranks. I want now to consider in what sense the mythical narrative can be said to be 'explanatory' of ethical behaviour in the kinds of life that we know; in particular, I want to consider whether any claim to explanatory value that might be made for it is disarmed by the large element of *luck* that Socrates builds into his story. Thus, if we ask why souls fall to earth in the first place, we are told that they 'meet with some mishap' (*tini syntykhiai khrēsamenē*) and are 'weighed down with forgetting and wrongdoing (*lēthēs te kai kakias*)' (248c6–7); but we are not told what that mishap might have been, nor is it clear whether 'wrongdoing' (or is it 'weakness'? – an alternative translation) is distinct from 'forgetting' or simply a gloss upon it, nor indeed whether 'forgetting and wrongdoing' are distinct from or simply a gloss upon the 'mishap' (as if one were to say: to forget the Forms is wrong; but this can just happen). We flounder as we seek the firm ground of moral responsibility in this concatenation of events; much as the souls themselves floundered and fell (at 248a6–b1) in their search for full understanding (the vision of the Forms) – the very event that we are trying to understand. Similarly, when the soul enters upon successive lives – in the cycle of reincarnation that is set in motion by the fall to earth – its future status depends partly on its own 'choice' (*hairesin*, 249b2), as

133

conditioned by the kind of person it has previously been (thus a philosopher must choose the philosophic life three times running in order to escape the cycle; see 249a1–5), but partly also on its luck in a 'lottery' (*klērosin*, 249b2).[32] For Hackforth 'the meaning is of course that our lives are partly predestined, partly self-chosen' (H. 88); while Thompson sees here 'a mythical mode of reconciling freedom and necessity' (Th. apud 249b).

Indeed; but I want to ask whether calling this mode of reconciliation 'mythical' is just a polite way of denying that reconciliation has been achieved. Hackforth seems to have thought that the myth does no more than *state* the truth for which it purports to account. But I believe it offers something more. Clearly, as a way of mapping the limits of ethical choice, it fails to satisfy; for it merely reduplicates in the next world the historical combination of fortune and fallibility that characterises our lives in this world. But I take my lead from the fact that, far from glossing over this explanatory weakness, Plato fearlessly advertises it. When describing the difficulty that some find in recalling during this life the vision gained in the afterlife he offers two reasons: their disembodied vision was only brief; or they have been 'unlucky' (*edystykhēsan*) in the company into which they have fallen on earth, whose bad influence has led them to 'forget' (*lēthēn . . . ekhein*) their vision (250a1–4). We have seen that both mishaps and reprehensible mistakes combine, in a somewhat cloudy mixture, to limit achievement in the afterlife; and here that account is simply coordinated with a similar blend of factors in the ethical life we know. For if it is bad luck that people grow up among or meet with bad company, this does not prevent us – or prevent Socrates, at any rate – from describing the result to which chance has thus contributed as a *moral* failure, a 'turn towards injustice' (*epi to adikon trapomenai*, 250a3–4).

When making moral judgments, we commonly take into account what is and is not within the control of the agent, and restrict properly moral agency to the former domain. It strikes us as unsatisfactory, then, that in a myth which pretends to account for how *good* a life we lead in this world, Plato sees fit to introduce a large element of chance. We expect, perhaps, a story like that of Adam and Eve, which traces the harsh necessities of life back to a voluntary commission of sin, with its unequivocal burden of guilt. Some such feeling, I take it, underpins the claim – implicit in Hackforth – that Plato's myth is no more than an *expression* of the state of affairs in this world, and does not function even in mythical terms as an *explanation*. This is a mistaken claim; not because the myth is anything other than an expression of the state of affairs in this world, but because the claim neglects how the very act of expression can impinge upon that state of affairs.

By injecting chance into the fall of souls, Plato inoculates us against feelings of pure moral guilt over our fallen state; yet clearly he does not wish us to feel liberated thereby from all moral burdens relating to it. As a result of the unspecified mishap, these souls lose such understanding of the good as they managed to achieve (their glimpse of the Forms); but they can hope to recover their memory of it in this life, in which each person – barring further mishaps, such as the influence of a vicious environment – can fulfil the ethical potential with which he or she was born.[33] The wrong for which these souls are accountable just is their ignorance – their failure of knowledge.[34] And, given the mechanism of reincarnation, these are *our* souls. We are not allowed to remain mere spectators of the cosmic débâcle, but are being asked to take on its burden, to feel responsibility; not, however, a straightforward sense of guilt, and the sinner's urge to repent, but rather a sorrow, and a yearning that it had not been so – that *we* had not been so.[35] We are not to feel guilt over our embodiment, since after all Plato's point is that we should view it as a contingency, an accident; yet we are not therefore simply to exonerate ourselves from all sense of responsibility as human agents in this matter, for if we do, we shall perpetuate the very ignorance which the myth asks us to acknowledge as a factor in the fall. And this for the following reason: that the perfect understanding of the good, which human souls vie to attain and which the gods securely possess, consists in a perfect integration of distinct desires and concerns, and in the gods' case is partly manifest through the complete ease with which they cope with the contingent; and so too, ideally, in our own case. We are not to consider ourselves moral agents only to the extent that we can be thought independent of contingency, but must welcome as proper to the best human life – a proper result of our moral choices – those (by now familiar) goods, such as the company of friends, which however are proper to the best human life – not just accidentally related to it – only by virtue of the more ultimate contingency of our embodiment; and which moreover are straightforwardly subject to good or bad luck in our upbringing and environment, our brushes with the world.

It is most plausible to discount luck from moral evaluations if our ethical theory (to adduce a standard contrast) is 'act-centred' rather than 'agent-centred'.[36] Act-centred theories – including both major theories in modern ethics, Kantianism and utilitarianism – ask first after rules to decide the moral worth of particular acts (what ought I to do?), and define the good person as one disposed to perform morally correct acts; while agent-centred theories – such as those of both Plato and Aristotle – reverse this order, beginning with the question 'what sort of person am I to be?', and assessing particular acts according to their notion of what the good person would do. If we focus on particular acts, it seems clear that acts performed involuntarily or unintentionally (at least where negligence is not involved) should be exempt from moral blame. With this neither Plato nor Aristotle disagree, of course. But agent-centred theories take as their unit of moral evaluation the whole course of a person's life; and here it makes sense – as would not be the case with particular acts – to talk of the moral fulfilment to which it attains, and to recognise the part that luck may play in its attainment. So for example in the *Republic* (VI 496d5–497a5) Plato does not hesitate to declare the life of the virtuous philosopher worse when spent in an unworthy society than in one befitting his nature: worse in terms of his own 'personal development' (*autos te mallon auxēsetai*, 497a4) as well as in terms of the good that he can do at large. This can only refer to his development as a philosopher, which for Plato includes much that we would describe as distinctively moral; yet this happy event will not come about, Plato feels, without a measure of good luck.[37]

Thus for Plato our moral lives are not led *in spite of* contingency (in Kantian fashion), but become complete through proper dealings with contingency.[38] So too we saw in the previous chapter that Socrates is not happy with his non-lover's puritanical hostility towards pleasure as such, as being external to the virtuous life and to the place of love within it; and I contrasted in anticipation how in his mythic hymn he would attempt to learn from and integrate into the scheme of a philosophic life the powerful effects of such goods as physical beauty and stirring poetic myth – goods which, taken metaphysically, result from the contingency of our embodiment. We shall presently consider how Socrates finds a place for the erotic in the philosophic life; but for now we are still immersed in the eschatological myth proper, and examining it as a tool for coping with the contingent. Nevertheless, it is important to grasp here that the myth is being told in order to provide a framework of explanation for the effects of erotic passion – thus at 249d4–5 Socrates declares that 'the whole discourse' so far has been working towards an account of what happens when the philosophic type comes face to face with beauty in this world (physical human beauty, as 251a2–3 makes clear). For this means that the myth on the one hand makes a place for the contingency of worldly beauty in the philosophic life, but on the other hand (as we have seen) is itself a product of contingency: something to which Socrates, the philosopher, has recourse only as a last resort, and describes as required by our humanity, our fall from heaven (246a4–6). The myth is required, then, as a result of the very event that it narrates. And this 'fact' reveals the sense in which, as I claimed, it does more than simply *express* the state of affairs in this world that it purports to explain, but also copes with it. Just as an understanding of the soul in general, we saw, has the power to change the character and life of the particular investigator who has gained that understanding, so to tell a story in which we become burdened by the contingency of embodiment, and to tell it as one's best stab at the truth, just *is* to take on the contingency of embodiment as a burden. In that sense, saying it makes it so. Of course, in order for the story to have such an effect, the storyteller must believe in it; but then: in what sense can we say that Socrates believes in his eschatological myth? Not in its literal details, certainly – his own caveats make that clear (246a4–6; 265b6–c3; cf. *Phaedo* 114d1–7). In which case, are we back with the notion that his story simply expresses the state of affairs in this world? No; for the story does not simply offer an impersonal description of the human condition (though it does do that), but takes up an ethical stance; one which can be opposed to other ethical positions, and which, if accepted and lived by, will make us into very different persons than we would be if we adopted those other positions.

But, we ask, granted that the myth offers us a way of coping with the situation that it describes, *why* should we accept its offer? Does it amount to no more than a statement of faith? How are we to choose between its ethical stance, and those with which it contrasts? Plato is offering us myth where we want argument. But just that, surely, is his point. It is not that he can give no *reasons* for adopting one stance rather than another. He has shown us, in the speeches of the non-lovers, what developments of character are promoted by ethical stances other than that which Socrates puts forward in the palinode, and we are about to see the kind of life to be led by philosophic lovers who have a conception of the good that is distinct from pleasure, yet integrates pleasure into that conception. He is giving us psychological insight into the different kinds of person we would become according to which positions we live by; and our reactions to those models are surely as strong a reason as any for determining our choice. We choose our ethical stance on the basis of whether we want its effects; and we can of course argue with Plato over his characterisation of the effects of the different stances; but, ultimately, the choice cannot be that of an impartial and purely rational observer. For we cannot determine the *value*

138

of those effects independently of whether we *want* them. We can change our structure of goals, hence too our desires, but we cannot, as it were, create them from nothing. This, I am saying, is what Plato figures *within* his myth by tracing the forms of life that we lead in this world back to natural endowment and chance (never making clear whether he means to distinguish the two); and this is the view that he shows he accepts, and the consequences of which he puts to positive work, by writing *as* a myth.[39]

CHAPTER SIX

LOVE AMONG THE PHILOSOPHERS

The place of beauty

Socrates' declared purpose in telling his eschatological myth, as we have just seen, is to make a place for the passion of love – hence for the contingency of physical beauty – in the philosophic life. But it is important to see that he does not, as it were, clear a space for it on a neglected shelf in philosophy's larder; rather, he portrays the life of philosophic lovers as the fullest realisation – or at the very least as one of the fullest realisations – of the philosophic life in general. Thus we recall that he described the highest of the nine ranks of life as that of 'a seeker after wisdom or beauty, a follower of the Muses and a lover' (248d3–4) – a life he subsequently glosses as that of 'one who has practised philosophy without guile, or combined his love for a boy with the practice of philosophy' (249a1–2).[1] And at the close of the speech he asserts that his exemplary pair of philosophic lovers have gained a good 'than which neither human moderation nor divine madness can furnish a greater for mankind' (256b5–6). In chapter four I indicated that in his palinode, by contrast with the speeches of the non-lovers, Socrates achieves an integrated account of the conflicting impulses in the soul, learning from and harmonising all its voices. That psychic harmony should be the philosophic ideal comes as no surprise to any reader of the *Republic*; yet all the same, the integration is here achieved within the limits of a purely erotic context. We might wonder, then, why Plato seems prepared to allow that context to seem virtually coextensive with the philosophic life at its best. An important clue is provided by the special place among the things that make life worthwhile that is now assigned by Socrates to beauty, as he proceeds to relate his mythical framework to the phenomenology of philosophic love. In

THE PLACE OF BEAUTY

turning to this issue, I shall be pursuing in the erotic realm what I have so far been examining in the mythical: Plato's attention to the personal meaningfulness to philosophers of their attempt to gain the cosmic or impersonal perspective.

When the philosophic type encounters a physically beautiful youth – when he sees 'a godlike face or bodily form that is a good image of beauty (*kallos eu memimēmenon*)' (251a2–3) – he is reminded of his disembodied vision of the beautiful itself, of which, as a philosophic soul, he caught a fuller glimpse than most. That is why he reacts differently to the encounter than do more down-to-earth types, seeing in the youth an object of reverence rather than an opportunity for sexual pleasure (249e4–250a4; 250e1–251a5). The massive punch that physical beauty delivers to his sensibility is mythically traced to the splendour of the place beyond the heavens. And it is a punch more powerful than any other that he experiences. Beauty was not, to be sure, the only object of his disembodied vision;[2] but here on earth its likenesses 'shine most clearly', and are apprehended through 'the clearest sense', namely sight (250d1–3). 'Wisdom' (*phronēsis*) cannot be seen with the eyes – if it could present itself with the clarity of a visual image, the love (*erōtas*) it would inspire would indeed be tremendous – nor can any other of the 'objects of love' (*erasta*) be seen, except beauty (250d3–6). Socrates is here using strong language of wisdom and the other objects of love, since terms derived from the *era*- root properly connote sexual or passionate love, rather than love in the most general sense (for which the *philo*- root serves).[3] The striking choice of term seems to follow from his previous description of justice and moderation at 250b1–2 as 'valuable to souls' (*timia psykhais*); that is, as things that we care about and which give meaning to our lives.[4] Such things demand strong language. And of these too he claims that their earthly likenesses do not have the brightness that belongs to the images of beauty; moreover, we have only 'dull organs' (*amydrōn organōn*) to press into service for apprehending them through those likenesses (250b1–5). Beauty, by contrast, is not only blessed with clear images, but 'was bright to see' among the other Forms at the time when we enjoyed our celestial vision (250b5–d3).[5]

To what is Socrates referring when he attributes greater 'brightness' to the likenesses of beauty in this world? Interpretations currently in the field take this as a point about the quality of the relation between the Forms and their likenesses. Thus de Vries explains that in the case of justice and the like 'the realisations ... which we see around us, are always far from adequate. Real justice is seldom found', whereas the realisations of beauty are likenesses 'to a very high degree, and, moreover, strongly evocative' (de Vr. apud 250b2–3); the point, then, would be that the beauty we encounter in this world more accurately resembles the corresponding Form. Robin, on the other hand, takes the point to concern not accuracy but immediacy of resemblance: that while particular likenesses of other Forms offer a 'mediate opportunity' ('*occasion médiate*') to think of the Form and measure its distance from the likeness, the likenesses of beauty imitate the Form 'without mediation' ('*immédiatement*') (R. xcvi n.1).

But I do not think either interpretation is right. To begin with, notice that before Socrates distinguishes the likenesses of beauty from the rest, he underscores the *general* inadequacy of *all* earthly likenesses to bring before us, in all clarity, that of which they are likenesses. For we read that when those whose philosophic 'memory' is sufficiently developed catch sight of a likeness of 'the things up there' (*tōn ekei*, 250a6), they 'are amazed and beside themselves, but do not know what is happening to them because their perception is too weak' (250a5–b1); in other words, their memory of the celestial vision is strong enough to be powerfully stirred, but not so strong as to bring with it a crisp awareness of its original force (so too we may know, of an odour caught fleetingly in the air, that we have smelt it before in some very particular set of circumstances, and perhaps even feel again something of what we felt on that earlier occasion, yet be quite unable – though we come so close, so close – to identify what those circumstances were). Even the philosophers, after all, are fallen

142

souls, condemned to remember rather than revisit the Forms. Within this fundamental limitation, Socrates proceeds to distinguish the 'brightness' of worldly beauty from that of other likenesses (250b1–e1).[6]

So far, then, Socrates has indicated that all sensible instances of the Forms are inadequately discerned just to the extent that each can be called a 'likeness' of the corresponding Form. Does anything in what he proceeds to say compel us to the interpretation that the sensible instances of beauty are somehow, even if fundamentally inadequate in so far as they are likenesses, nevertheless *better* likenesses of their corresponding Form – more accurate, more immediate? I think not; moreover, such an interpretation is difficult to reconcile with Socrates' valuation of physical beauty and sexual passion. For however we are to understand the claim that the resemblance between the Form and its sensible likeness is more *accurate* in the case of beauty, it would at least entail that I will stand a chance of *knowing more* about the beautiful itself as a result of seeing its instances than I will know about justice itself from an inspection of *its* instances. But then, given that beauty is a *bona fide* resident of the place beyond the heavens, and that the goal of philosophers is to recover their awareness of that place as far as is possible, why should the dominant pursuit of philosophers in this world not be to seek out the sight of physical beauty, as their best (most accurate) avenue of recollection? Yet, of course, it is not. Philosophic lovers, as we later learn, seek out above all those who are like them in character: 'philosophers and leaders of men by nature' (*philosophos te kai hēgemonikos tēn physin*, 252e3). The fostering of such qualities of leadership cannot but involve the pair in the pursuit of justice; and Socrates is quite explicit that, although both the lover and his boy are sexually attracted to one another, they are neither to foster nor, ideally, to indulge their physical passion (255e2–256b7). Over the course of their lives, these philosophers will actively *pursue* beauty only in the enlarged sense of that term, familiar from the *Symposium*, in which one can speak of the beauty of souls. However, in the passage under discussion Socrates is

143

very clearly speaking of the relative 'brightness' of the boy's physical beauty, and of the physical sense of sight; and my point is that, were he to be marking by this metaphor a greater accuracy in our apprehension of the corresponding Form than is attainable in the case of justice, this would be a reason for the philosophic life to develop in just the opposite direction from that in which Socrates in fact envisages it developing. So we should look for a different account of what he means.[7]

In order to give a more satisfactory account, I must appeal again to the way in which the philosopher 'walks into the background', and especially to the ethical turn which is given it in this speech (as explained in the early pages of the previous chapter).

First, let us take note of a non-metaphorical detail of Socrates' claim (one which can therefore be considered without begging the question as to what he means by 'brightness'): namely, that in the case of such values as justice and moderation, 'few' (*oligoi*) can detect the Form through experience of its instances, and then only 'with difficulty' (*mogis*) (250b1–5). The unstated implication would be that, as a result of the 'sharpness' of sight and the 'brightness' of physical beauty which is among its objects, the beautiful itself is likely to be detected with greater ease, and by a broader range of people. Now, consider in this context the well-known passage in Book VII of the *Republic*, in which a distinction is made between things which do and do not 'awaken thought' (*Rp.* VII 523b–524d). Holding up three fingers before Glaucon's eyes, Socrates explains that the fact that each is a finger can be adequately judged by sight, since a finger will not seem to be other than a finger regardless of, say, the position from which it is viewed, or of its fatness or thinness. However, there is something about the fingers that is not adequately judged by sight, and so stimulates thought. By this remark Socrates does not allude, as Glaucon at first supposes, to the possibility of optical illusion, or the problem of identifying objects such as fingers at a distance; rather, it turns out that he is referring to the very fatness or thinness, bigness or smallness that pose no obstacle to the task of identifying the fingers as fingers, and simply means to indicate that, because they are abstract properties, we do not *just see* the distinction between the big and the small as such in the way that we just see that there are three fingers of different sizes before our eyes, but we must ponder, in the abstract, the criteria of their distinctness – and so embark on a characteristically philosophic train of thought.[8] It is only in this sense that sight is inadequate to judge the bigness and smallness of the fingers, and sees the two as 'mixed together' (*synkekhymena*, 524c7). Not, of course, that we cannot *just see* that one finger is big, the other small, and the third middling in size – this, surely, is Plato's point in having Socrates hold up three fingers rather than just one (and securing Glaucon's immediate assent to the sight of them), and in having Glaucon initially presume that by the inadequacy of sight Socrates refers to 'mechanical' problems of vision. That is, simply to understand that there is some problem worth pondering here, given that no actual mechanical problem of vision is in question, is *already* to have awoken to philosophic thought. It is to have become aware of the background to our immediate and unproblematic perception of differences; to flag the properties that we invoke – normally without further thought – in describing the differences we see, and ask of *them*, what makes them different from each other.

So, then: careful philosophic questioning is needed to prompt an awareness in Glaucon (despite his readiness to engage in philosophy) that his immediate visual experience could give rise to enquiry other than by being unsatisfactory in purely optical terms. But here a contrast with beauty becomes apparent. Beauty is a value (one of the things 'valuable to souls', 250b2); and in this respect it is like justice and moderation, and unlike bigness and smallness, fatness and thinness.[9] But as a value – here unlike justice and moderation – it is bound up essentially with immediate visual (or, more generally, sensory) experience. Beauty must be seen (or otherwise sensed) to be appreciated.

Consider now what is likely to happen when you encounter

someone beautiful. The sight of their beauty gives you an immediate reason to care about them, in so far as they are the cause of this visual experience and, without them, it cannot continue or recur. You wish you might see them again; or, if that is unlikely or impossible, console yourself with the thought that at least you have seen them once. Of course, the sight of justice being done can also be powerful and inspiring (Socrates says as much at 250a5–7, in describing the startling effect of *all* likenesses of the Forms when encountered by a person of philosophic bent); but its power to inspire, unlike beauty's power, will not derive from the quality of the visual experience that it causes. Thus, beauty has the peculiar potential to bring that quality to our attention, by making it the object of our concern; and from here there is but a short step (one that I shall scrutinise more closely in the course of the chapter) to the question of why it is worthy to be the object of our concern. In terms of the example of the fingers, it is as if Glaucon, seeing the big and small fingers, were also immediately to feel (and want to question further) how the differences which he perceives are related to his concerns and interests as a human being in an environment of middle-sized objects to be grasped and handled. Instead, he just sees three fingers; and it takes patient philosophic prodding from Socrates even to initiate in him the line of thought which might eventually lead him to consider all that he sees in the light of the 'Form of the Good'; that is, of what makes anything – sober and just actions included – worth *caring* about (see *Rp.* VI 505a3–4). But beauty, unlike bigness and smallness, announces itself, as it were, as an object of concern; it is salient, and will not stay in the background. And this is something we all readily feel (hence the contrast with the 'few' who can detect justice itself through its likenesses).[10]

Nevertheless, Socrates does not say that we are all therefore philosophers, or even potentially so. He envisages two quite different reactions to the encounter with a beautiful person: on the one hand, a 'surrender to pleasure' (250e4), issuing in an attempt to achieve sexual gratification and/or the begetting of children; on the other, a kind of 'reverence' (*sebetai*,

146

251a5), stemming from the memory of the beautiful itself, and leading to the relationship of philosophic love (250e1– 251a5). Yet in both cases, notice, the visual experience points the beholder beyond the immediate pleasure he takes in the spectacle of beauty, prompting him to situate the beautiful person in the structure of his future concerns. To be struck by someone's beauty is naturally (at least, provided you are aware that what you see is a *person*) to consider that person as *lovable* – even if only in that one feature, and even if only hypothetically (that is, it is not a condition that you must yourself be seriously planning a relationship with that person – though Plato chooses to describe only such cases).[11] Put another way, a person's beauty naturally prompts you to care, not just about their beauty, but about them-as-beautiful. However, some horizons of care are very much more limited than others. The philosophic character, prompted by the boy's beauty to think of him as lovable, cannot (we shall see) justify loving him on the grounds of his physical beauty alone, nor on any grounds short of the possibility of jointly pursuing with him the worthiest kind of human life. But these are justifications *after* the fact of being struck by the boy's physical beauty.

The point is that both reactions, the philosophic and the unphilosophic, because neither are simply isolated sensations of aesthetic pleasure but rather locate that sensation within a forward-looking structure of care, are – or have the potential to be – discoveries of self. You can learn who you are by considering your unconsidered reaction to an encounter with someone beautiful, and thus gain the opportunity to foster and justify the life appropriate to the kind of character you take yourself to be. You discover, then, what you have been *given*. That is why the apparatus of myth is used. To say that the philosophic type has a sharper memory of the beautiful itself (see 250e2) is less to explain why his character is different than to describe his discovery of a difference not susceptible of further explanation. Mythically, it is because this soul saw more of the beautiful itself that he is a philosopher; but that is a way of saying two things at once: first, that in terms

147

of his life in this world it is rather because he is a philosopher that he sees more of the beautiful itself (that is, sees beautiful human beings in terms of the beautiful itself), and second, that this less mythical statement of the case is no more 'explanatory' than its mythic counterpart.[12] The reaction of the philosophic type to the boy's beauty allows him to *recognise* (or confirms him in his recognition) that the life he wants to lead is the philosophic life; for, since that is a life partly constituted by extensive reflection on the best life for human beings, and since he has not found himself placing his encounter in the least reflective and most automatic structure of care (although, we shall see, he is aware of a tug in himself towards this reaction too – but aware of it as a *tug*), consideration of his unconsidered reaction is therefore as it were *built into* the reaction itself – the philosopher just 'naturally' has a complex reaction to the boy's beauty, one which subsumes rather than bypasses the unphilosophic reaction.[13] This, I take it, is what is meant by saying that he does not just see the boy's beauty but is sharply reminded of the beautiful itself. Moreover, from such beginnings he will recognise that although he must, and can give reasons to prefer his way of life to the unphilosophic, these are all, in a sense, justifications after the fact. The philosophically reflective life of justice, moderation, and wisdom turns out after all to have something deeply in common with the sight of beauty. Beauty, we agreed, must be seen to be appreciated; and so too the philosophic life – and I take seriously now the comparison with more 'basic' skills and practices as presented in the opening chapter – can only be fully appreciated and understood in the actual living.

But this quality only *turns out* to be common to the 'things valuable to souls'; that is, it is learnt in the course of a life. And now it should be clear how I interpret beauty's greater 'brightness'. Physical beauty is not a more 'accurate' or 'immediate' likeness of the corresponding Form than are instances of justice in relation to *their* corresponding Form. Whatever exactly Plato meant by describing this relation as 'likeness' (a question which it is beyond my brief to attempt to settle here), I agree with those scholars who understand it to be all-or-nothing – not susceptible of degrees. The difference in brightness is not to be explained through the relation between Forms and their likenesses, but through the different modes of access permitted by the different sorts of likenesses. Just and moderate actions can only be fully appreciated in the context of a whole life, and a life not merely theorised about but actually lived in the light of theory; but the philosopher's discovery (or confirmation) that this is the sort of life he wants to lead can be intensely savoured in the context of a moment, in his immediate visual encounter with the beautiful boy. In that sense, the likenesses of beauty are brighter; their value is more immediately and readily appreciable. With the likenesses of justice, only a slow and painstaking process of living the just life can bring their value to light. I submit that this interpretation makes far better sense of the place of beauty in the structure of the philosophic life. It enables us to understand what the other type of interpretation renders inexplicable: why the philosophic character who is so stirred by physical human beauty does not go on to put it at the centre of his life. He does not do so because this beauty, in its brightness, has awoken him to the very limitations of such brightness in the structure of the fullest human life; it points him, in its immediacy, towards what is not immediately appreciable.[14] Yet its function and value is not therefore purely instrumental; for beauty is as much a value in itself as are the others, and has its place among the Forms. Rather, Plato seems to think of it as the value that has *in addition* to its intrinsic worth the function of arresting and directing the attention to the totality of values in a human life – hence its place in the earlier stages of the philosophic life. Beauty is the integrator; it has the capacity to make all aspects of the best human life, sensible as well as intelligible, into a whole.[15] And so we begin to see (to return to the point with which I opened this chapter) why Plato should suggest that the life of philosophic lovers is the philosophic life *par excellence*. For, while it would be highly implausible to think that the philosophic life simply could not be lived except by one who has had the opportunity to fall in love with, and nurture philosophy in, a physically beautiful youth (and indeed, I see no reason to attribute any such view to Plato), it makes more sense to hold that this type of life is most complete – more integrated and blessed as a human life – when graced with such an opportunity.

The love-mad philosopher: mixed pleasure

Beauty is the integrator – well and good. But I must not too readily bask in the glow of so optimistic a conception. We are none of us dwelling now in the pure light of that place beyond the heavens, and Plato takes pains to warn us that fashioning the wholeness of a philosophic life from the initial encounter with worldly beauty is no smooth task – indeed, from his vivid description of that encounter we might say that he felt beauty to be less a cohesive than a potentially explosive force in the philosopher's life. To that description I now turn, and in particular to the following question. Socrates is meant to be urging the benefits of love-madness. Yet he paints its effects on the philosophic lover with a decidedly sickly complexion of mingled pleasure and distress – of just the sort, indeed, that Plato elsewhere devalues as too 'impure' to deserve a place in the good life, not only in dialogues that can be assumed to pre-date the *Phaedrus*, but also in a work as late as the *Phile-bus* (on which more below). The puzzle here is twofold. Why should Socrates, now that he has decided to find the good in love, display its effects in anything less than a positive light? And given that Socrates does envisage a positive outcome from this 'impure' beginning, how are we to square his assessment with Plato's attempts elsewhere to exclude such impurity from the good life so far as is possible?

The philosophic lover's first reaction on meeting with the beautiful boy is fear. He 'shudders' (*ephrixe*), experiencing anew the 'dread' that overcame his disembodied soul in the presence of the Forms (*tōn tote ... deimatōn*) (251a4), since the boy's physical beauty has triggered his memory of the beautiful itself. And he feels a more mundane fear also, of public opinion: as he gazes longer on this physical loveliness

150

he feels reverence, as if before a god, and were it not that he 'feared' (*edediei*) being thought quite crazy, he might even offer sacrifice to the boy (251a4–7). Soon he will learn to fear public opinion less, throwing over his concern for propriety in order to be with his beloved constantly (252a1–7); but his fear in the presence of the beautiful is more problematic. Can it be fear *of* the beautiful itself, as of a direct danger? This would hardly square with the glowing description, in the vocabulary of religious ecstasy, that Socrates accorded our disembodied vision of beauty. Our souls, it seems, were wholly happy at that time (250b5–c6). Perhaps, then, the emotion referred to is closer to 'awe'? But I feel, rather, that we should not take the rhapsodic description of the disembodied vision as our only guide; since it seems to play down the negative aspect of that episode (much as in the feeling of awe the component of fear, though present, is not uppermost). For it is painful to be brought up against your limits. On a minor level, we have seen, the lover is brought up against the limits of social propriety by his passion, and is apprehensive of the consequences; but later overcomes his fear. But to tremble in the presence of beauty itself: this is his goal, not something to be overcome. We should not forget that even for the best human soul the vision of the place beyond the heavens was stressful. Not only did the unbalanced chariot-team make the aerial climb a struggle (247b3–6), but even at the sky's rim continually harassed the charioteer, who could barely keep his head above heavenly water, craning for his glimpse of hyperuranian space (248a1–5). Plato here puts at the pinnacle of human achievement, in his eschatological myth of the greatest prize for human souls, not a mystic union with the divine, but a full confrontation with our human limits – and a soberingly farcical picture it is.[16] Yet the struggle and the comedy is then obscured behind the solemn halo of beauty's mystic revelation, for which we were 'whole' and 'free of the evils that we endure in a later time' (250c1–2) (where, we ask, are the kicking horses?) – only to re-emerge in the present passage, in which the facing of limits dramatised in the charioteer's struggle now appears as an acknowledgment of the 'dread' that would accompany the religious ecstasy before only positively described; and through which, as I shall later emphasise, we are permitted a wry smile at love's agonies.

This wavering of tone is readily explicable if we think of Socrates' relationship to the eschatological vision he narrates as being psychologically analogous to the lover's early relationship with the beautiful boy. The clue lies in Socrates' apology for the unnecessary length of his evocation of the joyous vision of beauty, which was a 'tribute to memory (*mnēmēi*)', he says, spoken 'in longing (*pothōi*) for things past' (250c7–8). Compare how the philosophic lover, separated from his beloved and painfully 'longing' for him (*pothousa*, 251e2), takes pleasure in his 'memory' of the beautiful boy (*mnēmēn*, 251d6). This mixture of pleasure and pain he finds unbearably strange, and rushes to assuage himself with the boy's presence (251d7–e3). Yet his memory seems rather fond here; for the original encounter with his beloved was hardly an unmixed pleasure. We have already seen that the thrill it gave was a thrill of fear; and as we look further we shall find the lover's sensations in the presence of the boy compared to an itching or tickling (251c3–5) – the classic Phileban example of a mixed pleasure (*Phlb.* 46a8 sq.). Yet once smitten, the lover cannot make cool comparisons, nor can he simply wish his desire away. So too with Socrates. If his memory of the beatific vision seems inconsistent with his account in the myth proper, we must allow him the licence of a lover. His myth, we saw, both expresses and helps us cope with a philosophic perspective from which the fact of our embodiment and mortality seems, metaphysically, the merest contingency; yet, because it is not just any contingency but (heaven help us) the human condition, expressing the desire to escape it, and attaining that desire, are two different things. In particular, this longing condemns Socrates to the use of myth, when myth is the mark of the very limitations he wishes to transcend – a problem represented within the myth itself by his acknowledgment of the charioteer's struggle; as if even the highest human state, born of the aspiration to transcend the human state (to follow the god), must nevertheless – indeed,

152

for that very reason – be a state of preoccupation with humanity, given over to its humanity. Yet once smitten by such a longing, he cannot just wish it away, despite the difficulties into which it leads him – this is confirmed by his over-indulgent memory of the vision of beauty. He cannot wish it away, because it is what he has been *given*; it has been given to him to see the fact of human embodiment as a given, a contingency. In order to hold this view, then, he cannot but represent it to himself as a truth transcendent to human embodied experience, including his own. Yet at the same time he must recognise in himself a propensity to hold it that is itself a contingency of embodiment – *must* recognise the contingency of this, for he sees how he differs from other people in holding the metaphysical views that he does. Through one and the same enterprise, then, he discovers himself both *personally* (that is, in his full idiosyncrasy) and *as a person* (that is, as one among others).[17]

But these discoveries would seem to take the soul off in opposing directions (so that on the one hand it merges, as it were, in the sea of human nature, and yet, like some diving dolphin, reflects the sun off its vanishing flanks in a moment of wild and individual beauty – only, for the philosopher this moment should be a lifetime, and even beyond, in myth). And the question is whether an integrated psychological life can be forged from such materials. Plato attempts an answer to this question in his account of the growth of philosophic love from its seeds in the mixed feelings of the philosophic lover. I have backtracked here to the subject-matter of the previous chapter in order to relate those feelings to Socrates' need for mythmaking, and thus set them in the context of the larger philosophic life. In so doing I have partly anticipated my response to the puzzle put forward at the beginning of this section. With the reader thus forewarned, let me return now to the diagnosis of the lover's symptoms.

I choose the medical metaphor advisedly; for after the first shiver of dread the lover becomes unusually hot and breaks out in a sweat (251a6–b1), showing the symptoms of a fever.[18] The description here has been compared to that of the feverish lover who speaks Sappho's famous poem[19] – a comparison the more readily made because at 235c3–4 Socrates names Sappho and Anacreon as the most likely sources of his inspiration to speak on love. I take the significance of the comparison, however, to lie above all in the radically different way in which Socrates relates the symptoms to the sufferer. Sappho's speaker feels the symptoms directly – is cold and hot, sweats, shivers – whereas Socrates has no sooner attached these symptoms to the philosophic lover than he displaces them. The lover's hot sweating is described as the effect of the stream of beauty incorporated through his eyes, which warms and moistens the rooting-points of his soul's feathers, softens their sealed lips (long hardened-over since the beatific vision), and makes the quills swell and shoot to overspread the soul (251b1–7).[20] The physical heat and moisture generated by the lover's excitement is diverted to drive the turbine of allegory.[21] The bodily symptoms mount up in grotesque, and surely comic, detail: throbbing, itching, tickling, prickling, pressure, inflammation, and the whole syndrome of love-madness compared to the irritation in a teething infant's gums (251c1-d7). But the body in question is a winged soul, and this enables Socrates to be at once physically graphic and allegorically coy. The moistened lips, the hot and swelling stump – strong stuff?[22] And yet this sexual response, because of its impossible androgyny, is curiously disembodied.[23] So too the gorgeous array of pangs and tingles stirs our blood the less for having to imagine as its cause the sprouting of sprite-feathers. Despite Socrates' careful placement of each sensation, we are apt to lose our bearings in considering the lover's response, unable to say just what *he* – rather than his caged bird – is feeling. At one point, indeed, Socrates describes more straightforward travails that could only be undergone by the whole man. Unable to sleep at night or stay still during the day, he is portrayed as rushing off to where he thinks he will see the boy (251e1–3 – although the only expressed subject for this sentence is, significantly, 'the soul', mentioned at 251d6). Characteristically, however, his reaction upon finding the boy is once more assessed through allegory; for the

154

stream of desire is channelled to the pores where the feathers bud, re-opening them (for they had temporarily dried up again and closed over in the boy's absence) and bringing intensely pleasurable relief (251e3–252a1).

What is the point of this allegorical displacement? To find an answer, we must consider more closely the quality of the feelings displaced. The predominant sensation as the feathers sprout is initially an inflamed itching or tickling (hence the comparison with teething), registered primarily as a painful irritation (*aganaktēsis*, 251c3; *odynēs*, 251c8). Pleasurable relief follows as the moist heat of the boy's beauty continues to stream in through the lover's eyes (251c4–d1). It is important to notice that the ultimate cause of the irritation and of the pleasure is thus one and the same: the stream of beauty flowing off the boy. This is readily understandable, given the allegorical model. The lover is growing out of his carapace, and moist heat can do double duty in promoting this growth: both exciting the push and relaxing the resistant diaphragm; first stimulating and then eliminating the pain (again the sexual imagery is patent; with the crucial difference that thrust and yielding take place not between the partners, but in the single person of the lover). In order to overcome the irritation, then, the lover's soul must embrace its cause. Though there is fear and resistance at the outset, still this is a thrill of fear, a teasing, itching resistance – not repellent, but inviting exploration. That is why Socrates now identifies the hot stream of the boy's beauty with 'desire' (*himeros*, 251c7; cf. 251e3), adopting an extravagant etymology for this purpose (as if the word derived from three others meaning 'rushing stream of particles'). A strange identification, it might seem; for while the vision of the boy's beauty is clearly something the lover receives from without, is desire not something kindled within him, and then directed out in turn at the boy? But no; in this case the demarcation between stimulus and response is not so clear-cut. The very irritant (the stream) turns out to be desire; alternatively put: desire is the irritant. That is, the stimulus feeds off itself and steps up its own charge.

This curious feature bears instructive comparison with

Freud's account of sexual pleasure. Freud points out that feelings of sexual pleasure differ from other pleasurable feelings in that they characteristically give rise to the need for greater pleasure of the same sort, thus building towards the release of orgasm; and he insists that this impulse, in its urgency, is a kind of tension, and that tension always contains an element of unpleasure.[24] The feelings that Socrates describes have the same sexual urgency. From the outset, the warm current of beauty is said to 'feed' the budding feathers and promote their growth (251b5–6); in other words, is described as satisfying an appetite in a way that would normally give pleasure. But Socrates focuses instead on the element of irritation that accompanies growth (251c1–5), and allows the pleasure to emerge only as this irritation is relieved (251c8–d1) – relief obtained, however, through ingesting more of the very same food that is causing the irritation, since only by continued growth of the feathers can the irritation be escaped. In Freud's account, sexual excitement is what continually grows, requiring as its motor an unpleasurable tension, a need for more – although the sense of unpleasure is overwhelmed by the far greater pleasure that it generates. In Socrates' account, the lover's memory is awakened into aspiration towards beauty, as allegorised by the ever-burgeoning wings; and it is because this plant needs constant watering from its source in the boy's presence, because it seeks, not satisfaction merely, but growth (as in Freud feelings of sexual excitement include an impulsion towards *change* in the psychological situation), that unpleasurable irritation takes up a place alongside pleasure in the allegorical phenomenology.

The pivotal difference between the two accounts is, of course, that Freud is assessing how pleasure and unpleasure develop in a single sexual bout; Socrates, how they develop in the course of a relationship – indeed, of what will turn into a whole life of philosophic love. That is why the equivalent of orgasm is conspicuously absent from Socrates' story. Certainly, he talks of the pain of teething being 'relieved' (*lōphai*, 251c8) by the moist heat of desire; but this is not the relief of orgasm – an escape (however temporary) from the urgency of desire. We must not forget that in the allegory it takes the soul a whole life – a cycle of three lives, in fact, at the very quickest – to grow its full plumage and escape reincarnation (248e6–249a5; cf. 256b3–5).[25] Falling in love, the soul is re-born – this is the implication of the analogy with teething infants. However, our dentition will not be filled out within the mortal span that makes up but one phase of the new life. So the hot stream of desire brings pleasure by softening the gums and easing the irritation associated with continued growth, but not by causing a breakthrough to completed growth (the orgasmic pattern). Rather, a breakthrough occurred at the very onset of desire, when the swelling stem parted the moistened lips; but this was to break *into* the urgency of growth, not to discharge it.

For that reason, however (because there has indeed been a breakthrough), there is no easy return to the psychological state that preceded the onset of desire. If lover and beloved are separated, the pores of the lover's soul dry up and re-seal themselves; but the budding feathers now press and throb against the walls of their prison, making the soul frantic (251d1–6). Memories of the beautiful boy temper the pain with a joy of their own (251d6–7); but this swirling together of pleasure and distress is too bizarre to be stable, and drives the lover back into the presence of the beloved (251d7–e3), there to re-open the parched lips and 'gain a breathing-space, a surcease from the goading birth-pangs; and the pleasure he enjoys for that moment is sweet beyond compare' (251e3–252a1). Here we encounter not just a soothing but an actual discharge of built-up tension: temporary relief of an orgasmic type. But notice that what is described is a return to the original breakthrough of desire; and this was a breakthrough, not to the sheer pleasure of discharge, but to the painful pleasure of urgent growth. The lover returns to his boy in order that his soul's plumage can continue to grow, not cease to grow; and the opening up that he now feels as intense pleasure he previously felt as an irritating itch. Indeed, what he feels in the presence of the boy is a compound with the same bizarre formula that crazed him in the boy's absence: an irritant throb-

157

bing and a happy memory of something beautiful. The memory in this case is not of the beautiful boy, but of the beautiful itself;[26] and we have seen reason to believe that, just as the encounter that prompts the lover's joyful recollection of the boy's beauty was not in fact an unmixed pleasure, so Socrates' happy evocation of the disembodied vision of beauty (the very condition of the lover's mixed experience) was itself a little dewy-eyed – suggesting that there is no escape to be had from the urgency of philosophic love merely by attempting to talk of it from the outside and sum it up in a myth. However that may be, what Plato has clearly done here is to take the pattern of recurrent sexual appetite, of tension and release, and apply it not (as might be expected) to what happens to the lover when the two partners are together, but to the effect on him of the boy's alternate presence and absence; so that when the two are together, by contrast, the effect on the lover can follow the pattern of mounting sexual excitement (as delineated by Freud) but *without* the release of orgasm.

It might be wondered how closely the lover's excitement here does in fact follow the Freudian pattern, given that Freud makes no attempt to deny that sexual excitement is felt above all as pleasure, and finds evidence for the component of unpleasure only in the structural background of mounting tension; whereas Socrates insists that the itching and tickling of growth is felt, especially at first, as a pain or irritation. If we again adduce a comparison with the *Philebus*, and consider the vivid description there (at 46d7–47b1) of how pleasure and pain oscillate in a person dealing with an itch, then the excitement analysed by Freud is akin to that stage in the oscillation when the pain is present only as a mild undercurrent of tingling irritation, but is far outweighed by the sensations of pleasure, which, we are told, can make a person leap about, pant and groan and take on all manner of complexions and contortions; while in the *Phaedrus* the tickling felt by the soul as its feathers sprout is more akin to the stage when distress is uppermost, when itch has the edge on scratch. But it is actually by considering this discrepancy that I can bring out the full value of the comparison with Freud, and draw together the threads of the questions – about the purpose of the allegorical displacement and of the mixed emotions that mark the inception of philosophic love – which have been left dangling unanswered so far.

The love-mad philosopher: contingency and necessity

We must not forget that Socrates is speaking in allegory; that the sensations he describes must be imagined as felt by the lover in the pores and feathers of his bird-like soul. This gives Plato a licence not available to Freud. Freud is reviewing the stimulations that arise directly from the physical meeting of erogenous zones; so he can only narrate what is actually felt during the sexual act. But in Socrates' account, a mixed pleasure of the body – which, however much it has in common with the mixed pleasure of sexual excitement, is clearly a different pleasure: to wit, the pleasure of handling an itch or tickle – is used to represent what in that same stretch of the *Philebus* (at 47e1–3) is called a mixed pleasure of the soul: the anxious pleasure of love (*erōs*). Although the lover is indeed sexually excited by the boy (this fact becomes unequivocal when we later read of how his 'dark horse' is aroused in the encounter, at 254a3–7), the sexuality of his excitement does not emerge directly, but only through the imagery of throbbing stem and softened labia. Moreover, the explicit object of this imagery is not sexual excitement as such, but something more exalted: the emotional turmoil of falling in love. Thus, for all that the special qualities of sexual arousal make up the blueprint on which Plato builds Socrates' narrative, at no point (unlike Freud) need he faithfully transcribe how it actually feels to be so aroused. Rather, I take his direct announcements, within the allegory, of what the fledgling soul is feeling – the catalogue of tingles and tickles – to constitute as much a commentary upon, as an evocation of, what the philosophic lover actually experiences in non-allegorical terms.

Consider why the philosopher's soul, in the process of re-

growing its feathers, feels pain at all: only because the feathers must work their way through a skin that has become
calloused with time and yields stintingly, by the slow lubri-
cation of desire. And why this obstacle? Because the soul has
succumbed to embodiment, denying its feathers proper
nourishment – the vision of the Forms (248b5–c2) – and
allowing the pores to dry and close over. The allegorised irritation felt by the philosophic lover on the surface of his soul
would therefore represent a confrontation with his embodiment. Which is to say, a confrontation with contingency.[27]
Here I come back to and elaborate what in the opening section of this chapter I described as the natural complexity of
the philosophic lover's reaction to the boy's beauty; for it is
this complexity, I am about to argue, that prompts Plato's
recourse to allegorical displacement. We have seen that to describe the boy's beauty as awakening in the philosopher a
memory of the beautiful itself is to say at least this: that in that
moment the lover does not simply find the boy beautiful, but
finds that – how to put it? – beauty matters. For all its depen-
dence on the accident of physical endowment, the con-
tingencies of life-history, the chance encounter – this moment
of beauty has value in a person's life and in so doing shows
that life can have value beyond the moment. The tension here
is familiar enough. To fall in love with someone (or to sense
the possibility of falling, as in the first encounter with the
beautiful boy) is to allow (or contemplate allowing) that
person to become an essential and dominant part of your life
– only to lay yourself open then to such questions as: why *this*
person? Could this other person have taken – or still take – his
place, her place? Does the answer turn on nothing more than
which of them I met when? There is something awful in the
contrast between the contingency of your having met the
other, and the necessity that the other has become in your life.
The questions just posed focus this worry on the figure of the
beloved. They threaten to make of the beloved no more than
the lucky embodiment of a shopping-list of attractions, and to
prompt in him or her the diastrous complaint: you don't love
me for myself. Yet the worry is hard to avoid.

Now, Socrates' account of the philosopher falling in love gives a very significant twist to the issue. Rather than being centred on the beloved, the worry is turned back and inward on the philosopher himself. This is characteristically Platonic. One of the most striking aspects of Plato's investigation of justice in the *Republic* is that he analyses a virtue which pertains to our relations with other people in terms pertaining only to ourselves; for the psychic harmony which justice turns out to be is a condition of the individual soul.[28] Similarly, here in the *Phaedrus*, the supremely other-directed feelings of love are assessed primarily in terms of what takes place within the individual souls of lover and beloved rather than with reference to the structure of the relationship between them: at first in terms of the allegorical re-fledging of the lover's soul, and later (we shall see) of turmoil among the internal parts of the soul of lover and beloved respectively (at 253c7 sq.). Thus Socrates does not dwell on the charms of the beautiful boy; indeed, from his initial description the boy appears to us as no more than a body-part: 'a god-like face or bodily form that is a good image of beauty' (251a2–3); and so too he appears to the lover, who, gazing at him, is gripped by the urge to offer sacrifice to him 'as if to a statue and a god' (251a6). In the lover's eyes (and ours, so far as Socrates lends them vision) the boy seems both more than he is – a god, or beauty itself – and less than he is – a face, a shape, a block of stone. In the next section I will show how Plato responds to our fear that the boy himself might be lost from view in this split-image; we shall see that the initial shock of double-vision stimulates the lover to bring the image into proper focus; that is, to nurture and educate the boy in such a way that, so to speak, he deserves his beauty.[29] But my point now is that in their first encounter the boy does not yet live as a character, but is animated for the lover by the memory of beauty that he stirs; and this 'memory' is clearly something personal to the lover, not shared with the beloved (although in so far as the beloved is himself a potential philosopher he too is at least in 'possession' of such a memory). By this means our attention is diverted from the contrast between the boy's contingent beauty and the Form he mirrors to that between the lover's contingent memory and the Form he remembers. In the first instance the lover encounters his own contingency, not the boy's; for in seeing the boy as a manifestation of beauty itself, he sees, so to speak, his own vision made visible.

The foil here is the standard homosexual asymmetry underlying the speeches of the non-lovers: namely, that beauty should be the exclusive possession of the beloved, and its admiration the exclusive prerogative of the lover (while the beloved is expected to admire in the lover a quite different set of qualities). The philosophic lover, by contrast, sees and loves in the boy's beauty a vision of beauty itself which he, the philosopher, can regard as definitive of himself; as his own achievement, in terms of the myth. Not that Socrates simply substitutes a beauty that belongs exclusively to the lover for one that would be the exclusive possession of the boy. The beauty that the lover sees is no one's possession. The point of contrast is rather that, whereas in a conventional relationship the older man would come to the boy as a developed individual who nevertheless has certain needs, among them an emotional and sexual desire for the boy, in return for satisfying which he can offer him the edifying companionship of a well-disposed adult, the philosophic lover, even if he comes to the boy as a self-contained adult, discovers through the boy that he is not, after all, whole. Indeed, it will turn out that only by taking an interest in the boy's personal development can he himself now develop as philosopher (see 252e5 sq., and the next section of this chapter). But at the outset he is aware only that his reverence and need for the boy is predicated on the fact that the boy's beauty allows him to recognise in himself a reverence and need for beauty as such.

However, to revere and need is not the same as to understand; indeed, since (as we have seen) the philosopher here tastes in an instant the value of a life – the life of reflection – which can only be fully appreciated and understood (if then) in the living, this must be a moment in which his *lack* of understanding becomes vivid for him. For all who encounter it, beauty, we said, tends to set the beautiful person against a horizon of care; but whereas the conventional lover sees the horizon clearly (be it sexual gratification or the family life, 250e4–251a1), the philosophic lover, rather than simply see through the boy's beauty to the horizon in this way, feels more keenly the *fact* of beauty's transparency or brightness – thus rendering it more opaque. The conventional lover also feels the contrast between the moment of encounter and the life for which it might become pivotal, between the contingency of meeting and the project that aims to wrest a pattern from chance; but for him the feeling issues smoothly in a plan of action, and its pains are those attendant on the possible frustration of that plan. Only the philosophic lover lingers over the contrast itself; only he can feel pain at the very fact of his contingency.

Here, then, is my understanding of the philosophic lover's pain. In Socrates' narrative, the immediate effect of the boy's loveliness on the philosopher is not an urge to seduce and the formation of a plan to that end, but a private process of growth. We have seen that the sexual imagery of the passage endows the lover's soul with both thrusting stump and resistant diaphragm, so that he penetrates himself, not the boy; and the penetration is not part of a plan, but a state of mind which he cannot control, nor remove. That is why the effect is a kind of madness (249c8–d3; 251d7–e1). For while the ordinary lover can dissipate the urge that comes upon him by briskly furthering his clear intent, the philosophic lover has no ready outlet of this sort; for his encounter elicits, not the prospect of a well-established goal, but an aspiration towards a way of life, the goal of which he must learn to specify as he goes along. We must not forget that, for all their brightness, likenesses of beauty in this world are inadequately discerned, just in so far as they are likenesses, and so produce agitation and perplexity in the philosophic beholder (250a5–b1). The likenesses of beauty shine brighter because they can be appreciated in an instant; so that what is overwhelmingly vivid and clear for the philosophic lover in that moment is the fact of his aspiration, but not its object – he sees more clearly what he will *not* do, than what he will. Hence, while the other man makes his peace with contingency by simply seizing his chance, the philosopher is thrown into something more like a confrontation with it. He is brought up short against the limits of his understanding, and recognises this awareness of lack as a gift; like Oedipus, he takes responsibility for his contingent ignorance. He makes the contingent essential to himself. The struggle that this inevitably involves – inevitably, because the task can only be born of a confrontation with the limits of understanding – shows up in the allegory as the pain experienced by the fledgling soul.

But I said earlier that in the allegorical description of the soul's pain I found as much a commentary upon, as an evocation of, what the lover actually feels in non-allegorical terms; and I have emphasised how Socrates' use of allegory poses an obstacle to our appreciation of just what the lover, rather than his caged bird, is feeling. We are now in a position to grasp the purpose of this allegorical displacement. For if the philosophic lover is not seeing clear through the boy to the horizon of intent but becomes caught up in wonder at what the vision means for him, then the use of allegory perfectly captures his struggle to come to terms with himself. That is, if we have trouble figuring out just what the lover is feeling, this is because the lover is having trouble figuring it out for himself. Of course, he has direct access to his feelings; but since he feels himself (to retreat to allegory) growing out of his carapace, or (to retreat to paraphrase) re-identifying himself with what is best in him (as will emerge more clearly in subsequent sections), his problem is not so much one of knowing what he *feels* as of knowing what *he* feels – knowing who he is. Thus, as the lover is brought up against the limits of his understanding in the face of the beloved, so Plato, and we, come up against the limits of what we can articulate in the face of his experience. For although the characterisation that I have just given of the lover's feelings comes readily enough to the tongue, it is intended as an admission of defeat; or rather as a last-ditch attempt to articulate the full complexity of the lover's experience – and so, perhaps, snatch a devious victory – by savouring the full complexity of the allegorical displacement that it requires for articulation, and saying: now understand this allegorical complexity, in retrospect, as embryonic in the lover's initial reaction, and the source of its peculiarity.[30]

I can clarify this point by reverting to the comparison with Freud, and now bringing out its full value. Freud's argument that sexual excitement, while undeniably felt above all as pleasure, nevertheless includes an element of unpleasure, rested on the underlying urgency with which that pleasure builds towards the end-state of orgasm. Only from the perspective of an entire sexual episode as structured by its end-state is the element of unpleasure revealed. So too with Socrates' allegory. Only from the viewpoint of the life towards which the philosophic lover and his beloved will develop – although this goal, we saw, does not have the clear-cut finality of orgasm – does it make sense for Socrates to have recourse to the metaphor of teething in order to portray the lover's feelings of excitement and captivation; that is, to portray them as growing pains. In a way, then, he understands what the lover is feeling better than the lover himself yet does, and through the displacement of allegory can clarify those feelings by characterising them – as the lover cannot – in terms of their goal. And this is what I mean by insisting that his description of the lover's allegorical pain is as much a commentary on what the lover actually feels as a direct evocation of it. Compare how, under a certain type of psychotherapy (for Freud is relevant to this text in more ways than one) a patient will learn to specify a previously unacknowledged pain – feelings of anger, say – as the cause of a disturbing set of behavioural symptoms, and by that very act of specification help allay the pain specified. By his use of allegory, Socrates can gather within the single sweep of his evocation of the lover's experience those feelings which function as causes as well as those which function as symptoms, and mark them as such.[31] The lover's sleepless turmoil and general craziness he treats as symptoms of which the pain and subsequent pleasure of psychic re-fledging is the specific cause (for example, he says at 251d7–8 that it is 'from' (ek) the mixture of this pain and pleasure that the lover is 'perplexed and crazed'). And so he includes within his description of the lover's initial experience a pain that the lover must gradually *learn* to acknowledge and specify – as does the patient under therapy – in the course of the philosophic life. And this is to speak from a viewpoint beyond the immediate turmoil of the moment – a distance which the allegorical displacement of emotion both confesses and measures at once.[32]

Now that I have myself taken the measure of this distance, I can answer the twofold puzzle posed at the outset of the previous section as to why Socrates displays even divine love as an 'impure' mixture of pleasure and pain, and whether this can be squared with Plato's decision in the *Philebus* to exclude such impurity from the good life so far as possible (and so I gather in the last of my threads). I can be brief, since all that is required is to make clear how the answer is contained in the preceding discussion. What we have witnessed in the philosophic lover is not just *any* mixture of pleasure and pain, but an allegorical description, in terms of a mixture of pleasure and pain, of an emotional turmoil which eventually confirms the lover in a way of life as resistant as anything in the *Philebus* to mixed pleasures, not just of the body (for we have seen that the philosophic lovers refuse physical consummation of their love), but also of soul; for the allegorical mixture of pain and pleasure is actually caused, or at least exacerbated, by such resistance. Only in so far as the philosophic lover feels the contingency of his embodiment and ignorance as a burden, yet one which he must shoulder as his own (discovering himself, as I have put it, both personally and as a person), can he be said to experience psychological growth as pain. But at the same time he accepts the opportunity for such growth as a gift; that is, he would not have it any other way. Thus he can be said to experience it as pleasure. He learns to cope with contingency, then, as a result of the very ambivalence of his attitude towards it. But that his feelings should be ambivalent in this way is itself the very mark of contingency on his soul (in the large sense in which embodiment can be thought of as a contingency). It is an experience that keeps him from the complete spiritual integration of a god. And thus his love is actually fuelled by a measure of hostility and resistance – no less, I think, than with Socrates in the *Philebus* – to the mixed pleasure of soul that love is.

Lover and beloved: beauty distributed

I began this chapter by showing that the function of physical beauty in Plato's notion of the philosophic life is that of integrator: of fashioning all aspects of that life, sensible as well as intelligible, into a whole. In the two sections immediately preceding I have qualified this claim. Beauty does indeed integrate the philosophic life; however, it does not fulfil its task smoothly, but by causing the philosopher to struggle to make sense of his decidedly mixed reaction to it. Through Socrates' allegory of that reaction we gauge the depth of the philosopher's initial turmoil; but we have yet to see the lover work at making sense of his feelings. This Socrates now shows us in the remainder of his speech, in two distinct ways: he describes how the lover constructs along with his beloved a shared project of living; and takes us back within the lover's soul, this time to witness not just the maelstrom of his emotions but how he *learns* from the struggle within. In this and the next section I turn to the first of these two topics.

With Socrates' account (at 252c3–253c6) of how the relationship between the lover and his boy develops we emerge from the interior of the lover's soul into a more regular environment. In this passage Socrates no longer tells the story through full-blown allegory but contents himself instead with metaphor, to produce a generally more straightforward description of the lover's behaviour. He manages the transition with a well-placed joke. Setting the seal on his evocation of the lover's travail, he abruptly turns to the young boy who is the fictional addressee of his speech (252b1–2) and quotes at him what he claims is a little known (or perhaps apocryphal)[33] Homeric couplet in circulation among the rhapsodes, warning him that, because of his youth, he will probably laugh when he hears it.[34] The couplet appears to be a parody of Homer's habit of disclosing that certain objects and persons which we mortals know by one name, the gods know by another. So here with the god we know as Eros. The immortals look to his success at causing the soul's 'feathers' (*ptera*) to sprout, and call him: Pteros (252b8–9). Socrates also takes the trouble to point out that the addition of these two consonants to the god's name 'makes a mockery' of the metre (*hybristikon pany*) in the second line of the couplet (252b5–6).

I have already suggested that the drama of the lover's 'teething' has an element of the comic–grotesque. Socrates' Homericism now brings this aspect to a head. We are clearly being invited to laugh along with the boy; but equally clearly, we are being warned – if we do not want to join him in immaturity – also to reflect upon our laughter. Laughter is, often enough, a reaction to what we do not understand. If the boy laughs, it is because he is young and will react only to the overt silliness of the jingle Eros–Pteros; but we have seen that we too can be tempted to smile at the antics of the lover's soul, and for much the same sort of reason: namely, through reacting to the less than dignified exterior of the allegory – to the teething and tickles and tingles – rather that to its deeper psychological import. But whereas the boy can readily learn to overcome his giggling and look beyond the rhyme to the reason why the 'winged' nature of Eros is worth incorporating in his name, we, who are already doing that, cannot so easily get beyond the analogous obstacle encountered at the deeper level. Beauty, we said, has to be seen (or otherwise sensed) to be appreciated. Inevitably, then, in simply hearing of the boy's beauty and of the lover's reaction to it, rather than experiencing it ourselves, we are brought up against the difference between how the experience feels from the inside and how it seems from the outside; and this is a gap which laughter may help us contemplate, if not bridge. We cannot rest content with laughter, just as Socrates will not rest content with merely evoking the lover's turmoil through allegory, but wants to assess how the lover stabilises that turmoil into a pattern of life. Yet we had better be capable of laughing, also.

For a whiff of the grotesque will always accompany such large philosophic aspirations as are here evoked; the god, with all those extra consonants, is just too big a name to fit mere human measures.[35]

But let me turn, now with a lighter heart, to the attempt to make something of this philosophic love. It is at once apparent that the relationship between boy and lover develops through the lover's attention to the boy's character rather than his physical beauty. Not that beauty drops out of the picture; instead, it is taken for granted. Socrates simply states that it will be 'from among the beautiful' that the lover seeks a partner of a certain preferred disposition (252d5–6). Physical, not spiritual beauty was the tonic which made the lover's wings sprout new feathers; and Socrates does not attempt to quash this fact in what follows. Nevertheless, it must be admitted that the transition here is somewhat disingenuous. Indeed, Plato seems deliberately not to say too much about what I have been labelling 'physical beauty'. The lover is roused, as we have seen, by 'a god-like face or bodily form that is a good image of beauty' (251a2–3), and such beauty merits the label 'physical' simply in that the boy's flesh-and-blood presence is required to stir the lover's memory. Socrates does not actually say, however, that the boy has good looks in the conventional sense; he does not actually *identify* the boy who rouses the philosophic lover with the beautiful creature in whose presence the conventional lover would be stirred to attempt seduction (250e1–251a1) – although that suggestion is natural enough – and thus his words leave open the possibility of an interpretation such as this from Aryeh Kosman (in the context primarily of the *Symposium* rather than the *Phaedrus*):

Love on this view is *recognition*; it is seeing another as what that other might be, not in the sense of what he might be other than himself, but how he might be what he is. It is, in other words, coming to recognize the *beauty* of another. (Compare great portrait painters, who evoke the beauty of their (often plain) subjects not by artifice or camouflage, but by their skill in capturing the subject in just that attitude, in just that light, in which their true beauty is revealed.) (Kosman 1976, 64)

169

The physicality of the boy's beauty, then, would consist not necessarily in its conforming to a certain template but just in the fact that it can be seen only where the boy is. In either case, the element of contingency in meeting and being with the boy is preserved, and it is this, we have seen, that gives the philosophic lover pause; and, to be sure, what he sees in the boy confounds too neat an attempt to separate out the 'physical' from the 'spiritual' in his beauty. Still, I cannot help feeling that Plato's very reticence here stems from an awareness that the poignancy and self-consciousness of the philosophic lover's reaction would be all the sharper – all the more distinct from the conventional, and all the more blessed – if the beloved were not quite 'plain' but possessed of a more widely recognisable beauty. This would be painful for him to confront too directly, just because not every philosophic life is necessarily a life of philosophic love, and because the difference seems a matter of luck. The tale Socrates tells of the Zeus-like couple in the *Phaedrus* remains that of an exceptional pair[36] – so in the *Theaetetus* we hear him say, more comfortingly: 'You are beautiful (*kalos*), you know, Theaetetus, and not ugly as Theodorus said; because anyone who says something beautiful (*kalos*) is himself beautiful and good (*kalos te kai agathos*)' (*Tht.* 185e3–5).

The lover's shift of attention from the physical beauty to the character of his beloved resembles a stage in Diotima's account, in the *Symposium*, of the ascent through love to apprehension of the beautiful itself: when she says that the lover, who has at first been aroused by physical beauty, will 'next consider the beauty within souls to be more worthy than that of the body' (*Smp.* 210b6–7), so that he could fall in love with a person of only modest physical attractiveness provided he should have an outstanding character and mind. To be sure, the story in the *Phaedrus* is significantly different in that Socrates focuses on the joint development of a loving couple, a pair of individuals, over the course of a lifetime (as emerges most clearly at the end of his speech, 256a7–e2), Diotima on the development of a single individual – which, moreover, she narrates as an emancipation from concern for the beauty (physical or spiritual) of any other *individual* (*Smp.* 210c7–d6). In the *Phaedrus* the beautiful boy is earmarked by the lover for the philosophic life, rather than that the lover should progress in the philosophic life by ridding himself of a concern for, among other things, beautiful boys.[37] This contrast seems of a piece with Socrates' acknowledgment in his critique of rhetoric on the value of recognising particulars and adapting to the occasion, and would support the idea that the *Phaedrus* belongs with those later dialogues in which this strand of Platonism is more salient (as mentioned in chapter three). But I do not wish to become embrangled in this question.[38] My purpose in adducing the comparison with the *Symposium* is to show up how in the *Phaedrus* we are given more insight into *why* the lover should make what, in Diotima's account, seems the great leap, much in need of elaboration, from concern for physical to concern for spiritual beauty.[39]

A convenient path towards this insight is in fact provided by a metaphor common to both stages of the lover's relationship with the boy: that of the statue (*agalma*). The lover's desire to sacrifice to the boy 'as to a statue and a god' (251a6) was initially inspired by the boy's 'likeness to beauty' (251a3); but now this imagery returns with a different set of divine connections. The lover, we read, 'treating [the boy] as if he were actually a god for him, fashions and adorns him like a statue, in order to honour and worship him' (252d6–e1). Once again the boy is both statue and god; but now the god that the lover worships in him is, more specifically, the particular Olympian in whose train he, the lover, followed as a disembodied soul. And Socrates assigns to the gods of his heavenly myth the job of representing differences of character and ambition among their mortal retinue – thus the philosophic type is a follower of Zeus (a point first brought to our attention in the account of the beatific vision of beauty, at 250b7), the martial sort a follower of Ares, the kingly a follower of Hera, and so on (252c3–d2; 253b1–4).[40]

Accordingly, in fashioning the boy as an icon of the god

whom they share as a model, the lover might seem at first glance to be taking over the inspirational lead in the relationship; for whereas before the window on the divine realm was pierced by the boy in his beauty, now the divine model represents a type of soul, and one more fully instantiated by the lover than by the as yet embryonic character of the boy. But the recurring metaphor reminds us that even when the lover first beheld the boy's beauty, the boy's beauty was not all that he beheld. He saw a statue and a god – saw, as I said earlier, his own vision made visible. So that already the icon of beauty, as well as the icon of Zeus, is in part a creation of the philosophic lover; for only because of his philosophic character is he struck by the boy's loveliness in the peculiarly complex way analysed in the previous two sections, and summarised under the head of seeing the boy not just as beautiful, but as an image of beauty. Thus the structure of the relationship does not undergo a radical change between stages. The inward turn that we witnessed in the lover's reaction – from the beauty of the boy to his own memory of the beautiful – prepares the ground for his subsequent attention to the building of character and lifestyle jointly in himself and the boy; for since what the lover glimpses in the boy's physical beauty is none other than the value of the reflective, philosophic life, it seems only natural that from such a seed – provided one can accept Socrates' account of that first stage – the relationship should develop as it does. Diotima's 'leap' is not so much avoided as taken at the very outset, in the philosopher's memory of the beautiful.

In this sense, then, the lover can take the boy's comeliness as in part his own achievement; but, conversely, Socrates is careful to stress that the couple's philosophic development, which one might be inclined to credit to the lover in his role as elder and mentor, is in part the responsibility of the boy. Although the lover actively sculpts the boy, he has come across him, so to speak, as an effigy in the rough. Lovers of each sort, says Socrates, look for similar characters to love (252d5–6); so that philosophic types look for someone with a 'philosophic and commanding' nature (*philosophos te kai hēgemonikos*, 252e3); and when they have found him and fallen in love with him, they 'do all in their power to make him such a one' (*pan poiousin hopōs toioutos estai*, 252e4–5). Making and finding are fused in the lover's actions; for the lover's sculpting hands would fashion nothing from recalcitrant material.[41] But the boy's contribution is far more than merely to offer himself as suitable clay in which the lover can mould his preconceptions. In his eagerness to bring out what is best in his beloved, the lover brings out what is best in himself. So we read (252e5–253a6): now is the time that the lover, if he has not yet done so, will seriously engage in the practice of philosophy, and look within himself for the traces of his god,[42] which he will find the more readily for 'being compelled to look concentratedly upon the god' – namely, we are to understand, because he is captivated by the vision that the boy induces; therefore, to the extent that he succeeds through memory in being 'possessed' by the god (*tēi mnēmēi enthousiōntes*) and in modelling his behaviour after that ideal, he gives the credit for this achievement to the beloved, and loves him all the more for it. As a result of this reaction he directs the force of his inner encounter with the god back outwards to the boy, and transmits by example his enthusiasm for the philosophic life, somewhat as religious fervour spreads by contagion among a group of Bacchants: 'even though it is from Zeus that they [lovers] draw off their inspiration, like Bacchants they pour it onto the soul of the beloved and create in him the closest possible likeness to their god' (253a6–b1).[43] Thus, at the very point in the relationship where the philosophic lover might have been in most danger of retreating contemplatively within himself – as he grows to fit his own ideal and inevitably becomes more aware of how much it is *his* ideal (this I take to be expressed in the lover's 'touching' his god through memory, 253a2–3) – he instead finds in the fact of his development all the more reason to love the boy by whose agency he has developed, and focuses his efforts on their growth as a couple (cf. also 253b5–c2).

It is important to see that the lover does indeed credit the boy as an *agent* in his development, and not just with being a

cause of it. What inspires him, he judges, is not some accidental attribute of the boy but his philosophic 'nature' (*physin*,
252e3), from which the boy's major choices as a human agent
will spring. Hence the lover can rightly be said to be grateful
to the boy for his development (he 'loves him all the more' for
it, 253a5–6) rather than grateful to his lucky star – grateful
simply for the opportunity. (Whether the lover is even so not
grateful to the boy 'for himself' but only for certain traits in
his character is a question I shall broach shortly.) Nevertheless, since a large part of what the lover sees in the boy is
potential, his gratitude becomes fully justified only in retrospect. Thus we read later (at 255b3–7), when Socrates comes
to describe in turn the boy's reaction to the overtures of the
philosophic lover, that the effect of the lover's 'kindness' or
'good will' (*eunoia*) towards him, when experienced at close
quarters, is to startle him into seeing how much more this
'divinely inspired' (*entheon*) lover has to offer than all his
other suitors. As a result of this revelation the boy's soul
begins to grow its feathers. He returns the lover's affection
and aspires to emulate and share in his kind of life (255c5–d3;
256a1–b3). This, then, is the psychological process figured in
the lover's finding himself a statue to sculpt. The lover's good
will towards the boy is an expression of his confidence that he
has found an effigy of his god, a potential philosopher; and
since the effect of this confidence is to open the boy to his own
potential and confirm him in the philosophic life, it acts as a
sculptor's chisel on the still rough-hewn stone. In other
words, by demonstrating from the outset his faith in the boy's
philosophic character and therefore in his agency as an in-
spirer – by giving him in a sense more credit than he initially
deserves – the lover brings it about that his beloved will grow
fully to deserve that faith and that credit. At the same time,
not just any boy is able to allow the lover's confidence to
work its effect (of course, not just any boy would have
aroused it in the first place). It is an achievement on the part of
the beloved to recognise the inspired good will of the philosophic lover and to distinguish it from that of the run-of-the-
mill suitor; just as it was the philosophic lover's achievement

to react to the boy's beauty, which all could see, in his own peculiar fashion. Thus Socrates notes that the beloved is himself naturally disposed to feel good will in turn towards his admiring lover (255a3–4), and that the boy's increasing maturity (*hēlikia*, 255a7) – that is, his coming into his own character – will draw him almost inevitably towards the similar qualities and congenial company of the other (255a7–b2). At every stage in their relationship, then, Socrates emphasises that the pair are conjointly responsible for its development.

Lover and beloved: the clarity of confidence

I want now to put some weight on an aspect of this loving relationship that counterbalances somewhat the burden of the previous section. We have seen in some detail how Socrates takes care to distribute a portion of responsibility between lover and beloved at every turn in their dealings with each other. But this distribution is not perfectly symmetrical. It is undoubtedly the lover who bears the heavier load of responsibility, especially at the initial stage – above all, by virtue of that 'confidence' in the boy which we have just seen him exhibit. For consider what he achieves by its means. The boy, we are told, will at first be wary of the lover, obedient to the conventions of the chase which threaten dishonour for those who associate too freely with their suitors (255a4–6); so that the lover must be patient and wait for time and tentative exposure to his company to clear a path through the social niceties (255a7; 255b7–8). Here his faith must be at its strongest, if he is to avoid retreating within himself, and leaving the relationship stillborn.

In this section I will pose two questions about the lover's confidence. The first is, quite simply, how does he get it? Or more specifically, what enables him to persevere in the face of the boy's wariness? And the second is, does the lover's greater confidence threaten to overbalance the relationship and lead him to domineer over the boy?

The first question in a sense hits bedrock, and invites the reply: what enables the lover to persevere is love. In other words, to say that the lover's gratitude to the boy expresses itself as care for the boy's development is just to say that he is in love. Still, there is a little more that can be said: namely, by noting that the lover, unlike the beloved, has the spectacle of physical beauty to reinforce his faith. In order to explain this point I must consider again the boy's response to the lover, but this time not in general but in its sexual aspect; for it is through the contrast between the manner in which sexual desire is eventually aroused in the boy and the manner of its arousal in the lover that the importance of physical beauty in relation to the lover's confidence becomes clear.

That Socrates should explicitly envisage the boy becoming aroused at all is a further novelty of love among the philosophers, since we saw when considering the speeches of the non-lovers that the conventional expectation was for the boy to remain aloof from the lover's sexual throes. But if the boy is to order his soul like a philosopher he must experience the same range of feelings as his lover; only so, having gone through the same struggle for self-control (see 255e4–256a6), can they lead a life together 'as of one mind' (*homonoētikon*, 256b1). Nevertheless, Socrates maintains the asymmetry between lover and beloved to this extent: that although the boy has a desire for all degrees of sexual contact that is quite 'comparable' (*paraplēsiōs*) to that of the lover, still it is 'weaker' (*asthenesterōs*) than his (255e2–3). This relative weakness is what I want to consider; for it is to be explained by the place of physical beauty in the relationship.

Since Socrates is evoking an experience of radical confirmation in the boy similar to that which the boy previously elicted in the lover, he wheels back the familiar props of his allegory for this purpose. The boy's feelings are weaker because, says Socrates, they are like an echo. That bountiful stream of beauty and desire which, as we know, opened the buds of the lover's soul, although it flows originally from the boy to his beholder, is in part deflected back, like wind off a rock, to the soul of its originator – where it does a similar job of exciting the growth of his feathers and filling him in turn with love (255c1–d3). But there is an important difference between his reaction and that of the lover. The boy 'is indeed in love, but with what, he is at a loss to say' (*erai men oun, hotou de aporei*, 255d3); in fact, he cannot even tell that what he feels is love, let alone discern its object clearly. He is like a person who has contracted ophthalmia 'but cannot diagnose its cause' (255d4–5);[44] hence he will not properly acknowledge his sexual arousal even to himself, thinking of his feelings under the category not of *erōs* – passionate love – but of *philia* – friendship (255e1–2). And as for the object towards which those feelings are directed, he fails in particular to realise that when he looks at the lover 'he sees himself, as if in a mirror' (255d5–6).

The boy's inability to find his emotional bearings reminds us of the general effect on philosophic types of confrontation with a good likeness of the Forms, in which they were similarly said to have a hard time identifying either their feeling or its object: 'they do not know what is happening to them because their perception is too weak' (250a7–b1). But we also recall that this general limitation preceded an account of the special 'brightness' of the physical likenesses of beauty, which offer the prospective lover far readier access to the corresponding Form than is possible with those values such as justice and moderation which must be appreciated in the context of a whole life. For this reason the lover's feelings are much less confused than those of the boy. While it is true that the lover was thrown into a tizzy by the boy, 'maddened' (*emmanēs*) and 'at a loss' (*aporousa*) to cope with the strange cocktail of his sensations (251d8), this state should be distinguished from the boy's being 'at a loss' (*aporei*, 255d3) to say what he loves. The lover does not quite know how to manage the intensity of his emotions; but these are emotions stirred in the first place by the relative *clarity* with which the sight of the boy recalls him to his divine vision. So too, as the relationship moves forward the lover 'finds it all the easier' (*euporousi*) to model himself on that vision because, so to speak, the boy glues him to the celestial screen (253a1–5). It is not *cognitive* confusion that he suffers. The boy, on the other hand, fails to understand what it is that he sees and feels; and I

177

propose that his perplexity is an example of 'dull organs' (250b3–4) in action. For what awakens the boy's love is not physical beauty (the conventions of the time would block him from looking for this in a lover) but genuine demonstrations of kindness and good will (*eunoia*, 255b4); the kind of ethically fine behaviour, that is, which was contrasted with beauty as harder to appreciate (250b1–5). It takes time and frequent association for the boy to pick the philosophic suitor out from the rest; and even then his apprehension is relatively dull. The lover, on the one hand, sees straight because he sees double (the kind of oxymoron, this, that the phenomenon of 'beneficial madness' invites). That is, he clearly sees the boy's beauty as an image of the beautiful; sees both statue and god. The boy, on the other hand, is in fact seeing double but has not yet seen this fact. Where the lover sees the divine model, the boy sees the loving mentor on whom he will model himself; and where the lover sees in the boy an image that he has himself fashioned in part, the boy sees reflected in the lover an image of himself, an image, then, for which he himself is responsible – though again only in part, for his beauty is itself in part a creation of the lover, and this to-and-fro of origins has its ultimate source only in the place above the heavens. But, unlike the lover, the boy fails to recognise the image he has made (255d6).

Now, this amounts on the boy's part to a failure (as yet) to emulate the lover's achievement in integrating sexual desire with philosophic aspiration. We have seen that even though the boy feels sexual desire for the lover he does not admit this to himself but calls what he feels 'friendship' rather than 'love'; for he has yet to emancipate himself from the conventions of his day. And indeed why *should* he be erotically aroused by the lover's kindness and companionship, in the absence of physical attraction? The allegory of desire provides a theoretical answer: that the boy's erotic feelings have their origin in physical beauty after all, to wit, the boy's own beauty as reflected in his lover's eyes.[45] This account borrows some plausibility from the fact that to excite a person sexually, and to know it, can in turn arouse (or increase) one's own excitement. Merely sexual excitement, however, is not what the philosophic lover demonstrates – although in associating with the boy in gymnasia and other such places he does 'touch' him (*haptesthai*, 255b8), to this extent following the traditional gestures of courtship. Rather, he shows that peculiar excitement which derives, as we have seen, from his having to cope with a combination of sexual impulse and philosophic awakening, and which so distinguishes him, as 'divinely inspired', from the throng of suitors (255b5–6). The boy can recognise this much: that there is something special about the excitement that *this* lover is showing (and moreover that he, the boy, is its cause); and he duplicates it instinctively (in the automatic way that sexual excitement can be picked up), because, I take it, it is his nature to be susceptible to this contagion (see 255a3–4). But since he duplicates it unthinkingly, he is himself surprised by the compresence of ethical appreciation and sexual readiness in his attitude to the lover, and becomes confused. In failing to recognise his own image, he fails to understand that what distinguishes the philosophic lover's good will from that of the others is just that it arises from an attempt to integrate his sexual reaction to physical beauty with his higher ambitions (rather than to satisfy them separately – which leads to the problems seen in the speeches of the non-lovers). Instead, the boy actually understands only what his 'dull organs' can detect: the lover's kindness and congenial conversation. The rest – his own beauty transmuted in the lover's reaction – he sniffs at and gets hooked on, but does not at first confront; retreating instead to that label for his feelings ('friendship') which convention would dictate. The lover, by contrast, cannot fail to confront the task of integration from the outset with the full power of his understanding; for it was the boy's physical beauty, there before him, not reflected in another but direct and undeniable (although, of course, itself undeniably a 'reflection' of the Form), which aroused and confirmed his philosophic ambition in the first place, and so left him no avenue of re-interpretation in terms of conventional propriety.[46] For the philosophic lover, this love – as a project of integrating sexuality and philosophic ambition – was unconventional from the start; an unconventionality which the boy, however, can only gradually learn to appreciate. He gets his chance because of the lover's faithful perseverance; to which the lover is in turn committed because of the epiphany of the boy's physical presence. And this, I propose, is Socrates' final word on the place of beauty in their relationship.[47]

At this point I should square the present proposal with my earlier account of the lover's behaviour. I have emphasised the relative clarity of the philosophic lover's double vision by comparison with that of the boy. But let me not forget that by seeing double at all the lover is prey to the general inadequacy with which likenesses of the Forms are discerned; so that, when I discussed the horizon of care against which the beloved is set, it was the relative opacity of the philosophic lover's view of the distance that I contrasted with the clear-headedness of the conventional lover. There is no contradiction here; only the verbal ramifications, entwined around 'clarity', of the freakish-seeming notion that the philosopher – reason's servant – is mad. In the speeches of the non-lovers, the madness of love was presented as a temporary disease of the mind which the lover is unable to prevent, and during which he is incapable of deliberating for the best, either for himself or for his beloved, and so will repent of what he has done when he returns to his senses (see esp. 231c7–d6; 237d5–238a2 with 241a2–4). Socrates corrects this account at the start of his palinode by pointing out that the results of madness are not necessarily divorced from what is best. Soothsayers are known to have offered excellent counsel; 'faith-healers' have lifted family curses; inspired poets have edified future generations by glorifying the past. In these cases madness does not muddle the clarity of one's senses (not where it counts, at least) and so prevent action for the best; yet, like the love-craziness described by the non-lovers, this madness is beyond the full control of those she visits, and her visits are temporary – associated with fits or trance-like states.

The erotic madness of the philosopher, however, is different again. We have seen that it too comes upon the philosopher in a way that he cannot control: as a discovery of a self which he has yet to make fully his own, but on which he cannot renege. This is its title to be called 'madness' (and I postpone more detailed discussion of this phenomenon – in particular, how it differs from merely being overwhelmed by appetite – to the following sections on the struggle in the soul). But unlike those already established forms of benign madness, philosophic madness does not come in spurts. The lovers, we saw, awake to the prospect of an entire life of inspiration; and in mythical terms the process of re-growing the soul's feathers can apparently not be completed even within so long a span as that. I drew attention to something similar in the figure of Socrates back in my chapter of orientation: his being the man without sandals, always at leisure to find philosophy where others see nothing to remark upon.[48] And the great span of philosophic madness is to be connected with a peculiar feature of its 'clarity', one which I discussed earlier: namely that, initially at least, the fact of the philosophic lover's aspiration is more vivid to him than its object, so that he sees more clearly what he will not do, than what he will – whereas each bout of those other kinds of divine madness issues in a determinate and positive result or product. This too has its analogue in Socrates' behaviour. He is inspired to set out on the experiment of his palinode, we recall, by a visitation of his 'daemonic sign'; and the peculiar quality of the prophetic power thus evinced – 'I am a soothsayer, you know', says he, 'but not an entirely serious one' (242c3–4) – is just its negativity: 'always, when it comes, it holds me back from what I am about to do' (242c1). Socrates cannot, like the Sibyl, just tell the Greeks what they must do to set the future right (see 244a8–b5). When it comes to prophecy he is 'like those people who are bad at their letters: I'm only good enough for my own purposes' (242c4–5). But mistakes, at least, he can see 'clearly' (*saphōs*, 242c5); and knowing what he will *not* do or tolerate, he can proceed with the slow attempt to spell out the truth.

So I come to the second of the two questions announced at

the beginning of this section. Does the older man perhaps take advantage of his greater 'clarity' and conviction in order to impose his ideas on the boy? Is the force of his inspired example, despite his genuine good will, nevertheless surreptitiously manipulative – saying to the boy in effect: you must become what I am? And is it true that, as Gregory Vlastos puts it: 'Depicting [the boy] as an adorable cult-object, Plato seems barely conscious of the fact that this "holy image" is himself a valuing subject, a center of private experience and individual preference, whose predilections and choice of ends are no reflex of the lover's and might well cross his at some points even while returning his love' (Vlastos (1969) 1981, 32)? This nexus of objections to 'Platonic love' draws strength from an ideal of love as – again quoting Vlastos (p. 19) – 'wishing another person's good for just that person's sake, looking upon the loved one's individual being as something precious in and of itself'. In so far as this ideal borrows from the *agapē* or unconditional love of the Christian god[49] its value as an ideal has itself been questioned, to my mind rightly, on the grounds that to love an individual unconditionally, just as the individual that he or she is, is to love him for what he *happens* to be, and so to make it accidental that *he* is the person loved.[50] What is loved in such a case, it seems – here turning the tables on those who see Plato's philosopher as being in love with beauty rather than with the beautiful boy – is not so much the individual, more his individuality. Whereas surely to wrest a life and a character of one's own from the lottery is an achievement, and it is for our achieved 'selves' in *this* sense – or in the boy's case, for the promise of achievement – that we want to be loved?

Even accepting this reply, however, the worry persists. For, granted that to love persons for themselves is to love them for what they essentially are and can fully become, can we be sure that the lover in his eagerness to bring out what he takes to be best in the boy is not limiting the boy's horizon to what he himself can see and directing into a ready-made channel of aspiration what might otherwise have taken a subtly different turn? It should be clear from my account of how their relationship develops what response Plato has to this worry. He accepts it. That is why he is so careful at every stage to emphasise the joint responsibility of the partners in furthering their love. The lover cannot even surreptitiously be saying to the boy: become what I am; because, as we saw, he learns who he is in part by loving the boy. Indeed, it is because he is in this sense lacking and unsure of himself (fallen from heaven) that he is open to love in the first place (susceptible to having his memory stirred). Conversely, the boy could not be squire to the lover's quest unless such were indeed his destiny; that is the point of Socrates' stressing his achievement in picking the philosophic lover out from among his suitors and the affinity of character betokened thereby. Of course, this is simply to propound an ideal of love; it is not to offer some kind of guarantee that between two persons of philosophic mien the progress of love cannot but be smooth and free from manipulativeness. But my point is that in propounding this ideal Plato shows every concern, *pace* Vlastos, for the fact that the boy is 'a valuing subject, a center of private experience and individual preference'; for he makes it clear that the relationship can only be a success if the boy already shares as a matter of individual preference the values on which the lover wants them to build together. And he would not insist on this if he were not himself already sensitive to the worry that critics of 'Platonic love' offer to supply.

Nevertheless, I should not pretend that there isn't a genuine divergence of ideals here. Recall how the quotation from Vlastos continues: '[a subject] whose predilections and choice of ends are no reflex of the lover's and might well cross his at some points even while returning his love'. This makes an attractive picture: that through love two people might each foster the other's nature even in those areas where their goals are different, and learn to tolerate, trust and respect those differences. But what Plato would find truly alien in this view is the suggestion that respect for such differences is in part actually constitutive of love; that to love a person is to be prepared to foster him or her in their very difference from oneself. Plato's view, by contrast, is that love and the nurture of

LOVE AMONG THE PHILOSOPHERS

what is common to the partners grow in step. Naturally, both
lover and beloved must be tolerant and patient of their slow
development, and both must trust that they have a future
together; but to the extent that the need for such tolerance or
trust is occasioned by divergence in their characters and goals,
Plato gives no sign here of thinking that this divergence could
work otherwise than *against* the fruition of their love, or at
least, that in no sense could it provide, even in part, a positive
focus for their shared project of life. The strength of his
account is that it gives full value to the intuition that to love
another is above all to want to create with that person something *joint*. It is the intuition that Hermias voices, I think,
when he says of the philosophic lovers' generosity towards
their beloved: 'what they want for themselves, they want also
for the beloved; for their life is one' (Hermias apud 253b). Of
course this desire would be still-born unless accompanied by
'imaginative sympathy and concern' (returning to Vlastos, p.
32) for what our partners 'themselves think, feel, and want';
and I have just argued that Plato acknowledges as much. But
where Vlastos puts this sympathy *as such* at the core of the
loving relationship (it is 'what love for our fellows requires of
us ... above all', p. 32), Plato sees it as a necessary condition
for an enterprise that must be otherwise – and more positively
– specified; so that this sympathy is itself conditional on just
what it is that the lovers can think, feel and want, and
especially on their thinking, feeling and wanting it together.
The other view, for all its nobility, seems to me too negative. It
allows consideration for the otherness of the partner to usurp
the commanding position that ought to be reserved for the
commonality of nature which gives such consideration its
point.[51] Influenced perhaps by a Kantian ethic, it holds up for
our admiration a relationship between individuals who value
each other primarily as ends-in-themselves. Fine as such a relationship can be, it yet bears a curious likeness to the kind of
liaison which in the speeches of the non-lovers is taken to its
logical extreme: one contracted between agents for the furtherance of their separate goals. This may be mutual and even
affectionate respect; but can it be love?

184

The struggle in the soul: sheep's clothing

The reader will recall that I announced two paths by which Socrates investigates how the philosophic lover stabilises and builds upon his turbulent feelings for the boy: one, which I have discussed in the previous pair of sections, traces how lover and beloved come to mesh in their aspirations; the other, to which I now turn, leads us back to the interior of the lover's soul, there to witness the process by which he tames and at the same time learns from his feelings.[52]

What prompts Socrates' return to the allegorised happenings within the lover's soul is the need to explain how he manages to win the boy over to his love (253c5–6); that is – given what we saw in the foregoing section – how the force of the boy's beauty is transmuted by the lover into a passionate good will towards the boy so distinctive as to sweep aside all competing suits and awaken in him a reciprocal love. What goes on within the lover's soul as he effects this alchemy? Socrates makes his assessment by dramatising a struggle between the three figures that structured the progress of the soul-chariot through the heavens in the first part of his speech: the charioteer and the good and bad horses. The horses he now paints for us more vividly: the one straight and well-boned, high of neck and shining white, 'a passionate lover of honour, tempered by restraint and modesty (*timēs erastēs meta sōphrosynes te kai aidous*)' (253d3–6); the other dark and squat, thick-necked, hairy-eared and bloodshot in the eye, 'a friend to wantonness and imposture' (*hybreos kai alazoneias hetairos*) (253e1–4). In the face of such heavy caricature, one could be forgiven for expecting the distinction between the three players to come through quite as black-and-white as the horses' coats; but the expectation is confounded in the narrative that follows. In the charioteer and good and bad horses respectively we can discern, as is commonly agreed, at least an approximate correspondence to the reasoning, spirited and appetitive parts of soul (to give them their usual labels) familiar from the analysis in the *Republic*.

185

But the special contribution of the account here in the *Phaedrus* is a curious feature of the give-and-take between two of the figures, the charioteer and the bad horse (a feature which, so far as I can discover, has as yet passed without adequate remark among scholars): namely, that although the charioteer seems to stand for the control of reason and the bad horse for brutish, uninhibited lust, in the struggle between the two it is the bad horse who adopts persuasive language and the methods of reason, while the charioteer maintains control by sheer strength and wordless violence.

I take this feature to be central to a proper understanding of the lover's achievement, and will begin by delineating it in this section through a close reading of the passage, savouring the strangeness of the moment as charioteer and bad horse pilfer from one another's wardrobe.[53] Only then (in the following section) will I address myself to interpreting that strangeness.

At the outset of the drama a telling metaphor unexpectedly associates the charioteer with the lustful rather than the well-behaved member of his team. The good horse, we are told, can be led by word of command alone and never needs the whip (253d7–e1);[54] but the bad horse 'barely yields to the whip and goad (*kentrōn*)' (253e4–5). Both means of power are exercised by the charioteer. Yet when the charioteer himself comes to feel another's power – the attraction of the beautiful boy – he is metaphorically described as sensible, not to the power of words and reason (as with his natural ally, the good horse), but to the 'goad (*kentrōn*) of itching desire' (253e6–254a1); and his next action (at 254a3–4) is to attempt to restrain the lustful horse, without success, by means of whip and goad (*kentrōn*, again). The goad that pricks the charioteer, as commentators correctly explain, is not the goad with which he belabours the bad horse but the 'goad' that pictured the growing pains in the lover's soul earlier in the speech, when the swelling feathers pricked at their sealed carapace (at 251d5 and 251e4). The conjunction of literal and metaphorical instances of the term in these lines is no less remarkable for that.[55] It enables us to appreciate not only that the charioteer, the voice of reason in the soul, has desires all his own,[56] but also that the goading and whipping he inflicts on the lascivious horse directly transfers the force of the goading he receives from the boy. The desires of the charioteer and of the bad horse conflict, to be sure (notice that the goad felt by the charioteer is a stimulant, that felt by the horse a depressant); but they are comparable in their intensity.[57]

However, whereas the charioteer's desire is described in a way that associates it with lust, and finds overt expression in his lashing of the bad horse, the bad horse's intentions in turn – which are no less direct and brutal than the lashing he receives[58] – are described in gentle euphemisms and given overt expression primarily in his persuasive use of words. It is true that upon becoming aware of the beautiful boy the prurient animal ignores the whip, 'compels' (*anankazei*) his partners to approach the youth, frisks at the reins and bolts in an abundance of natural 'forcefulness' (*biai*) (this in summary of 254a3–6); but everything hangs on how that force and compulsion is dramatically realised in the scene as a whole. After all, the sense of shame even in the good horse 'forces' him, we read, into modest behaviour (*aidoi biazomenos*, 254a2); while the memory of the Forms 'compels' the charioteer to virtue (*ēnankasthē*, 254b8). There are other ways to force and compel than by brute strength, and what is remarkable in this scene is that not until the very end does the bad horse again attempt to coerce his fellows with the sheer muscle power that we see him flex at the start.

What happens in between? The tone is set by the surprisingly circumspect coda to the sentence in which the bad horse capers and bolts. He presses the others to approach the boy and 'give him a reminder (*mneian*) of the favours of Aphrodite' (254a6–7). And a similar circumspection marks his second approach, which is made 'in order to renew the proposal (*logous*)' (254d5–6). In short, Socrates muffles with the vocabulary of verbal exchange a transaction that the lewd beast intends, if he gets his way, to conduct primarily in the language of the pelvis. So much for the euphemistic description of the bad horse's intent. As for the overt actions by

187

which he expresses his desire: the charioteer and obedient horse, reluctantly allowing themselves to be led by him, succumb not to his brute strength but rather 'agree to do his bidding' (254b3).[59] Accordingly, when they have come within sight of the boy's flashing glance, and the charioteer in awe and horror at what might be done falls back, jerking both horses to the ground in consequence, the bad horse treats this action as a breach of promise. He becomes angry and administers a rebuke that despite its harshness is not gratuitously insulting (254c7–8),[60] but – of all things – righteously indignant, in that he upbraids the charioteer and his yokemate 'for their cowardliness and unmanliness in deserting their post and breaking their agreement' (254c8–d1). The sentiment is lofty, and expressed not violently but through persuasion – the rhetorical pose seems to be that of a commander in the field exhorting his faint-hearted troops.[61]

Indeed, not only does he use persuasion, this animal that we have seen fuming at the traces, but he allows himself to be persuaded in turn when the other two beg him to delay a while (254d2; 'barely' persuaded, to be sure; but he has a right to be truculent – who broke their agreement, after all?).[62] He then waits patiently until the 'agreed deadline' comes around (254d3); and only when his partners welch on their promise yet again and this time stoop to guile, pretending to have forgotten and ignoring his reminders, does he resort to brute force. He drops his persuasive inflections and speaks with the voice of a horse – we hear his 'whinny' for the first time (*khremetizōn*, 254d4: the first properly equine predicate ascribed to him since his initial 'frisking' at 254a4).[63] And now indeed he becomes the incarnation of violence. Hunkering down, thrusting out his tail,[64] he bites the bit and 'shamelessly' drags the chariot along (254d5–e5). But it should now be clear that his culminating violence is no simple and immediate outburst but is prompted by a failure to secure his ends through the unquestionably rational means of verbal contract; a failure that in turn derives from an apparent refusal by the voice of reason and his ally in the soul to stick to reason's rules.[65]

If we approach this exchange of roles from the other direction, it is equally clear that the charioteer's actions throughout are portrayed in such a way as to tone down his rationality and highlight his use of violence and muscle.[66] What is more, his violence is, ironically, of an especially equine sort.

We have already seen how in applying the goad to the bad horse the charioteer outwardly expresses the goading he receives from the beautiful boy. Then for a while he and the obedient horse exchange words with their licentious partner – although the verbal exchange is not of their instigation (254a5–b3). When next the charioteer takes the upper hand, his action is not verbal but violent. On catching the 'lightning-flash' (254b5) in the boy's eye he is rudely startled and 'rears back' (*anepesen hyptia*, 254b8) – horse-like behaviour.[67] We hear more about this reaction when it recurs on the second approach (254e1–2): that it is like 'rearing back' (*anapesōn*) from the starting-line in a horse race.[68] The phrase presumably pictures how charioteers must lean back on the reins to control their horses as they chafe at the starting-line.[69] Plato has thus selected as a movement expressive of the charioteer's control one that in its visual shape resembles closely the backward-rearing of a horse that is unable to contain itself. This is appropriate enough, in so far as the violence that we have seen the bad horse avoid is present in the charioteer's gesture from the outset; for he does not simply rein the horses in but brings them to their haunches (254c1–2), on the second approach bloodying the jaws of the lecherous steed, crumpling his legs beneath him, and 'giving him over to agony' (254e4–5).[70] But Plato sharpens the irony by portraying this movement, which purports to establish the charioteer's command, as nothing more than an involuntary consequence of his shock. The flashing glance of the beautiful boy, we read, reminds the charioteer of his disembodied vision of the beautiful itself; so that 'he is afraid, and in reverence rears backwards, and in that same motion is compelled (*kai hama ēnankasthē*)[71] to pull back on the reins' and drag the horses to the ground (254b7–c1). The gesture of mastery seems more like a compulsive reaction of aversion. It is as if the charioteer pulls on the reins only because he is still holding them as he gets thrown backwards.

The struggle in the soul: philosophic madness

So much by way of establishing the 'fact' that the struggle in the soul is narrated in such a way as to make it appear that the charioteer and bad horse, in their respective attempts to re- alise their desires, each adopt methods more appropriate (given the content of those desires) to the other. But what is the philosophic function of this 'fact'?[72] It seems to me to offer further insight into just what the peculiar complexity of the philosophic lover's reaction to the beautiful boy consists in – how he can be said to learn from his sexual response and integrate it with his philosophic aspiration, rather than simply spurn it – and how it can be that the love which nou- rishes the philosophic life, the life of reason *par excellence*, merits categorisation as a kind of madness.

The first point to settle is that by attributing rational behav- iour to the lascivious horse Plato is not out to increase our regard for the beast but rather to display the limitations of the only kind of reasoning it can use: prudential calculation of the means to a predetermined goal. The bad horse has a single desire: to gratify his lust; and he calls on his reasoning powers only in order to skirt the obstacles that keep him from that goal. That is why brute strength is indeed his first as well as his last resort; only when the charioteer and good horse resist his initial bolting does he attempt to reason with them.[73] And what is crucial here is not that Plato assigns the lustful horse only a single desire – which may well be an accident of the erotic context – but that, regardless of how many desires he has, the animal is portrayed as being able to deliberate only about how to satisfy his desire, and not about whether that is the desire he wants.[74] Thus, when he lectures the charioteer and good horse for breaking their agreement (adopting his most thoughtful and righteous voice) the fault he lays at their door is simple failure of nerve: 'cowardice and unmanliness' (254c8). That is, he interprets their motivation as operating only on a first order; as if in deciding what to do they have merely taken the path they are most strongly inclined to follow (namely, by indulging their disinclination to accost the boy). This is to see only part of the truth; for the desire actually motivating the charioteer is a result of his concern over what desires should move the whole person. Reason in the philosophic lover is not merely prudential but deliberates between and selects ends; so that the charioteer's 'fear' – and this would relate to the lover's initial *frisson*, at 251a3–4, upon seeing the beautiful boy (as discussed in the opening section of this chapter) – is not a simple failure of nerve when up close to the boy but a reverential trembling before 'the nature of the beautiful' (*tēn tou kallous physin*, 254b6). In other words, it is the result of a valuation of what is beautiful – as represented by the conscious act of comparison (however instantaneous) between what he sees (the boy) and what he remembers (the beautiful itself).

There is an asymmetry of understanding, then, between charioteer and lustful horse. The charioteer fully understands what motivates the beast (that is why he is so frightened at what might happen), for his task is to assess and direct the desires of the whole soul (notice that he is described at the outset as 'suffusing the *whole* soul with a feeling of heat', 253e5–6).[75] But the beast cannot in turn properly understand what motivates the charioteer.[76] This is presumably why the philosopher's second-order choice of desires is attributed within the allegory to a human being, but his lust (the satisfaction of which, if requiring deliberation at all, requires it only on a first order) to an animal.[77] And indeed, the fear the bad horse ends up conditioned to feel in the presence of the boy (254e5–8) is, ironically, of just the sort that he wrongly ascribed to the charioteer, avoidance rather than pursuit of sexual contact having now become, simply (and not, of course, through deliberations of his own), the option he is most strongly inclined to take.

It is this asymmetry of understanding, and the fact that the charioteer and bad horse are contrasted (in the matter of reason) not as the rational to the irrational part of soul but rather in terms of the level at which their reasoning takes place, which give insight into how the charioteer actually learns from the fractious creature. For consider the following remarkable feature of the narrative. Although the charioteer feels the goad of desire at the first sight of the beloved, and indeed (as mentioned in the preceding paragraph) is as it were the furnace that transfers the heat of this reaction to the other parts of the soul, nevertheless only *after* he and the good horse have been worn down by the persistent urging of the lustful horse and approach the boy does the charioteer, catching the full 'lightning-flash' of the boy's glance,[78] return in memory to his vision of the beautiful itself and fall back on the reins in awe. In other words, only through the agency of the bad horse does the charioteer come into full re-possession of his birthright; for he would not otherwise have come close enough to be dazzled.[79] Moreover, while he is joined by the noble horse in first resisting and then yielding to their skittish team-mate, the ensuing memory of beauty itself comes only to the charioteer – after all, only he had managed to hold his head above the celestial rim in order to glimpse that vision in the first place (248a1–3).

In less mythical terms, one and the same feature explains the difference between charioteer and good horse and the profit that the charioteer derives from the bad horse's importunacy: namely, that only the charioteer has the power and function of caring not just for his own desire but for the desires of the whole soul; only he holds the reins. In this asymmetry the good horse is involved on the side of the bad. He gets tugged to his haunches together with the bad horse, except that, unlike him, he 'willingly' obeys the charioteer's gesture, since he is 'always' self-restrained (254b8–c3 with 254a1–3). The good horse, then, is just doing what comes naturally, and what he has always done; he learns nothing new. That is why, for all his self-restraint, he is nevertheless represented as an animal rather than a human being, no less than the bad horse; for he too does not deliberate about what he should want.[80] The charioteer, by contrast, actually benefits from the experience of conceding to the lascivious horse;

for he is enabled thereby to recognise the full force of his 'reverence' (254b8) for the Forms. That is, he sees how much he cares, in a self-conscious way, about following the virtuous model. In so far as his subsequent reaction is to resist the forward tugging of the bad horse – to hold back on the satisfaction of sexual interest – it does not differ from that of the noble horse; but whereas the latter's resistance stems from his natural self-control, 'self-control' (*sōphrosyne*) appears in the charioteer's vision 'enthroned' alongside beauty 'on her holy seat' (254b6–7). This is to say that only the charioteer treats self-control as a project – appreciates that the 'self' to be controlled is the one that results from the interaction of all three parts of the soul.

Moreover, the phrasing suggests that he is confirmed in this project just to the extent that he connects it with his vision of the beautiful; and again the asymmetry of understanding between the charioteer and his animals allows us to see why. For the charioteer's task of controlling the whole self, although animated by a desire to integrate all parts of the soul, does not have as its goal integration *tout court*; this the contrast with the bad horse's use of reason makes clear. The bad horse too, after all, takes the trouble to ensure cooperation among all parts of the soul – bargains his partners into a contract. But this just shows that not every integration of the soul is worthy. Or, to put it another way, what the bad horse achieves is merely the integration of symptoms, not of underlying causes;[81] and this is all that he seeks to achieve. That is, being single-minded about his goal he cares only that the others should go along with him; he does not care about the means by which he secures their agreement, nor does he care to take their interests into account, but wants to reduce them simply to extensions of himself. The charioteer, on the other hand, comes into his full power just when he recognises and accepts that the soul's division is fundamental, and that his task of integration must begin from that fact; a recognition which beauty, of all values, is best able to induce. For the boy's beauty is something to which the lustful horse can respond as intensely, albeit on his own limited level, as does

193

the charioteer; so that the charioteer is brought into vivid confrontation with the beast and sees that he simply cannot give sexual desire full rein. He is at once confirmed in his values, and in how he must realise them: namely, by defeating that which, if dominant, would make the soul over in its manipulative image.[82] And his subsequent efforts to curb the lustful horse merit the title of 'integration' rather than mere 'manipulation' or 'repression' because they are the result of following through on the soul's sexual interest far enough to see where the line must be drawn. The charioteer cannot be content simply to resist the desire of the bad horse, but cares that it should find its proper place. This, then, is the sense in which he actually learns from the experience. (No such development affects the good horse: his role is mostly that of a foil to the other two – to whom the curious 'exchange of roles' is accordingly confined.) Notice, however, that the charioteer is indeed resistant to the bad horse from the outset; he does not go along with the creature in a spirit of experimentation, but unwillingly, and only because his resistance has been worn down (254b1–3). This is what we should expect if, as I have said, integration of the soul's characters is not in itself the charioteer's goal; for it is rather (always given the team to which he finds himself hitched) the inevitable expression of his goal. For the same reason, there is no straight answer to the question whether on this picture sexual interest, as that which enables the charioteer to regain his full memory and properly take up the reins, is being given a merely instrumental role to play. Yes: because the vision to which the charioteer reverts was one which the bad horse originally did nothing but hinder him from attaining (by dragging the chariot down: see 247b3–5); and no: because the task to which the charioteer's memory recalls him includes as an essential part (he has no choice in this matter, for it follows on from his falling back on the reins) the proper training – not the eradication – of the recalcitrant member of the team.[83]

Thus the use to which the prurient horse puts his powers of reasoning points up an asymmetry in the respective capacity for understanding of himself (together with the noble horse)

194

and the charioteer, one that elucidates how the charioteer can be said to learn from his experience of resisting the other's persuasion. However, I have yet to take properly into account the extreme violence and apparent involuntariness of the charioteer's jerking on the reins – the gesture by which he comes to dominate the soul. To detect in such actions an experience of 'learning' might, indeed, seem euphemistic evasion. I propose, however, that Plato is here more closely scrutinising the awkward fact that, as we have seen, the encounter with the boy inspires in the philosopher a clearer view of what he will *not* do than of what he will. His evocation of the charioteer's experience is a juggling-act. He wants to capture both how the philosopher is compelled to action, in that he comes up against a limit he finds himself unable to transgress (sees clearly what he will not do), and yet how, by being so compelled, he is doing what he most wants as a creature capable of deliberating over what desires should move him, and is in that sense rational and free (and able to steer himself towards a philosophic life).[84] The need for so complex an analysis is set by the fact that the struggle to which we are privy here is not just over what action the lover should take in his present encounter with the boy, but over what desires should motivate his life: what kind of person he should become. This indeed is the nub of the asymmetry between the charioteer and his horses. The charioteer motivates action always with a view to his desire for how the life of the whole person should go, a desire which will therefore seek to control other desires; while the horses motivate action from desires which, because they have no intrinsic connection to the other desires of the whole person, are not oriented beyond the action to the life of which it is a part (except in so far as this might affect the satisfaction of their desire).

Now, if the lovers' lustful horses were to win the struggle and have the lovers consummate their passion, we could say that both persons had been overwhelmed by their sexual appetite – had found this urge impossible to resist. These ways of speaking make sense of a person's feeling *compelled* to do something that he nevertheless *wants* to do by dividing the person into distinct psychological elements with which the person as a whole can identify to a greater or lesser extent. Thus when Socrates comes to consider such a pair of weak-willed lovers at the end of his speech – lovers of the second rank, not philosophic but 'honour-loving' types (*philotimōi*, 256c1), who let their unruly horses take control in a drunken or otherwise unguarded moment[85] – he points out that although they will likely continue to make love on occasion, they will do so infrequently, 'because what they do is not done with the consent of the whole mind' (*hate ou pasēi dedog-mena tēi dianoiai prattontes*, 256c6–7).[86] The quality of compulsion in what they do derives only from the fact that one part of the soul has mastered the other (which therefore feels unfree), and so applies only at the level of the whole soul. By contrast, the quality of compulsion in what the philosophic lover does, although within his soul too one part (the charioteer) will have mastered the other (the bad horse), derives not from the charioteer's victory but from the effect on the charioteer alone of his memory of the Forms – for this it is which determines his falling back on the reins – and so applies primarily at the level of one part of the soul (the charioteer) rather than the whole. In the case of the second-rank lovers, it is not the charioteer who is overwhelmed by 'his' lust (for the charioteer has no lust): the person is. But in the case of the philosophic lovers it is precisely the charioteer who is overwhelmed by his own memory of the Forms; he not only feels the desire to hold back from the boy but is compelled to do so.

The difference is crucial. For consider a soul in which the bad horse dominates. The bad horse himself is not compelled to do what he does; he just does it because it is his only desire; and the person as a whole is indulging his strongest desire. To the extent that this person feels overwhelmed and compelled so to indulge, it will be because he is aware of a pull in himself towards other options which are being quashed – that is why the second-rank lovers are said not to make love with the consent of their whole mind. Now consider the successful philosophic lover. The charioteer has mastery in his soul; but unlike the unruly horse, the charioteer has not acted simply because such was his desire, but because that desire has been fortified in his encounter with other options: options to which he naturally gives regard because his concern is for the life of the whole person. The charioteer jerks back on the reins – thus closing off the option the bad horse would have him allow – as a not fully voluntary consequence or side-effect of his fear and reverence at the memory of the Forms; that is, the gesture is a part of his natural reaction to that memory simply by virtue of his being the one to hold the reins – of his being that in the psyche which is concerned for the good of the whole. What this gesture expresses, then, is that controlling the options of the other parts of soul is an intrinsic component of the charioteer's desire.[87] The consequence on the macroscopic level for a soul in which the charioteer has achieved dominance over the bad horse is this: that the individual feels a 'compulsion' to act as he does not because, as with the second-rank lovers, he is aware that a call within himself towards another option is being muffled, but because all other options have already been closed off, and as it were taken up into his dominant desire, so that having no other course to take he cannot do otherwise than work towards the philosophic life.[88] He feels that he has no option (although this is not through simple unawareness of the options, or tunnel vision), and as if compelled from without, because it is the call not of his present but of his future self that he hears; yet – and this for the same reason – he is acting wholly for himself (which is not to say: selfishly); is enrapt by his project. And it is in this sense that his vocation comes upon him as a kind of *madness*.[89] Hence it should now be clear that in following up his philosophic desire he is not simply indulging his strongest appetite. Nor, however, do his actions stem simply from a sense of moral compulsion: the recognition of duty; for he is not only recognising what he must do but what he most truly wants to do. That is why he is both captivated and yet free.[90] The philosophic lovers, we read, 'have enslaved that in which the badness of soul was engendered, and have freed that in which the goodness has its origin' (256b2–3). Thus they live as free a life as is possible within human limits.

For when the bad horse enslaves the charioteer, the life that results (depending on how thoroughly the charioteer is enslaved) will not only be compelled but *compulsive* – the reason being that the beast has no intrinsic concern for its fellows and so will repress and manipulate rather than integrate them. Hence it is (so to speak) 'made' to be a slave; and the charioteer's 'enslaving' violence towards it is no act of repression but our best chance, on Plato's view, of achieving a life in which, on the contrary, nothing in us need be repressed. I take it, then, that by allowing the lecherous horse to speak reasonably and by painting the charioteer in the colour of blood Plato is describing the deceptive signals that our souls can send to tempt us into calling freedom 'repression' and indulgence 'good sense'. He is saying: this looks like violence, but isn't; this sounds like the voice of reason, but isn't – and so indicates in both cases what *is*.

This deceptiveness, and this struggle within the soul, are writ large in the competition between the three speeches on love, and the spuriousness that Socrates eventually unmasks in the claims of the non-lovers.[91] In a final address to the fictional boy of his palinode Socrates warns him of dire results from association with the non-lover, mixed as this will be not with divine madness but with merely 'mortal temperance (*sōphrosynē thnētē*), niggardly dispenser of mortal benefits, and which gives birth in the dear soul to that ignoble unfreedom (*aneleutherian*) which the crowd extols as virtue (*aretēn*)' (256e5–257a1). In an earlier chapter I displayed the bad faith of the non-lovers: how Lysias' man couches his appetite in the language of good sense, and how Socrates' man unctuously masks infatuation with a sermon. We can see now that the deceptively sweet reason of the former is just that of the prurient horse – devoted exclusively to the prudential maximisation of his pleasure (and that of the boy), but not at all to consideration of what his pleasure should be. Recall, for example, that a major argument of Lysias' speech is this: that whereas lovers will welch on promises made in the heat of the moment, the non-lover, who feels no passion and can remain prudent, will keep his word (231a2–3; 234a5–8).

198

Lysias' non-lover is thus as emphatic about the value of verbal contract as was the bad horse in the face of his own partners' attempt to wriggle out of their bargain. Moreover, he applies to this situation the same limited understanding that we saw the bad horse bring to bear; for he attributes lovers' promise-breaking simply to a cessation of desire (231a3; 234a7) – as if a single engine were pulling them along the tracks towards their goal, and had now gone into reverse. The account that Socrates' non-lover gives of the same event shows what he has to add to the Lysianic perspective; for he argues that the lover, having suffered a change of heart, will be too ashamed to admit this openly when he is reminded that he has broken his agreement (241a2–c1). This is to speak with the noble horse's sense of shame, and with the idea that the train has an engine at both ends (the lover's change of heart is the result not just of desire fizzling out but of the ascendancy of a new master: good sense, 241a2–4); and notice that it also corresponds rather better to, or is able to capture more of, the psychological struggle described in the palinode – in which the charioteer and good horse do indeed pretend to have forgotten when the time to keep their bargain comes around (254d2–4). This improvement can be put down to the fact that Socrates' non-lover has progressed, one might say, to the conception of the two-horse chariot. But he has forgotten the driver. Hence what he proposes is no less 'niggardly' an association after all than that of Lysias' man, if for different reasons. The latter economises through prudence, and is 'unfree' both in the sense that his perspective is hopelessly crabbed and because he experiences this economy as a necessary limitation on his desire; while the former economises through resistance to pleasure as such, and is unfree both because his psychological conception too, as we have seen, is limited in its own way, and because this economy results from the defeat of his ever-resentful desire. And both deck out their unfreedom in the finery of good sense and what they think of as virtue.

We can see, then, that there is a parallelism between the way in which the charioteer gains mastery of the philosophic soul and the way in which Socrates in his second speech finally overcomes the inadequacy of the previous two speeches. Just as the charioteer succeeds by virtue of his concern for all voices in the soul, so Socrates succeeds not by dismissing the voices heard in those other speeches but by integrating them – thus quite changing the effect of their timbre – into his polyphonic song of the charioteer's success. In appreciating this point, we can understand more fully what I anticipated in outline in the opening pages of my chapter on the speeches of the non-lovers: how Socrates' philosophic ethos shows through his speeches much as Lysias' rhetorical ethos shows through his. In particular, we can now see why it matters that Socrates should come into full voice only gradually: because his is the ethos of the charioteer who learns through struggle.

As I began this discussion of the clash between the parts of the philosopher's soul I pointed out that they are thought to correspond at least approximately to what are known as the reasoning, spirited and appetitive components of the tripartite soul most fully described in the *Republic*. Quite clearly, however, these labels have only limited application to the conduct exhibited by the charioteer and horses. These allegorical figures are actual characters (even if of a rather vaudevillian sort), each with his own appetites and capacity for deliberation. But the correspondence with the *Republic* is not disarmed; for interpreters have long found that these labels do not adequately apply even to that work's description of the behaviour of the parts. There are two main camps over this issue. Many have been influenced by the assumption that each 'part' of soul ought to stand for a single faculty (say: reason, emotion, desire), and that the complex behaviour of a whole person is best explained by the interaction of these simple faculties. The discovery that Plato's various descriptions of such interaction imply complex behaviour in each of the supposedly simple parts they accordingly see as sapping the explanatory power of the theory. This has been the more traditional approach. Other interpreters, in response, have worked from the assumption that Plato was never aiming at a theory in which (to put it baldly) reason simply reasons and

200

desire desires; that the parts of soul are better construed as a type of agent rather than faculty; and some among them have explicitly defended Plato's theory so construed against the accusation that it lacks explanatory force.[92]

I generally agree with this response, and in my account of the altercation between the three characters in the soul have unabashedly entered into the spirit of Plato's allegory, treating them as agents with plans and desires of their own, and not attempting to re-construe them as representatives of simple faculties. The essential point of contrast between the charioteer and rebellious horse is not that between a faculty of reason (without desire) and a faculty of appetite or desire (without reason) but, as we have seen, between that in us which aims at how best the life of the whole person should go and that which looks only to as immediate a satisfaction as possible.[93] Certainly these aims are to be correlated with reasoning and appetite respectively – after all, the labels 'reasoning', 'spirited' and 'appetitive' are not exegetic creations but translations of some among the labels that Plato himself uses in the *Republic*.[94] Thus for the charioteer deliberation is essential: how else could he plan for a whole life? He does not just *use* his power of deliberation, as does the lecherous horse, but is, so to speak, *devoted* to it (have we not seen him act with the violence of a zealot?). These labels apply, then, to what the characters represent not exclusively but *par excellence*; 'reason' and 'desire' are symptomatic of their behaviour. Similarly, the fact that the charioteer's desire operates on a second order by comparison with those of the horses derives from and is symptomatic of his aim rather than being in itself the decisive difference between them.[95]

This method of psychological explanation has evoked unease among representatives of the more traditional approach; for surely, it is argued, to account for the complex behaviour of a person by appeal to sub-units which themselves behave like little persons endowed with multiple faculties – *homunculi* – is not properly to explain the behaviour of the person but merely to reduplicate it, and so threaten a regress? In reply it is urged that there is nothing inherently objectionable about psychological explanation in terms of *homunculi* (rather than faculties) provided their behaviour is more limited than that of the whole person, and not subject to the very conflicts for which they are designed to account – conditions fulfilled by the 'parts' of the Platonic soul.[96] I find this response sound, but feel that a significant aspect of Plato's psychological method is missing from it, which as a result of the foregoing account we can now appreciate. The behaviour exhibited by the characters within the philosophic lover's soul is indeed in each case less complex than that of the person. However, by portraying them as allegorical figures Plato enables us to see that what we have here is not only a stretch of behaviour broken down into more limited components that nevertheless remain characterisable in terms of human behaviour, but also a stretch of behaviour seen as the turbulent intersection of the idealised forms of life to which it could give rise. In each case – not just in the case of the charioteer whose concern we have seen the whole life of the person to be – the allegorical figure represents the extreme kind of life to which its control of the person would lead, rather than simply the kind of behaviour by which it would establish control. So for example the lewd horse not only represents the pull of sexual appetite but offers a picture of what the whole person would become, how his life would degenerate into lechery, were the beast to gain complete control over him – a caricature (as we saw), more than a picture; for is any life going to degenerate to quite that pitch?[97] This would explain why the dark horse is labelled as unequivocally 'evil' (253d1–2) despite Plato's view in the *Republic* that the lowest part of the soul is not inherently either evil or good, but inherently excessive, and therefore prone to disrupt the person as a whole – who becomes evil to the extent that he fails to keep the lowest part under control. 'Evil' and 'good' would thus be terms properly reserved for the whole person. But my point is that the allegorical characters within the soul offer us just that: pictures of whole persons waiting to be summoned into being; hence the unequivocal ethical judgments.[98] Thus Plato resolutely refuses to give an 'atomic' account of the philosophic lover's experience – an account of the phenomena in terms of elements different in kind. Rather he describes the person that the lover is in terms of the persons among whom he must choose, or better: the person that the lover is in process of becoming in terms of the various persons he could yet become. These persons or lives are simpler than any life he might actually lead and so can function as explanatory elements; but they are not simpler in principle, but only as a practical matter; in the sense that the world is unlikely to allow anyone to lead so monolithic a life as each member of this trinity represents. And I think the reason for Plato's avoidance of atomic explanation in psychology is this: that he thereby sharpens in himself the perspective of the charioteer. For it is only the charioteer who tends naturally to appreciate the tugging and dragging within the soul in terms of the realised lives towards which it moves (the type of awareness which I have opposed to 'faculty'-psychology), while his partners concentrate on the efficacy of their pull. Thus it is characteristic of the bad horse that his energy is exhibited through distinct 'faculties' – first and last the force of naked desire, and in-between the calculations of reason – because with his goal in place he need diversify only in the mode by which he attains it; while the charioteer's reflection on his goal and overwhelming desire to reach it come in a single gesture as he falls – literally falls – in love.[99]

So I bring my celebration of these Platonic lovers to an end; the wedding-party draws to a close. I have understood what I can of their love, and leave them now to their private joy.

CHAPTER SEVEN

WRITING THE CONVERSATION

Theme or epilogue?

In this final chapter I return to the vantage-point of the first and assess the dialogue as a whole, knitting together its various concerns and indicating where and why the seams are meant to show. In my opening chapter I approached this task by considering Socrates' and Phaedrus' attention to their physical environment, which inaugurates both halves of the work, and by this means I oriented the reader towards what was to follow. In this chapter I will look back on the ground traversed through the filter of the critique of writing which is the final topic of their conversation. Apart from its connection with the dialogue as a whole, Socrates' devaluation of the written word in relation to the spoken in the closing pages of the dialogue has special relevance for the entire Platonic corpus, because he finds fault with all forms of written discourse, the philosophic included; therefore, apparently, with Plato's dialogues also (see 276b1–277a5). And this passage of the *Phaedrus* (together with a stretch of the less securely Platonic *Seventh Letter*, 341b3–345a1) is the major source for Plato's view on the matter.

We recall that Socrates announced his critique of rhetoric as an investigation into the conditions not only of good speaking but also of good writing (259e1–2).[1] His general recommendations for rhetorical reform would apply to both; but with the main argument of his critique complete he broaches the special characteristics of writing as an additional matter (at 274b6). What Socrates says about writing is less clearly an indictment than a warning of potential danger; he stamps its packing-case not 'radioactive' but 'volatile' – to be handled with care. Incautious handlers, encountering a written 'Art' of the sort the rhetoricians composed, expect something 'clear and firm' (*saphes kai bebaion*) to come of it, not realising that writing can serve only to jog the memory (*hypomnēsai*) of one who already knows what it has to tell him (275c5–d2). The reason is that the written word, like a painting, offers only the appearance of living intelligence; and if you attempt to converse with it you will discover that it is no more capable of reply than a person in a portrait, but has only one message, which it repeats over and over (275d4–9). What is more, it cannot choose the appropriate audience for that message but delivers it indifferently to those who do and those who do not receive it with understanding; and when it runs into the unfair criticism that one would expect in such circumstances it has no voice with which to defend itself but stands in need of help from its 'father' (*patros*) (275d9–e5).

Far superior is the spoken word (Socrates continues), especially as it figures in philosophic discussion (the 'art of dialectic', 276e5–6); for the speaker can select his conversational partner, and can implant his words 'with understanding' (*met' epistēmēs*, 276a5; 276e7) directly into the soul of the other,[2] words which can therefore 'help themselves' and defend their creator rather than require defence from him, and which avoid the sterility of the written word – its saying the same thing over and over – by generating fresh speech in the soul of the hearer (276a1–9; 276e4–277a4). One who appreciates this distinction will not necessarily abjure the written word but will treat its use as a 'game' (*paidia*), not seriously expecting to achieve anything 'clear and firm' by its means, but writing as a 'reminder' for those who know, and who are aware in particular that only in the living conversation about 'the just and beautiful and good' can we find what is 'clear and complete and worthy of seriousness' (*to te enarges einai kai teleon kai axion spoudēs*) (278a3–5). Moreover, when approached with this attitude the dangers of the written word are defused. One who is not reliant on the written word for understanding, who has no false expectations of it, and who is able to supplement its inadequacies in speech, may write about what matters to him – as Homer and Solon wrote about what mattered to them (278c2–4)[3] – and yet

205

merit the title 'philosopher' (278d4) (this in summary of 276d1–e3; 277e5–278d7).

These reservations about the written word need to be teased out further, and I shall explain my sense of them and of their place in the dialogue by contrasting it with three importantly different interpretations. One – which we may not unfairly call the prevailing or standard interpretation – is to take the passage as a serious and straightforward expression of Plato's distrust of the written word, his own writing included, and as an attempt nevertheless to annex a zone – legitimate, but of secondary value to that of the living word – in which to exercise his continuing urge to write. Hackforth and de Vries are representatives of this interpretation (see H. 162–4 and de Vr. 20–2). In polar opposition stands the 'ironic' reading which would have Plato mean the contrary of what he has Socrates say. Arguing from the fact that Socrates' condemnation of the written word itself occurs within a written work, it urges that Plato, far from thinking that philosophy derives its value from and is at its best in spoken discussion, is covertly claiming the highest place for his own peculiar mode of philosophic writing, the written imitation of spoken dialogue. This view has received extended treatment in Ronna Burger's work on the *Phaedrus*. She sees Platonic dialogue as the best resolution of the problem that, on the one hand, 'the self-moving motion of soul [as represented in living, spoken discourse] is always an obstacle to reaching the perfect fixity and stability of the beings', while on the other hand, 'the perfect fixity of the written word seems to exclude the possibility of living thought'; so that 'the ideal meeting point defined by the principles of dialectics, as the convergence of the two paths of *erōs* and death, of living speech and writing, is in fact represented by the Platonic dialogue itself' (Burger 1980, 108–9). On this interpretation Socrates' critique of writing is no epilogue to the *Phaedrus* but a revelation of its commanding theme, Plato's defence of his own mode of pursuing philosophy.[4] A third type of interpretation agrees that the critique of writing is no epilogue, but refuses to push the idea that Plato intended this irony. Rather, it takes Socrates' words to represent a serious attempt on Plato's part to argue the value of the spoken over the written word; an attempt which fails, however, for metaphysical reasons which go to the heart of Plato's whole philosophic enterprise, and which would cause any such attempt to undermine itself. On this view, then – which originated in the work of Jacques Derrida[5] – the critique of writing tries to be the epilogue to the *Phaedrus* but ends up, despite itself, as the theme.[6]

The problem with the standard approach – as the other interpreters mentioned have collectively insisted – is that it does not sufficiently take into account the apparent ironies with which Plato's presentation of the issue abounds. By this I do not primarily refer to the effect of self-referentiality and self-undermining in a written devaluation of writing – for, eye-catching though it is, I do not find this effect as dizzying or as truly paradoxical as some opponents of the standard view would have it be (on which more below) – but rather to the many expedients, both through the action of the dialogue and the turns of phrase that its characters employ, by which Plato is at pains to suggest that the barrier Socrates sets up between speech and writing should be seen as a membrane prone to osmosis; that speech too is liable to the dangers of writing, and that writing can partake of the advantages of speech.

For example, after Socrates has had his say about the written word he begins to set out the final judgments that result from the entire discussion of rhetoric; or rather he claims that in the course of their discussion it has been made clear enough what opinion they are to hold of the artistic and ethical legitimacy of Lysias' activity as a speechwriter (277a9–b3); but Phaedrus, alas, requires a little help to recover this wonderful clarity: 'Well, yes, we did think it was clear; but remind me again just how' (277b4). In requesting that Socrates jog his memory Phaedrus uses the very term (*hypomnēson*) that we have seen Socrates apply to the function he says is the highest of which writing is capable: that of 'reminding' (a point he harps on: *hypomnēsai*, 275d1; *hypomnēmata*, 276d3; *hypomnēsin*, 278a1). And the word was explicitly linked to

207

the inadequacy of writing by the god Ammon (in the myth with which Socrates fortifies his critique, and which I shall discuss presently), when he insisted that the newly invented technique of writing would not be an aid to 'memory' (*mnēmēs*) but only to 'reminder' (*hypomnēseōs*) (275a5–6).[7] Phaedrus' use of the term, embedded as it is in a characteristic example of how his sociable desire to please and agree with Socrates outruns his ability to follow him, should serve in turn as our 'reminder' of those dubious accomplishments of his which in my opening chapter I designated as the wiles of the 'impresario'. In particular, it steers us in this context towards appreciating how Phaedrus, as impresario, in effect risks dealing with the spoken word as if it were written.

This, indeed, is a topic of the opening scene of the dialogue – the scene in which Phaedrus' skill as impresario is most apparent – that I left unremarked in my chapter of orientation, choosing to reserve it for presentation at this point, where its connection with the dialogue's final scene can be properly made out. I am referring to the fuss and banter induced by that third, alien presence in the conversation, which Phaedrus, almost shamefully, keeps hidden under his cloak: the written scroll of Lysias' speech. Socrates punctures Phaedrus' feigned reluctance to retail the speech by shrewdly reconstructing how far Phaedrus' passion for words was likely to have taken him that morning: how, not content with prevailing upon Lysias to deliver his piece several times, he had doubtless got hold of the written script itself to learn it off by heart; which done, he had come out into the countryside to practise declaiming it (228a5–b6). Significantly, Socrates' caricature is in fact not extreme enough; he had not anticipated that Phaedrus would go so far as to appropriate the written text itself and bring it out into the country with him.[8] The would-be orator is betrayed only by the guilty bulge beneath his robes; guilty, because he had been about to launch into his personal re-creation of Lysias' performance, insisting that he had not managed to con the speech by heart (228d1–5). But once Socrates discovers that, as he puts it, 'Lysias himself is present', he refuses to offer himself as audience for

Phaedrus' rehearsal and demands to hear the written text read out (228d6–e2). Thus, although Phaedrus' acquisitiveness for the *ipsissima verba* of the master outstrips what Socrates can imagine, it is Socrates, not Phaedrus, who insists on having this scriptural treasure put into circulation. Phaedrus' behaviour reveals that what he longs for above all is to reproduce the *effect* of Lysias' speech; that he, a mere amateur, should acquire the dash of a professional wordsmith (as he tells us at 227d6–228a4). The written script is the means to this end and also a kind of talisman; for it is important to Phaedrus not so much for conveying what the author has said as representing the cherished ideal of his performance. That is why, for all his tenacious clutching at that scroll, Phaedrus tries hard to disown it and substitute his own improvised version. For although the upper bound of his efforts would be an exact reproduction of the written words, he wants, somehow, for the inspiration to be *his*; wants to re-create for himself the magical aura that those words trail with them (you can see Phaedrus – but I am being mean to him again – at any Elvis Presley convention; when the Elvis act-alikes take the stage and mug to the voice of the master, present only on vinyl). Socrates for his part, although no friend to the written word, nevertheless insists on a reading from the text rather than an extempore performance; but only because he can see that Phaedrus' 'orality' promises to be fake – a vain attempt to duplicate the lost original. Phaedrus is turning himself into text. Far better, then, to demystify the written word by bringing it into the open and reading from it directly; treating it only as tool, not talisman.

Phaedrus' behaviour – or rather what he would have done had Socrates permitted – clearly shows that the dangers which Socrates attributes to writing are not mechanically confined to the context of the written word. Yet it also shows that writing does at least promote these dangers; for what encourages Phaedrus to attempt to re-create in extemporised speech the magic of a lost moment is the illusion that the written text has frozen this moment for those whose enthusiasm carries enough heat to thaw it out. Conversely, the very text which as it were infects Phaedrus' orality with its writtenness also helps liberate the Platonic text in which it figures from some at least of the disadvantages of the written word. It does so by purporting to be written by someone other than Plato himself. For even if the contemporary Athenian readership knew for certain whether the speech was an actual piece by Lysias or not rather a parody of Lysianic prose by Plato (and Plato's contemporaries were already no contemporaries of Lysias), Plato himself, whether he turned an already existing speech to his own purposes or whether he made one to measure, can hardly have been unaware, given the attentiveness to the status of written texts which this very dialogue evinces, of the effect of his authorial gesture: namely, that the longer the embedded text lay preserved within the book written around it, the more likely it was that subsequent readers would find themselves unable to determine its authenticity. He would have known, in other words, that he was seeding his text with a question that was likely to prove unanswerable; for any internal argument to authenticity from the Lysianic style of the piece works just as well as an argument for successful pastiche,[9] while external testimony has indeed proved too scanty to satisfy those scholars who long to settle this point (the story is summarised in de Vr. 12).

When seen as a consequence of Plato's gesture, this longing, which has generated many pages of scholarly controversy, becomes ironic indeed.[10] For although few interpreters could fail to be at least a little curious about the historical question of the author's identity, have we not already heard some advice from Socrates about this type of curiosity, and in the very scene which brought the speech to our attention? I suggest we have, and that the effort to settle the historical question of authenticity resembles nothing so much as that of the scholarly 'demythologisers' to trace the tales of Boreas and his like back to their origin in historical fact – an effort from which Socrates was at pains to distance himself as he and Phaedrus looked for a spot to read that historically dubious speech (and I discussed his reasons in my opening chapter, in the section: 'Boreas and his interpreters'). Of course, we

210

have just seen Socrates insist on getting the authentic Lysias, verbatim, and not some Phaedran rehash; but he did this precisely to ensure that the 'author' should not become a despotic 'authority', his exact words an absent ideal. By contrast, were we to pursue our historical curiosity to the neglect of the philosophical, insistent to learn whether what we have is the real Lysias or a Platonic spoof,[11] we would swiftly be reduced – like the demythologisers (see 229d2–e4) – to weaving a filigree of speculation around irrecoverable fact, and so – like Phaedrus – elevate the recalcitrant text to the status of a fetish. But would it not be better to follow Socrates' example and turn from undue emphasis on the truth of events to concern for the truth about ourselves (see 229e4–6)? For then we could turn our thoughts to the question itself rather than its elusive answer, and to Plato's gesture in provoking it,[12] and so appreciate that writing does indeed have that dangerous quality which Phaedrus found so seductive: the quality of making a fetish of the truth of events, of giving the heady feeling that the creative moment has been suspended and can perhaps be revived. But we will appreciate this *for ourselves*: from our own experience as interpreters.

And it is in this sense that inclusion of a supposedly alien text goes some way (not by any means the whole way, as I shall soon make clear) towards mitigating the general effects of the written word in the particular case of Plato's own writing here. For the action invites us to ponder, as part of our interpretation of the work, our own performance as interpreters; and so the supposedly silent text steps out of its frame in the portrait gallery and finds a voice with which to answer us after all. The live voice that we hear is our own – the voice of the interpretive performer – not Plato's. (It is deflected back from the smooth page like an echo; and since we are a little older than the beautiful boy we do not mistake its source.) In other words, Plato devised his text (I *must* put it this way) such that for the event which we cannot experience – his creative performance as author – we may substitute our own performance as interpreters. We are touched by that heady feeling after all; but only as a result of first taking our distance from it as a phenomenon. In this respect the effect is one of many such, and we have encountered others in the course of this book each time I have allowed the cicadas to sing out; for their song has alerted us throughout to the importance, for what the text has to say, of the competence and performance of both the author, in getting it said, and of the reader in receiving the message.[13]

It should be clear from the foregoing that I do not disagree with the standard interpretation, but seek to supplement it. I too think Socrates' warning a serious expression of the reserve that Plato felt towards his own use of the written word. I have shown, however, that Plato takes pains to set this relatively straightforward point about the characteristic tendencies of written as opposed to oral formats (namely, that the written tempts us more forcibly to make a fetish of original performance) against the larger contrast of which it is only one manifestation: that between the concerns of the impresario and those of the philosopher – the one content with the mere effect of fine words, the other seeking the life which gives those words importance. And we saw as a result how the second contrast can overrule the first; how some writing can be philosophic, and some speech be limited by the aims of the impresario. For whereas the first is a contrast between mere tools of discourse, the second sets out the different structures of goals which give those tools their function (indeed, to prejudge the function from the tool alone would be once more to commit Phaedrus' error of judging the good by externals – the error against which the cicadas warned).[14] Now, the standard interpretation does not ignore this further point – Hackforth, for example, insists that 'it would be absurd to conclude from these passages that the content of the dialogues was, in the eyes of their author, of little value; it is surely plain that Plato writes for the most part in a vein of deep seriousness, with a sincerity at times passionate' (H. 163). But what it fails to see is that we do not need to rely on our sense of what would or would not be 'absurd' in this case, but that Plato duly qualifies an extreme reading of Socrates' words by means of the very action of the dialogue from which they arise.

On the other hand, nothing in the subtlety of Plato's presentation compels us to go to the extreme of the 'ironic' interpretation, which would have Plato indicate not merely that his own mode of writing avoids the worst effects of the written word but that it is in general the nearest to an ideal method of doing philosophy that we are likely to find, and which claims moreover that Plato wrote the *Phaedrus* primarily to defend this contention. Many more instances of the type of subtlety that I have illustrated could indeed be adduced. For example, having qualified writing as a 'game' (*paidia*) by comparison with the 'serious business' (*spoudē*) of philosophic conversation, Socrates brings his own philosophic conversation with Phaedrus to an end with the declaration, 'let this be the measure of our game' (*pepaisthō metriōs hēmin*) (278b7). And twice he actually conveys the advantages of oral communication through the metaphor of its contrary, saying that it gets itself 'written' on the soul of the hearer (276a5; 278a3).

It is by appeal to striking subtleties of this sort that Ronna Burger makes her case for the 'ironic' interpretation. These would be Plato's hints to the attentive reader not only that his own writing escapes the dangers of the written word, but that by just such complexity as is evinced in this enigmatic web of hints it claims its place as the proper form of discourse for the complex philosophic soul (Burger 1980, 103). I shall not tackle her interpretation hint by hint, for I think it open to the following more general objection. The collective effect of the various points of presentation that I have garnered here is to engage the mechanical distinction between the linguistic tools of speech and writing with the ethical distinction between the ways of Socrates and the ways of Phaedrus, and in so doing to point up the extent to which either tool is capable of both good and bad use. With this Burger agrees, for it is the wedge with which she begins to undermine and weaken Socrates' criticisms of the written word.[15] Certainly when we take these points of presentation into account we see that an extreme interpretation of Socrates' words, which would strictly confine the effects he describes according to mechanical boundaries of format, is not a plausible reading of Plato's intent. But why should we leap from this worthy qualification of Socrates' critique to the idea that Plato is covertly claiming thereby that his kind of writing, as opposed to philosophic conversation, is in fact the best way forward in philosophy as such? Surely, in fact, this is just the sort of move that those subtleties of presentation warn us *not* to make? That is, they indicate to us that what matters most is that we do philosophy rather than merely go for its effects, follow Socrates rather than Phaedrus, and that it is of secondary importance (which is not at all to say: of no importance) which tool of discourse – speech or writing – we employ. But a consequence of this message is that *no* practice of writing, however sophisticated and self-aware, is necessary in itself (let alone sufficient) to make philosophers either of those who engage in it or those who interpret it; and that if Plato intended through this dialogue to bind the future of philosophy to the raft of his special kind of writing, he was going against the tenor of the very devices by which he supposedly conveyed his intent. I conclude, then, that in order to make its case the 'ironic' interpretation would require arguments based on something other than those subtleties which collectively qualify Socrates' critique. But so far as I can see, Burger has none,[16] and there are none. By all means let us agree that in this dialogue Plato is out to make a place within philosophy for his brand of writing; but the indications are (and I have yet to elaborate them fully) that he thought this a secondary place, and its defence a secondary issue – though not simply extraneous to the major concerns of the dialogue. So that Socrates' critique of writing is, after all, what it seems: an epilogue.

The Derridean interpretation is also sensitive to the various means by which Socrates' critique of writing is to be qualified by its presentation and context. As with the 'ironic' interpretation, Derrida takes the qualifications to undermine the success of Socrates' criticisms; but he imagines this to occur for reasons larger than can be explained by Plato's individual intent, and which engage nothing less than a dominant scheme in the history of Western philosophy.[17] One of the ways in which Derrida makes his point is to home in on the Egyptian myth that Plato chooses to have Socrates cite as an authority for his reservations about the written word.[18] I will turn to that myth now myself, for I too consider important the fact that myth should be Plato's preferred means of presenting this issue. Unlike Derrida, however, I think that the larger philosophic questions engaged through the myth tend rather to support Socrates' critique than to tell against it.

Not only does Plato position his Egyptian tale prominently, setting it up as the first thing Socrates has to say about the comparative merits of speech and writing (at 274c1–275b2), but he also draws the reader's attention to its status as a myth. No sooner has Socrates finished the story – in which the Egyptian god Thoth, having just invented the art of writing, takes his new baby for the divine nod from the king of the gods, Ammon; who refuses to approve it, however, giving the reasons that we have seen – than Phaedrus impugns its value. It's easy enough, he says, for Socrates to spin yarns from Egypt or any other country he pleases (275b3–4). And his reluctance to accept the authority of the myth was to some extent encouraged by the opinion Socrates himself expressed as he began his story: that it was 'something one hears said' (*akoēn*) about the olden days, but that only those who lived then knew the 'truth' of it (*to d'alēthes*) (274c1–2). Yet Socrates will not tolerate Phaedrus' reaction. You modern men are so wise, he quips; but in an older time the earliest oracles, at Dodona, came from an oak tree, and people were 'simple-minded' enough (*hyp' euētheias*) to listen to what an oak or a rock had to say, provided it were true (*alēthē*); not to fuss, then, about who is speaking or where he comes from; just ask whether things are in fact as the story says (275b5–c2) – an admonishment which Phaedrus duly accepts, along with the truth of Ammon's words (275c3–4).

Derrida finds in Socrates' initial reservation about the truth of his tale a parallel with his subsequent warning about the effects of the written word; for just as writing, on the strength of Ammon's words in the myth, is accused of saying the same thing over and over without understanding (hence in need of its 'father' to come to its defence) (275d7–e5), so Socrates

215

here admits that he is duplicating a story without knowing the truth of it. In other words: 'We begin by repeating without knowledge – by means of a myth – the definition of writing: repeating without knowledge.'[19] This cleverly expresses a genuine kinship; but fails to acknowledge an important difference. As a linguistic product Socrates' tale has met with much the same fate through oral transmission (for it is announced, we saw, as 'something one hears said', *akoē*) as, say, the text of Lysias' speech through written transmission; belated recipients of its message, that is, can no longer tell whether it did indeed originate from what it claims as its source. Here we have yet another of the means by which Plato shows that the use of oral discourse as such provides no magic formula for evading the problems more especially associated with writing. But Derrida suggests more: that if the mode of speech by which Socrates establishes the distinction between speech and writing itself suffers from the very limitations that he attributes thereby to the written word, then neither Socrates nor we can adequately grasp and express the distinction.[20]

There is a truth lurking here too, but it needs careful teasing out. Socrates' re-telling of the story of Thoth and Ammon is indeed taken up in the very process that the story narrates, but not in the sense that it is subject to the fatal drawbacks that the tale attributes to the written word (it isn't; as I will later explain). Rather: it is a myth, and narrates the origins of myth. For writing is only one of a whole gamut of arts that Thoth has invented and takes to Ammon's patent office (see 274c8–d1). These people of old, then, these simple folk who can converse with oak and rock, are wise without knowing it; they live before the formalisation of arts.[21] What King Ammon fears for his subjects is the loss of their innocence: that the written word will tempt them to rely on external repositories of knowledge for reminder rather than learning for themselves and developing a self-sufficient memory (275a2–6); and so for the first time people will come to seem wise without being so – cramming themselves with information but learning nothing, and yet able to bring off a self-conscious 'conceit' of learning (*doxosophoi*)[22] (275a6–b2). We are thus witnesses through this tale to the opening of that gulf which we have seen to be of such importance in the relationship between Socrates and Phaedrus and in the critique of rhetoric as an art: the gulf between the pursuit of wisdom and the pursuit of the effects of wisdom. But an appreciation of just this distance also underlies Socrates' subsequent rebuke to Phaedrus that he should look to the truth of the story rather than worry about its pedigree; for a concern for pedigree – at least, when pedigree is irrelevant to truth – betrays an undue valuation of the effects of understanding (as when we ask: is this the book that 'everyone' is reading?) at the expense of the real thing. And a myth is just a story that has been accepted on the grounds of pedigree and tradition (because that is what one hears said; because they always tell it this way) rather than truth – whether or not those grounds, and their contrast with truth, are made conscious and explicit. It is in this sense that Socrates' Egyptian myth narrates the origins of myth itself. It describes the introduction of the very possibility of drawing that contrast between truth and tradition, truth and pedigree, to which Socrates appeals in the remarks which frame his tale at either end.

But, of course, in the world that Socrates and we inhabit considerations of pedigree often have every relevance to the question of truth; and the admonishment that Phaedrus accepts so submissively may strike us as reflecting rather too much of the innocence of an earlier age. Yet the reverse is the case: the tinge of idealism in Socrates' advice is what makes it a proper sentiment to espouse for his own world, rather than the world of the myth. To explain. The bygone race who could listen to oak and rock represent an ideal for Socrates: that of unconcern with questions of pedigree and status where this is irrelevant to truth. But clearly this is not an ideal those simple folk could themselves have held; for pedigree and truth had not yet been sundered in their society. Rather, their behaviour exhibits this ideal to our eyes only – the eyes of self-conscious late-comers to the world. That is why much that is appropriate for them is inappropriate for us, and vice versa.

217

'Simplicity of mind' (euētheia), a term of praise when applied to them (275b8), has become in our world the kind of 'simple-mindedness' (euētheias, 275c7) displayed by one who ignores Ammon's words and thinks to find clarity and firmness in writing;[23] and the collocation 'oak and rock' had itself atrophied to a proverbial phrase in Greek for that which springs from nowhere – as if not only can we no longer converse directly with oak and rock, we cannot even name these things without trailing indirect associations.[24] So too, it is proper in our world for the 'father' (patros, 275e4) of a written work to come to its defence, because any written work will undoubtedly encounter misunderstanding (275d9–e5); but for just the same reason it was not proper for the 'father' (275a1) of the art of writing itself to come to the defence of his creation (274e7–275a2).[25] Above all, it would not be appropriate – indeed, it would be impossible – for the people of that age to espouse Socrates' ideal, because their function for him is rather to display it; but despite this, it remains appropriate for Socrates to see his ideal in them – and, again, for just the same reason that it cannot be right for them to see it in themselves: because they simply exhibit the ideal.

The consequence is this: that Socrates' enunciation of his ideal in his advice to Phaedrus, though it appears rather too innocent and simple, in fact offers the best means of both incorporating and going beyond the lost simplicity of that earlier time. For consider: only if Socrates had attempted to justify his myth against Phaedrus' scepticism would he be making a fetish of it – delving into its sources like an antiquarian, seeking to stamp this stretch of talk with a seal of historical authenticity, as if that could somehow guarantee its truth.[26] Instead, he readily passes on from his story, considered as a linguistic product. Never mind where it came from, he says; do you think it is right? But to say this is both to enunciate and to put into action the very ideal that the people of oak and rock themselves exhibited, but could not enunciate. By refusing to linger over their story or make a fetish of their status, Socrates is in fact proving himself their most ardent follower. He has found a way to emulate their simplicity, without becoming simplistic.

We can see, then, that just as Thoth invented many arts, of which writing was one, so this myth engages more than just the narrow issue of the advantages of one mode of verbal expression over another. As a myth that narrates the origins of myth – better, of mythical consciousness – it sets the dangers of the written word against the broader horizon of the philosopher's struggle to cope with the consequences of his powers of reflection. This I discussed at some length in the second section of the previous chapter ('The love-mad philosopher: mixed pleasure'). We saw that neither Socrates nor the philosophic lover, once awake to their desire to transcend the contingency of embodiment, can simply wish this desire away, even though it leads them inexorably into actions (such as the use of myth and the fostering of one special person) which, so far from fulfilling their desire, tend rather to bring them face to face with the obstacles to its fulfilment – and leave them there to cope, rather than conquer. Similarly, for Socrates to see *expressed* in the simple folk his ideal of a truth free from the contingent trappings of pedigree is for him to have awoken to the value of the ideal, and so to have put himself forever beyond the life which would simply show the ideal in action.[27] Rather, he has awoken to the very contingency of his awareness. He sees that, and why, these people are now mythical for him; marks his own pedigree in relation to them; and stands on watch for the dangers of this belatedness. In the particular case of the valuation of speech over writing, the effect of Plato's presentation here is to show that we who now prize the capacity of conversation to encourage genuine rather than manipulative communication do so not in the belief that speech in its very orality can bring about this result at a stroke – to believe *that* would be to do exactly what writing encourages us to do: treat the external trappings of communication as a talisman – but rather in the belief that only after we have appreciated that speech does not merit its superior place on the basis of orality as such, does speech in fact come to merit its superior place. There is no such thing any more – certainly not in philosophy – as pure speech. Speech is always speech-in-the-light-of-writing – a tool self-consciously adopted. But that is good; because we need the virtues of reflection for our world. By contrast, it is now writing that represents the unreflective way of life – the 'simple-minded' trust in the intrinsic value of what can be set up and handed down in permanent form, the idols of the tribe (see 275c5–d2).

Returning to the Derridean interpretation which I have here used as a springboard of my own, I will make my opinion of it clear. Derrida is right to think that Socrates' critique of writing engages issues fundamental to the dialogue as a whole (and hence to the subsequent course of philosophy), and right to sense that Socrates' act of re-telling the Egyptian myth is to be understood in terms of what the myth itself has to say. But he is wrong to think that the effect of the mode of Plato's presentation of the critique is in any way to undermine its content, either considered in its aspect as a point about writing or in its larger metaphysical aspect. In the latter aspect, we have seen that Socrates – and Plato through him – has every right to continue to see his ideal in the people of oak and rock, and this not *despite* the fact that by so doing he puts himself irrevocably beyond them, but precisely *because* of that fact. So far from undermining the ideal presented, the ironies of presentation actually reinforce it. And as a point about writing, it seems to me that neither in the sense that Socrates 'repeats' his justificatory myth 'without knowledge', nor in the more general sense that Plato himself commits Socrates' critique of the written word to writing, is the critique undermined by its presentation. Through Socrates, Plato makes a serious but relatively straightforward, almost banal point about the written word (it would have seemed more novel, of course, in Plato's day). We have seen the point illustrated in Phaedrus' behaviour: namely, that although, as a tool, writing is to be thought good or bad not in itself but in terms of the goal for which it is employed (a point Socrates made at the very outset of the discussion of rhetoric, 258d1–5), nevertheless some tools are better adapted for certain goals or results than others; and writing, with its capacity to capture words in a permanent form external to and potentially independent of their user, is especially prone to encourage that fetishising of words which Phaedrus exemplifies and which is the antithesis of genuine communicative art. This I take to be a simple truth.[28] And here I find a place for that description of living speech as 'written in the soul' of the learner; for it points up how that much-touted benefit of writing, its fixity and permanence,[29] is in fact truly to be attained by human beings (in so far as they can attain it at all) only in the unshakeable conviction of a certain kind of life – in that sense, then, graven on their souls. The 'fixity' of a written text is a mirage; after all, there will be as many different interpretations of its meaning as there are interpreters (275d9–e5); hence too its 'clarity' goes up in smoke. And we can see that, since Socrates opposes the spoken to the written word as possessed of genuine rather than spurious permanence, the 'clarity and firmness' which he misses in the latter and so hopes to achieve in the former is not to be thought of – though the terms might tempt us to this thought – on the analogy of clear and unshakeable axioms, or self-evident propositions; for these could also be written up in one of those 'silent portraits' (275d4–9). Rather, he refers to the clarity and firmness of personal conviction – a conviction that he chooses to express through philosophic conversation and a wariness of the effects of the written word.[30]

But none of this implies that philosophy should not be written; only that it should not be written (nor read) without awareness of the dangers of writing, together with the sense that what ultimately matters is *neither* writing *nor* speaking but the way of life in which they can find a worthy place.[31] As a piece of writing, the *Phaedrus* conforms to these strictures about as well as any text could, and is neither undermined by nor itself undermines the critique to which Socrates gives voice. Socrates does not, after all, 'repeat' his myth 'without knowledge' in the same sense that writing 'repeats without knowledge'. His lack of knowledge is a conscious awareness of the limits of his knowledge; whereas writing 'lacks knowledge' simply because the very possibility of consciousness is inapplicable to it. And the fact that Socrates' pronouncement on writing itself appears in written form does nothing to invalidate it. For Socrates does not say that writing inevitably lies; only that its truth is liable to get lost.[32] We had better watch out, then; but we needn't give his message up entirely.

Yet even as Plato follows the advice that he puts on his master's lips (by writing so as to conform to his guidelines), he allows the distance between them to show. We have seen before (long before, in chapter two) how a certain courage in his own naïveté allowed Socrates to remain unsullied by the rhetorical ethos in his own essay into rhetorical performance (in his speeches on love) and into literary criticism (in his examination of Lysias' speech). But Plato, who, unlike his master, chooses to write philosophy as well as live the life of philosophic talk, is far closer to the dangers of professionalism, and needs to assess his relative position more guardedly.[33] It is fair enough, then, that Socrates, who does not write, should mention only the practical disadvantages of writing as a medium, and leave out its not insignificant practical benefit: the simple fact – horribly contingent and fraught with dangerous consequences though it is – that had Plato not written down his (and Socrates') thoughts, there would be no continuing conversation in the name of either. That Plato thought this benefit worth the risk of distortion is not something he needed to make explicit within his text (any more than he needed to script a reply for Thoth to Ammon's attempt to prevent the release of writing); for this is clear enough from the mere fact that we learn his opinion of that risk by having read it.

The writing on the soul

At the beginning of this chapter I promised to look back on the dialogue as a whole through the filter of Socrates' critique of writing. So far I have chosen to fulfil that promise in an indirect manner: by showing that although the critique engages, in its own special terms, the major philosophic concern of the dialogue (namely, the vindication of the philosophic life against a life that seeks only its effects), it does indeed make this contact as the epilogue that it seems to be. But let me become more direct, here in the closing pages of my book, and confront once again the variety of guises in which that major concern ramifies throughout the dialogue. It is this variety, of course, which gives the *Phaedrus* its own character; for to say only that the dialogue is out to vindicate the philosophic life against a life that merely seeks its effects would not distinguish it from almost any other dialogue that Plato wrote.

It is tempting to draw the threads tight by pointing out analogies; to begin from the lesser analogy between the relation in which self-aware philosophic writers (and readers) stand to their texts and the relation in which philosophic lovers stand to their beloved, and move on to the central analogies between the rhetorical ethos and that of Lysias' non-lover, on the one hand, and the philosophic ethos and that of the divinely maddened lovers, on the other. The text encourages such analogies; they are to a varying extent the common property of previous scholarship on this dialogue (most especially the more central analogies);[34] and I have not hesitated in the course of this book to invoke them myself. But equally important, I feel, is a pervasive disanalogy, which shows itself through the disjointedness of the two halves of the dialogue (and which has not received an equivalent attention from commentators). I will focus on this disanalogy in what follows; more precisely, I will argue that the analogy between the dialectician and the philosophic lover is less close than that between the rhetorician and the non-lover, and consider the consequences of this fact in terms of the overall structure of the dialogue.

Let me approach the issue through the less central analogy between philosophic writer and philosophic lover. The kinship between them can be set out as follows. By treating his text as a treasury of reminders (276d3), the philosophic writer displays a self-conscious caution about the risk of his activity as a writer usurping that primary place in his structure of goals which belongs by right to the way of life that such writing instrumentally promotes; while the philosophic lover, in so far as he treasures his boy for the reminder of the beatific vision stirred by his presence,[35] is swept up in a painfully self-conscious struggle against that in him which would neglect this vision, allow the boy to become a compulsion, and so succumb to the danger that the mere presence of the boy, divorced from the larger sense of beauty that he inspires, should become the addictive goal of his life. The good writer and the good lover, then, share a sensitivity to the common risk of obsession in their respective spheres of action. However, the difference in the objects upon which they operate is considerable. The status of the written text in a philosophic life, for all the benefits that it can bring, is simply that of an instrument – the burden of the previous section of this chapter has been to vindicate this basic belief in Plato's name. But I have argued at some length that the beautiful boy is no mere instrument of the philosophic lover's self-development. As a human being capable of living the philosophic life, he is cherished by the lover not only for the instrumental benefit, the vivid edge that he brings to the lover's project of life, but also as being of value in his own right – as a person whose good the lover desires to pursue in common with his own.[36] This difference has its effect on the manner in which the philosophic lover and writer pursue their ultimately similar goals. Writing, as an instrument the consequences of which depend on its good or bad use, must be handled with the utmost diffidence and transparency as to its potential danger; so that philosophic confidence in the written product stems from a thorough-going lack of confidence in the medium. But the beautiful boy is no mere instrument; his turning out good or bad cannot be gauged as a consequence of the lover's input alone. In other words: the boy is *alive*.[37] The result is that, initially at least, the lover will require a certain lack of transparency in his dealings with the beloved; will need, as we saw, to maintain a greater confidence in him than he may in fact merit. The lover – hence the beloved in his turn – must remain open to the not wholly predictable ways of this soul that chance has entrusted to his care.

With this point made, I can pass on to the crucial analogies between the good and bad lovers and good and bad users of language. For the reader will recall that the characteristic which I have just attributed to the philosophic lover – a searching openness to the twists and turns of the living soul – was also the characteristic by which Socrates distinguished practitioners of the true art of speaking from pretenders to that title (as discussed in the third section of chapter three: 'Symptoms and causes'). Where the traditional rhetorician was content to combine knowledge of the symptoms and routines of human behaviour (encyclopedic, but in principle closed) with the knack of manipulating those symptoms (a knack which simply comes from practice), the true orator gives those symptoms unity and purpose – brings them to life – by relating them to that of which they are symptoms. He refuses to approach actual human behaviour as no more than a target on which his encyclopedia is made visible and invites application. Looking again at the traditional rhetorical ethos, as represented by Lysias, we can see, then, that its analogy with the attitude of his non-lover (and therefore also with the voice of the dark horse) is exact. Both are wholly invested in the production of a certain event or effect of human behaviour: the adherence of the audience (in the case of the non-lover, the beautiful boy) to a particular belief – whatever belief the pair happen to want them to maintain. The rhetorical type will carefully scheme towards this goal if such steps prove necessary, but, in principle at least, it is all the same to him if the desired effect were to fall into his lap (this we can now see to be the first-order reasoning characteristic of the dark horse). Of course, such steps always do prove necessary, especially in the case of the professional orator. No speechwriter gets paid for beating the audience over the head. But these limitations are practical – a matter of playing by the rules. The reasoned steps which lead to the desired goal are therefore not intrinsic to it. And this lends an air of unreality to the care and labour expended in the climb; once at the goal, it is *as if* he had been whisked to the top by magic carpet; for it makes no difference how he arrived.

It is true that there is the following distinction to be made between Lysias and his non-lover: that whereas the non-lover himself believes what he asks the boy in turn to accept, a professional like Lysias is not committed to the truth of the belief which his compositions attempt to inculcate in the jury. But this difference leaves undisturbed the fundamental similarity of their behaviour. The crucial point is that in both cases speaker and audience have different goals, and rather than combat this asymmetry the speaker accepts it and puts it to work, bargaining and manipulating his audience towards at least a semblance of mutual satisfaction for both parties. For the advocate, persuasion is the primary goal, while that of his audience is truth; but this is just one among the many possible asymmetries of interest which gives rise to manipulative behaviour. Another is that between the non-lover and his boy: the one looking for sexual fulfilment, the other for a social mentor. The contact between them is no more genuine, no less manipulative, because the non-lover happens to believe that the type of relationship he urges upon the boy is indeed the most effective path to satisfaction of the boy's desire as well as his own; this belief merely greases the wheels of his argument with the lubricant of conviction. Conversely, Lysias as a person does not escape comparison with his non-lover simply because it is in his professional activity – and perhaps only there – that the resemblance is to be found. For manipulative behaviour does not somehow become worthy (although it may become more understandable) because adopted in a limited domain, nor because it gets results where they are needed and would otherwise be hard to come by (as in the lawcourts) – any more than the non-lover's proposal is justified because it offers the easy semblance of a result in a social context where genuine contact is hard to build.

All this concerning Lysias' likeness to his fictional character is ground already traversed (in chapters two and four). I have gone over it again in preparation for showing how the corresponding resemblance between Socrates as dialectician and the figure of the philosophic lover is significantly less complete. Before passing on to that point, however, I will take the opportunity to complete the portrait of Lysias, now that we have seen how the scroll of his speech makes him a third, vicarious character of the dialogue; or rather, I will consider why it is that Plato does not allow us a proper portrait of the man (which will lead me also to cap my assessment of the character of Lysias' greatest fan, Phaedrus).

We have seen that the fact that Lysias insists on keeping his private *mores* in quarantine from his professional activity does not prevent Socrates from criticising that activity, and Lysias for pursuing it, on ethical grounds. Nevertheless, Lysias is successful in keeping his personal character out of Socrates' spotlight. Socrates attacks the rhetorical ethos both in general terms, in his critique of rhetoric, and in terms of the particular example furnished by the non-lover. But the non-lover gives voice to the ethos only of Lysias the professional; the whole man might be different (although, to repeat, this fact does not afford Lysias an escape-route from comparison with his fictional character). Indeed, it is difficult to imagine a whole person quite so calculating and thoroughly of one piece as Lysias' non-lover – still less as the lecherous horse who echoes that voice. Much of the cleverness in Lysias' speech derives precisely from his making so unlikely a character sound plausible (see Phaedrus' estimation at 227c5–8); and similarly, the idea that behind the non-lover's suave and reasonable exterior we could find such a creature as the mis-shapen horse is meant to seem shocking and extreme. In re-ality, Lysias, or any practising rhetorician, is likely to be a more complex and less delinquent character.

Here Lysias' relationship to Phaedrus becomes relevant. At several points in the conversation Socrates refers to the pair, whether playfully or otherwise, as lovers – Lysias being the beloved to Phaedrus' lover.[38] This gives special significance to the fact that Phaedrus is called upon throughout to speak on behalf of Lysias and of the profession that he represents, both when he reads his beloved's speech with beaming pride (234d3) and when in the course of the critique of rhetoric he gives Socrates the standard line that he has heard from prac-titioners of the art (e.g. 259e7), and in general offers himself as respondent to Socrates' arguments. We know from Soc-rates' palinode that lovers of all kinds can be expected to seek out those of similar character to love (252c3–253c6); so that in Phaedrus we can be forgiven for making out a sketch of the elusive Lysias. It is also significant in this context that Lysias was a resident alien in Athens – a metic. The fact is brought to our attention on the dialogue's opening page. In response to Phaedrus' explanation of his morning's entertainment Socrates remarks: 'But Lysias was in town, it seems' (227b1); thus reminding us that the 'son of Cephalus' (227a2), for all his metic father's wealth, did not have the Athenian citizen's right to own land within the city, and so was established with his father outside the city limits, in the Piraeus. As a metic, Lysias was also not allowed to vote or hold a political position, nor – the point upon which I want to fasten – could he appear in person to defend himself if summoned in a lawsuit, but required the good offices of a native patron, a *prostatēs*, who would represent him before the citizenry. Here we have a nice irony: Lysias the professional speechwriter, the hidden voice behind so many citizens' appearances in court – just as he is the voice concealed beneath Phaedrus' cloak – cannot appear in that forum even when the summons is directed at him in person.

However, no more does he appear in person in this dialogue when his own profession is in the dock, even when the native citizens, Socrates and Phaedrus, have left the city and stepped onto his own turf;[39] instead, Plato sends Phaedrus to speak for him as his patron and lover. The implication I take to be this. Lysias, as a paid professional, is a metic in more than just the technical sense. His voice in the city is heard purely for its results, the verdicts it can elicit – the bottom-line. It is no free and living voice. Its symbolic landscape is the pretty countryside beyond the city walls. There Phaedrus goes to be alone and to orate to himself (228b5–6).[40] But rhetoric, wherever it occurs, is always just that: talking to oneself in empty, pretty spaces. Lysias goes to town, but turns the house of Epicrates into a place of entertainment, a restaurant of words (227b2–7); Socrates steps out into the fields, but brings the city with him – not letting Phaedrus talk with his echo, nor the cicadas lull them with words turned to musical chatter.

Lysias, then, has not just been excluded by birth from genuine participation in the city, but has excluded himself by profession; hence too he has no living voice in this dialogue between citizens whose ethical lives are not split by institution and who stand a chance of making those lives whole. But through Phaedrus we hear him, and feel the imprint of his character. I do not mean this as a quasi-historical point about Lysias' personality, but as a point about Phaedrus, in the general capacity of impresario (something which would have concerned Plato far more) – that is, as the type of character to whom the dangers of rhetoric are not apparent. We can take it that Lysias in person, thinking as he does that rhetoric figures only in the professional compartment of his life, is of similar mind to Phaedrus. But the truth about Lysias' character is less important than the difficulty we encounter in excavating it. The significant point, then, is that Phaedrus, by contrast with his beloved, shows up as a real character: not a caricature, like Lysias' non-lover or the lecherous horse, nor a mask, like that which Lysias has imposed upon himself, but a complex person who vacillates (257b5),[41] who can be persuaded (261a3–5), who is no calculating, dyed-in-the-wool cynic but cares about what he does, who has the right-sounding ideals (258e1–5), but does not understand how the sound is seducing him – I shall not repeat the estimate of his character that I gave at length in my chapter of orientation. I want only to say that the portrait of Phaedrus makes vivid for us what the critique of rhetoric dealt with in the abstract, and what in Lysias' non-lover we are invited to view from the far perspective of distaste. For do we not all fear – we who are 'sick for words' (228b6) – that there might be more of Phaedrus about us than we would like?

So much for Lysias and Phaedrus – those lovers of rhetoric, and rhetorical lovers. But what of the analogy between Socrates as dialectician – 'lover' of collections and divisions, who follows after those who share his love as if in the tracks

of a god (266b3–c1) – and the philosophic lover of his palinode – in whom the presence of the beautiful boy evokes a
memory of something divine? That there is an extensive
analogy to be drawn I have already agreed. The peculiarities
of the philosophic lover's love are recognisably due to his
character as a dialectician; for example, we saw in the opening chapter how Socrates' outburst on arrival at the arbour is
a little gem of the kind of eccentricity that gives the philosophic lover his struggle. But I want not to lose sight of the
special place love has in this dialogue; that is, Plato's acknowledgment of the blessed luck of those who find it. The relationship between the philosophic lovers as evoked by
Socrates is no mere allegory of philosophic discussion, no
mere pilfering of the language of love in order to romanticise
the exchange of ideas that went on under the plane-trees of
the Academy. It's *love* that Socrates is talking about in that
speech; and for those philosophic lovers of his, philosophy
and love must struggle to come to terms. But Socrates' speech
is not the whole dialogue, nor is the love of philosophic lovers
the whole of philosophy, or the only pattern for the philosophic life. That is why Socrates' great speech remains a relatively isolated outburst, a moment of glory in this and the
other Platonic dialogues; and why the *Phaedrus* has its
broken-backed structure. In the second part of the dialogue
Socrates retreats to the perspective of the life of philosophic
talk and action, rather than of philosophic love,[42] and the
lack of continuity between the two parts reflects – however
pale the reflection – the disturbing contingency of the experience of love described in the first. The philosophic lover
cannot simply seize his chance, but finds himself dwelling
upon it; so too Socrates does not simply succumb to the inspiration of his myth, but attempts to bring it into line with the
life it has burst upon.

In short, it is precisely because the dialectician and the
philosophic lover are indeed analogous to each other that the
course of their respective lives is distinctively different. Let me
elucidate this point by contrasting it with the analogy between
rhetorician and non-lover. From the viewpoint of the rhetori-

cal type, since he aims only at bringing about a certain effect, the intermediate steps which build to the desired effect, if they are necessary, are not intrinsic to the satisfaction of his desire. Once at the summit, he allows the story of his getting there to drop from sight. So that there really is no important psychological difference between the figure of Lysias and that of his non-lover; manipulative reason has flattened life for them into a seamless tissue of opportunism, whatever the object of the moment. But the philosophic type, as we have seen, is alive to and dwells upon the metaphysical contingency of his place in the world. He does not attempt to scheme and manipulate his way around it — as if to smooth it to a plane that can create no friction for his desires. Not that he is happy with his place; but, given his sense of having fallen to ground here, he does not simply turn his back on the world — does not escape to the courtroom or the contract, the domain of deals and pre-arrangements and clear results. Of course, when seen from that domain, turning his back on the world is exactly what the philosopher seems to be doing — that crazy bird of the palinode who gawps at the stars and longs to fly off, back to where he came from (249c8–e4). This is what Plato's philosopher wants, to be sure; but he wants it not just anyhow, but in the right way — through freedom, not self-deception. For which it is essential — always given the ultimate contingency of our place here — that he should not attempt to quash the story of his seeking that goal. For only so can he both orient himself towards a goal the goodness of which is independent of his particular desire, and yet not simply be compelled towards it, but make the journey, and so the destination, peculiarly his own; only so can he discover himself (to repeat the phrase from the previous chapter) both as a person, yet also personally. The meaning of what he cares for is thus essentially bound up with a *narrative*: the history of his attempt at seeking it. This we saw when considering the contrast between the freedom-through-captivation of the soul's charioteer and the simple slavishness of the bad horse: how, even after he has come to dominance, the charioteer does not allow the narrative of his learning — the to-and-fro with the members of his team – to drop out of sight, but incorporates and integrates that pattern into his desire for the whole soul.

We see, then, that precisely because the philosopher refuses merely to circumvent contingency (despite his longing to flee it), he must accept that there is a psychologically important difference in the lives of those among the philosophers who are lucky enough to find philosophic love. Their awakening through physical beauty, if successfully followed through, is an experience that not every dialectician can expect to have, and one that makes their lives more nearly whole than any other human life can be. Plato does not attempt to smooth out or spirit away this result, contingent though it is. He lets the rough edges of the world poke through the joints of his dialogue. Let us not struggle too hard, then, to unify the *Phaedrus*; for the real struggle is elsewhere.

NOTES

1. Orientation

1 That this is a live metaphor is strongly suggested by the emphasis in this opening scene on the theatricality of Phaedrus' approach to the speech of Lysias. He has brought the script with him into the countryside in order to get it off by heart (228a5–e2), and when he comes to deliver it is reminded of the importance of posture by Socrates, who himself makes a fuss over finding a good seat (230c3–5, e2–4). Compare Socrates' later description of a statesman leaving the assembly after passage of his bill: 'happy with himself, the poet quits the theatre' (*gegēthōs aperkhetai ek tou theatrou ho poiētēs*, 258b2–3).

2 Examples of the former case: *Gorgias, Charmides, Ion*; of the latter: *Cratylus, Philebus*.

3 This is to simplify. All three dialogues actually open with direct speech; but the body of each is narrated by one of the direct speakers (and in the *Symposium* this takes the form of the narration of a narration).

4 As, for example, in the *Protagoras*, where Socrates is both narrator and participant.

5 Compare *Smp.* 177d7, where Socrates declares that the art of love is the only art he knows.

6 In the course of this book I will have much to say about 'art', and, notoriously, no single English equivalent captures the meaning of the Greek *tekhnē*, to which 'art' here corresponds. This does not seem to me a sufficient reason for leaving the term untranslated. I prefer to employ a varied family of English equivalents (art, discipline, practice, skill, technique, craft) according to context, while making it clear that each needs supplementation by the others.

7 Notice here the emphasis on the concept of *kairos*: the 'appropriateness of the moment' (at 272a3 and 272a6–7).

8 This would give point to the otherwise puzzling repetition *idōn men, idōn* ('seeing, *seeing* him') at 228b7 (when Socrates is reconstructing Phaedrus' reaction upon meeting him). De Vr. ad loc. recommends deleting the second *idōn* despite its presence in many MSS, among them the oldest. He does so all the more readily because the reasons given by those who favour its retention are thin: they cite only a supposed 'pathetic effect' or 'poetical reminiscence' without explaining why such an effect or reminiscence would be suitable here. Why should Socrates choose to emphasise the act of vision when describing how Phaedrus

233

caught sight of a fellow fanatic for intellectual talk? On my interpretation, this emphasis makes good sense. Just as the competent orator must not only know the rules but also, and crucially, be able to recognise when he has a relevant case before his eyes (271e3–4), so the repeated *idōn* in Socrates' account of Phaedrus' reaction upon meeting him points up that Phaedrus has not simply *seen* Socrates in the street, he has *seen* what has fallen into his clutches: he recognises Socrates for what he is (or thinks he does) – to wit, a 'fellow fanatic'.

9 Notice the structural crescendo in Phaedrus' expectations: Socrates claims he can say 'other things no worse' (*hetera mē kheirō*, 235c6); 'no worse' becomes 'better' (*beltiō*) in Phaedrus' reformulation and is now paired with 'no less' (*te kai mē elattō*, 235d6–7); and in Phaedrus' second reformulation at 236b2 'no less' suffers the same inflation as 'better' did by becoming 'more' (*hetera pleiō kai pleionos axia* – and comparison of this final phrasing with Socrates' original *hetera mē kheirō* reveals Phaedrus' demand for *pleiō* as the interloper that it is).

10 Notice also that *en route* to the arbour Phaedrus comments on the pleasure that results from his convenient barefootedness (at 229a5–6).

11 Socrates need not, however, have been distracted in quite so outlandish a fashion as he is; here his own character as a philosopher comes into play.

12 I choose the translation 'intellectuals' as broad enough to encompass whatever distinctions we may wish to make between *sophistai, rhētorikoi, meteōrologoi, logographoi,* etc. Were I making a study of the historical figures who created the intellectual climate in late fifth-century Athens, it would be wanton of me so to bracket Lysias and Teisias with, say, Metrodorus of Lampsacus (who has been suggested as a typical demythologiser and possible target of Plato's remarks here – see de Vr. apud 229c6). But my object of study is Plato's *Phaedrus.* Consequently, I find wrong-headed any attempt to pin a distinct historical label on the *sophoi* of 229c6, just in so far as it would mask Plato's deliberate vagueness here. Compare how his list of contributors to the rhetorical art, the *sophoi... legein,* at 266c3 sq. contains, without distinctions of rank or field, not only those whom we think of as primarily rhetoricians (Theodorus, Teisias, Evenus, Polus) but all the most famous of the sophists (Protagoras, Gorgias, Hippias, Prodicus). Plato paints his 'wise men' with a deliberately broad brush in this dialogue because the art of philosophy he advocates is not only a formal discipline but also a theoretical stance available to (but unlikely to be taken up by) the practitioners of a wide range of traditional arts, including rhetoricians, poets, and lawgivers (278b7–d6); and *sophos* is both his often ironic catch-all term (see 258a8, 260a6, 266c3, 267b6, 273b3) and at the end of the dialogue the marker of a new ideal (278d3–6; cf. 273e9 and 245c2, which prepared for this revision of

vocabulary). I consider this to be adequate justification for my conflating the concerns of the demythologising *sophoi* of the Boreas passage with those of the rhetoricians and sophists who figure in the rest of the dialogue. Socrates' line of fire is wide enough to sweep them in a single arc. We might want to resist this conflation as historically blunt-nosed; but, by a curious twist, such resistance would in turn blunt the nuances of the text.

13 *Eikos*, the 'plausible', is the term that Socrates reports Teisias as opposing to truth in the second part of the dialogue, 272e2–5. I shall elaborate this connection in the final section of chapter three.

14 For this reason it is a mistake to take the demythologisers, as Hackforth does, to represent 'the allegorical school of poetical interpretation' (H. 26), or to suggest Metrodorus of Lampsacus as a possible target (see de Vr. apud 229c6). The relevant model is not Metrodorus' equation of Homer's Agamemnon with the aether, Achilles with the sun, Helen with the earth, etc. (see DK II.49.22–5) but, say, the naturalistic version of the story of Io in the opening pages of Herodotus. Conversely, allegorical re-use of a traditional mythic apparatus is precisely the mark of Socrates' second speech. To be sure, Plato is subtle and philosophically sophisticated where Metrodorus, so far as we can tell, was ham-fisted and ridiculous; but their tools are the same (indeed, Plato would be indicating both his superficial kinship with and vast superiority to the likes of Metrodorus if, as many commentators hold, he is indulging in some simple astronomical – as opposed to properly philosophical – allegory in his description of Hestia (Earth) in relation to the other Olympians at 246e4–247c2, for which see H. 73–4).

15 Of course, Socrates does not adopt myth simply as a suitable and preferred alternative to a prosaic account, but declares himself, as a mere human being, compelled to resort to myth when it comes to describing the soul (246a3–6). I will devote proper attention to this point in chapter five.

16 *Hē men gar poiēsis mallon ta katholou, hē d' historia ta kath' hekaston legei.* Aristotle's comment is the more pointed if by *historia* he refers primarily to the antiquarian strand of historical writing, the work of a Hellanicus or Hippias rather than Thucydides.

17 Notice that at 228a5–c5 Socrates has already refused Phaedrus the luxury of glossing over the enthusiasm for cultural entertainment that accompanies this skill.

18 See n.12 above for the deliberate breadth of reference in *sophos* here and throughout the dialogue. Professionalism is an important link between the various species of new intellectual there considered, and sets them collectively apart from the philosopher. See Guthrie 1969, 27–34 for the development in the usage of *sophos*, *sophistēs*, and

deinos. Notice that Socrates brings out the ironic flavour of the antiquarians' *sophia* here by qualifying it as *deinotēs* ('cleverness'; see 229d4); and *deinotēs* is later contrasted with the *sophia* of the true philosopher in Socrates' second speech, at 245c2.

19 Thus for the intellectual professional leisure is labour, play is work, and *skholē* comes to refer especially to learned activity (see LSJ sub voc. II); whence our word 'scholastic'. Is it work or isn't it? The ambiguous term *skholē* here conveys this issue in much the way the ironic use of *adoleskhia* does later in the dialogue and elsewhere in the Platonic corpus (270a1; and see de Vr. ad loc.).

20 See Lloyd 1979, 80–1 on the growth of professionalism in the art of speaking. Notice that Socrates qualifies the activity of the *sophoi*, the demythologisers, as *sophizomenos* (229c7): a word which has connotations of excessive subtlety (see LSJ sub voc.). So too Phaedrus declares Lysias' speech especially subtle (*kekompseutai*, 227c7; echoed by Socrates in his encomium of Phaedrus' own talent: *pantōn de kompsotaton to tēs poas*, 230c2). For the interest shown by sophists in all forms of social discourse see e.g. Protagoras' literary criticism of Simonides' poem at *Prt.* 339a sq. (and notice that at 319a he agrees that what he teaches is best described as *politikē tekhnē* – how to become a good citizen), or Hippias' stories of, among other things, 'the races of heroes and of men', the study of which he labels *arkhaiologia* (*Hi. Maj.* 285d6–e2).

21 See de Vr. apud 230b2, c1, c3.

22 For exhaustiveness as a mark of panegyric notice Phaedrus' approval of Lysias' speech in praise of the non-lover for saying 'everything that is worth saying on the subject' (235b2), and compare Gorgias' model strategy for encomium in the *Epitaphios* (DK II.285.10 sq.). Exaggeration is declared proper to panegyric by Aristotle (*Rhetoric* 1.9.38). Hermias (apud 230b) gives an extensive appreciation of Socrates' exhaustiveness here; and Socrates' belabouring of superlatives and emphatic modifiers in this passage becomes positively comical when traced (and here I leave the Greek untranslated because this really is a point – a minor point – that requires familiarity with the language for its appreciation): *mal'amphilaphēs* (230b3) ... *pankalon* (b3) ... *euōdestaton* (b5) ... *khariestatē* (b6) ... *mala psykhrou* (ibid) ... *sphodra hēdy* (c2) ... *pantōn de kompsotaton* (c3) ... *pankalōs ekhein* (c4–5) ... *hōste arista* (c5) ... What remains for Phaedrus to say but: *atopōtatos* (c6)?

23 Compare Socrates' claim before giving his second speech to be 'a prophet, but not an altogether serious one', *mantis men, ou pany de spoudaios,* 242c3–4.

24 Notice that it is introduced with an exclamatory oath: 'By Hera!', 230b2, as if Socrates were taken aback; and that he breaks off from

what he was saying as the place suddenly impinges on his attention, at 230a6–7, as if he cannot help but notice it.

25 In comparing Socrates' behaviour to that of the philosophic lover, I am not attempting simply to equate philosophic love with philosophic discussion, as if the former were a mere allegory of the latter. But the difference between them will take time to emerge (indeed, I shall not make it entirely explicit until we come to the final few pages of this book).

26 Eryximachus is doing just this in the *Symposium* when Aristophanes, seized by a fit of hiccups, banteringly recalls him to his professional role (*Smp.* 185d2 sq.).

27 Given the semantic stretch of the concept of *tekhnē* over our distinction between 'crafts' and 'fine art', the figure of the philosopher here delineated is perhaps the closest thing in Plato's world to that stock character of our romantic heritage, the artist who lives and breathes his art.

28 This metaphorical use of the term 'background' has seemed natural also to John Searle, who adopts it to denote 'a set of nonrepresentational mental capacities that enable all representing to take place' (Searle 1983, 143). I have been struck by the convergence between Searle's metaphor of a pre-intentional 'Background' that empowers intentional states and Plato's appeal to the scenic background of the *Phaedrus* as an emblem of the tacit or recognitional component in the enabling conditions of rule-governed human behaviour (as explained in this section). Of course, Searle's notion of the background remains in crucial respects distinct from the notion that I attribute to Plato: for one thing, Searle insists that 'there is nothing whatever that is "transcendental" or "metaphysical" about the Background, as I am using that term' (154).

29 For a general account of this issue in Plato see esp. Moravcsik 1978 and Wieland 1982.

30 I should point out that the contrast between propositional and non-propositional knowledge is not simply isomorphic with that between foreground and background in the metaphorical sense. For example, a dancer might make the technique of executing a nimble caper completely explicit (and so bring it into the foreground) by performing it in slow motion and pausing between its component movements – could do so with complete accuracy and yet be unable to convey those movements with a matching accuracy of description. Nevertheless, since the arts mostly in question in this dialogue are verbal, the contrast between the propositional and the non-propositional is especially characteristic of foreground and background in this case.

31 Notice that as sober an exegete as de Vries is alive to this double function of the passage: 'The "myth" of the cicadas ... serves as a relaxing intermezzo. But at the same time some fun is made of Phaedrus'

philologia ... Further Plato calls upon his readers to serve the Muses in the right way' (de Vr. apud 258e6–7); only, he does not connect the right way to serve the Muses with the right way to interpret this dialogue, as I am about to do.

32 Again, de Vries (apud 258e4–5) discusses with considerable sensitivity how Plato 'makes of [Phaedrus'] parading half-digested profundities almost a caricature'.

33 His first speech he compares to dithyrambic and epic verse (238d2–3 and 241e1–2); the second he judges 'to have been said in somewhat poetic language' (*tois onomasin ... poiētikois tisin ... eirēsthai*, 257a5–6).

34 This is not to deny that Plato could have serious reservations about the philosophic status of Socrates' 'mythic hymn' (as his second speech is called at 265c1); for it is especially characteristic of philosophy that it should question the status of the various modes through which it can be pursued, and that it should reckon this very questioning a legitimate philosophic pursuit. (I will consider this question at some length in the next chapter: see the section, 'The philosopher judges himself'.)

35 It may be relevant that the Sirens, to whom the cicadas are compared, produce the Pythagorean harmony of the spheres at *Rp.* X 617bc – a music rendered inaudible by its background constancy.

36 And the mind runs easily here to Kant's similarly questioning refrain in the introduction to the *Critique of Pure Reason* (as well as to the very different mode of answer that he gives): How is pure mathematics possible? How is pure natural science possible? How is metaphysics as natural disposition possible? How is metaphysics as a science possible?

37 This is itself, however, a somewhat rhetorical formulation. It captures the spirit behind the dialogue's structure; but for the sake of accuracy I will need to fuss over it in the course of the book. In particular, I do not mean to suggest that the first part of the dialogue is straightforwardly rhetorical rather than philosophic. Rather, as we shall see, it is problematically philosophic. In addition, the second part of the dialogue contains, as if it were an unexpected bonus, a theoretical account of dialectic as well as rhetoric (at 265c3–266c1). All this I examine in more detail in the next chapter.

38 *Pace* the widespread scholarly opinion that the distinctively philosophical achievement of the dialogue lies in its second part, above all in the methodological pronouncements on Collection and Division. Owen 1973, 249–50 urges that the middle Platonic paraphernalia of the dialogue's first part is superseded by the new dialectic of the second, and that all we are to salvage from the first part, at least in dialectical terms, is its exemplification of the method of Collection and Division; De Vries takes as unifying theme of the dialogue the 'persuasive use of words', the 'means' of which is beauty, the 'condition (unlike current

rhetoric's) ... knowledge' (de Vr. 23); so again it would be the dialectical part of the dialogue that turns to the foundational nub of the matter ('condition' rather than 'means'); Hackforth, commenting on the passage that introduces the methodology of Collection and Division, roundly declares: 'There can, I think, be little doubt that the plan of the whole dialogue is centred on the present section' (H. 136).

39 It is this idea – that Plato's attention to topography in the *Phaedrus* does not just run parallel to the larger philosophic concern of the dialogue but is, through the very fact of its parallelism, and through its status as a foregrounding device, a constitutive part of that concern – that distinguishes my interpretation from any other known to me in which more or less detailed parallels are drawn between the topography of the dialogue and its philosophic content: notably Helmbold and Holther 1952; Burger 1980; and Philip 1981.

2. From Argument to Example

1 The scholarly consensus to which I refer may be traced through e.g. Cope 1867, 7 n.1; R. xlvii-viii; H. 9 and 136–7; and de Vr. 23. To be sure, this is consensus only at the most general level.

2 The second and final stretch of argument, however, at 266c–274a, I will not consider until the next chapter, after I have set out the limitation under which both parts of the argument operate. This follows Plato's course of exposition in the second part of the dialogue.

3 So this case is more tricky than the example Alisdair MacIntyre picks to illustrate the distinction between goods external and internal to a practice (MacIntyre 1981, 175–6): tempting a child with candy in order to spark his interest in playing chess. The attractions of the intellectual life for Phaedrus are not wholly contingent to that practice in the way candy is to chess; yet they are not (by MacIntyre's own criteria) internal to it, either; for they can be had by other means than engaging the intellect. Aristotle's discussion of friendship in books VIII and IX of the *Nicomachean Ethics* registers the intriguing status of such goods more explicitly, perhaps, than any other ancient text.

4 This is Rhetoric's counter-move to Socrates' suggestion, in calling her a 'clever enemy' (260c4), that she is actively *averse* to truth. She did not mean that the student was *necessarily not* to learn what is truly just – but, we are to understand, only *not necessarily* (260d5–6).

5 This is substantially the position that Socrates' questioning prompts Gorgias to take in the dialogue that bears his name: see esp. *Grg.* 460a.

6 Here I draw on Kronman 1981. Kronman prefers to represent the tension in terms of the double function of the law professor alone, as a teacher of advocacy in the service of his students and as a pure legal

scholar serving himself (957). But, surely, even as a teacher of advocacy the law professor is primarily out to 'say something true about his subject' – a phrase Kronman applies to the literary critic to show that one can be out for truth even where no clear standard of truth exists (962). The crucial divide, then, remains that between the teacher and the practising advocate.

7 Much of their teaching, indeed, was by example – delivering the kind of display-piece that we see in this dialogue in Lysias' speech. See further Kennedy 1963, 167–73.

8 So it would be too simple to argue, with Burger 1980, 74, that Socrates' proposal to examine the truth of the slogan that tells us we need not learn truth constitutes 'an implicit rejection of the position'. Undoubtedly, we are meant to see the difference between the goal of the practising orator and Socrates' goal as its assessor; but Socrates' position is one that Rhetoric herself can and does occupy in her role as teacher. Merely to take up this position as teacher does not constitute a rejection of a maxim that applies only to rhetorical practice; for that, further argument is needed – and Socrates is about to supply it.

9 It is generally agreed that the title of 'Eleatic Palamedes' (261d6) refers to Zeno.

10 The point of drawing this consequence from the audience's point of view, I take it, is to show the connection between the general premisses about the logic of deception so far and the actual deceptive activity of the practising orator.

11 It is of course conceivable that one should remain unpersuaded by either side and thus be compelled to a vote of yes or no that does not express genuine conviction. Hence in modern law a jury is 'charged not with deciding what happened, but with deciding whether the party with the burden of proof has discharged that burden. A criminal jury that acquits is not deciding that the defendant is innocent ... but only that he is not guilty beyond a reasonable doubt' (Yeazell 1981, 96). Formally, then, although perhaps not in practice, the jury's primary task would be to judge the performance of the speakers – the power of their arguments to convince – rather than to announce what they believe true. Athenian jurors, by contrast, were offered no such escape-clause.

12 We have of course encountered this asymmetry already, in the contrast between the goals of the practising orator and of the teacher of rhetoric.

13 Of course, it does depend for its success on a distinction between truth and seeming truth which a hard-nosed relativist of a Protagorean sort might not accept. This caveat must also be entered against Socrates' second stretch of argument, and I shall consider it a little more fully at that point, in the next chapter.

14 Burger 1980, 76–9 is an honourable exception to the general run of

commentators in this context. In Socrates' irony she finds instruction concerning what she takes to be the overall thesis of the dialogue: to wit, Plato's project for a 'philosophic art of writing'. In this section I concur with her approach to that extent but disagree with her conclusions. So, for example, she holds that 'Socrates takes the speech of Lysias as the paradigm product of writing' (79); I would insist, by contrast, that Lysias' speech is a paradigm product of *rhetoric*, and that it is as rhetoric that the speech is criticised, not (primarily) as writing. I discuss Burger's overall interpretation at some length in chapter seven.

15 Thus there would be a *double entendre* in Socrates' phrasing of his request to hear the actual words of the text read out yet again: 'Let me hear it from the man himself (*autou ekeinou*)', 263e5 (we recall, perhaps, that in the dialogue's opening scene Socrates joked, upon discovering the manuscript of the speech hidden under Phaedrus' cloak, that 'Lysias himself is here', *parontos de kai Lysiou*, 228e1). Apart from Burger 1980, Th. apud 264a is the only commentator known to me who even hints that Socrates' criticism here is less than completely fair to Lysias, let alone that the apparent misunderstanding is significant.

16 As Burger 1980, 78 also sees.

17 *Pace* H. 130 n.1: 'He had in fact defined *erōs* in both speeches.' Of course, a re-definition of love as 'divine madness' is *implicit* in the content of the mythic hymn; but the relevant point is that there is nothing in the second speech to compare even remotely with the extensive insistence on and instantiation of formal definition that opens the first.

18 Notice that Phaedrus' acquiescence in this criticism is significantly limited and cagy: 'I will grant you this much (*ge toi dē*): that what he speaks of is what you would find in a peroration' (264b1–2).

19 This, of course, was an important and problematic feature of the ethical environment bequeathed to contemporary Athenian society, and which we find Socrates (among others) reacting against in such classic texts as the *Crito* and the discussion with Polemarchus in the first book of the *Republic* (see further Irwin 1977, 13–36). Compare in particular the following vision of simplicity in the orator Antiphon: 'If violence on the part of the young and self-control on the part of the old were as natural (*houtō kata physin ēn*) as seeing with the eyes and hearing with the ears, then there would be no need for you [i.e. the jury] to stand in judgment; the young would stand condemned by their mere age', *Tetralogy* III 4.2.

20 In an intriguing note, Thompson suggests something along these lines; but appears to conclude that Plato is simply being unfair here. The note is worth quoting in full (Th. apud 264a): 'Lysias doubtless plumed himself on his skill in plunging thus *in medias res*, instead of commencing *ab ovo*, as a novice might think it his duty to do. And even the confusion of which Plato complains he might justify on practical

grounds: the entire speech being an example of rhetorical insinuation, where more is meant than meets or is fit to meet the ear. But it does not suit Plato's purpose to place himself on the "Standpunkt" of his victim.'

21 See a contemporary work, Alcidamas, *On the Sophists*, esp. 13 (in Radermacher 1951, 137): 'Those who write speeches for the lawcourts shun accuracy and mimic the way in which people communicate when improvising; they think that writing best which least bears the marks of having been written.' And compare this later judgment on Lysias' work by Dionysius of Halicarnassus, *De Lysia* 1.16: 'His art is concealed beneath the semblance of artlessness.'

22 As commentators do not fail to note: see Th. apud 262c and de Vr. apud 262c10.

23 Notice that at 261d1–2 Socrates asserts that the love-speeches afford examples of how 'one who knows the truth might mislead his audience'.

24 Socrates' claims to naïveté are, of course, a common motif in the Platonic corpus, and often trail with them the sense that such naïveté is a positive and progressive force; not least in a passage of the *Republic* clearly recalled in the language of Socrates' first criticism of Lysias. Th. apud 264a and de Vr. apud 264a4–6 note, without further comment, that Socrates' image of Lysias 'swimming on his back, in reverse' (264a4–7) strikingly corresponds to that used in *Rp.* VII 529c to describe the activity of astronomers and ridicule the notion that the study of the stars 'elevates' the mind. My interpretation gives this correspondence a clear point; for astronomy is another study that, taken as an end in itself, becomes lost in the kind of superficial subtlety and complexity (the *poikilmata* of *Rp.* VII 529c7) that only a courageous act of philosophic 'naïveté' (*euēthikōs*, 529b3) can cut through – that is, by questioning the fundamental goals of the practice rather than the subtle detail of its results. Compare also the passage of the *Phaedo* in which Socrates dismisses the subtle explanations of Anaxagoras and others in order to insist 'plainly and artlessly and perhaps simple-mindedly' (*haplōs kai atekhnōs kai isōs euēthōs*) on the function of the Forms: that it is because of the beautiful that things are beautiful (*Phd.* 100de).

25 Notice that what for Socrates can be purchased only through a whole way of life – indeed, as it turned out, at the cost of his life – has its analogue, so to speak, in the bargain basement: in the concealing of art by art that takes place when the rhetorician writes a speech, as in Lysias' case, to read as if improvised.

26 Lysias is duly called the 'father' of his non-lover's speech at 257b2.

27 Of course, we have seen that Plato points out (and indeed himself makes use of) the stylistic niceties that Socrates passes over. But this is not at all for Plato, or for his appreciative reader, to *enter into the spirit* of such niceties. Rather, it is to make a spectacle of the spirit to be

avoided; it is the writer's and reader's follow-up to the closing hint at
264e5–6 that much remains to be drawn out from Lysias' speech in the
way of examples of what to eschew. The point, I take it, is that most of
us require more forceful dissuasion from the attractions of Lysias' way
than does someone as exceptional as Socrates.

28 There could be no argument because the attitude towards argument is
(in part) what is in dispute. Compare Bernard Williams' discussion
(Williams 1985, 22–9) of the difficulty of discovering an Archimedean
point for ethics. Compare also Julia Annas' account of the limitations
on Plato's arguments for the existence of Forms, in Annas 1981, 236–
40, esp. 237: 'It is thus a change of heart more than a mere sharpening
of the wits that is needed to make one realise that there are Forms.'

29 Th. apud 262d and de Vr. apud 262d7 are both struck by the
impatience of Phaedrus' tone here.

30 On this topic compare Myles Burnyeat's discussion, in the context of
Aristotle's *Posterior Analytics*, of the conviction that comes not from
further evidence but from what he calls 'intellectual habituation' (see
Burnyeat 1980).

31 By contrast, a piece such as Kronman 1981, discussed earlier in the
chapter, limits itself in its confrontation with a modern analogue of this
choice of lives (the academic *v.* practising lawyer) to explicit
considerations, designed to persuade us that the life of the practising
advocate tends to promote moral cynicism. In this it conforms, of
course, to standard academic practice. Kronman is not neglecting the
importance of example, however; his argument, indeed, is that
professors of law must set an example in their classrooms (see his
p. 959). But Plato is setting such an example even in his writing (as well
as in his teaching, no doubt); and part of his motivation for taking this
course would be to prevent such proposals as Kronman's from being
taken in a spirit of mere piety.

32 This is not to say that it must be conveyed specifically via the dialogue
form (that would be to commit Phaedrus' error once again).

33 The four are Apollo for prophetic, Dionysus for 'telestic', the Muses for
poetic, and Aphrodite along with Eros for erotic madness. It is true that
in the course of the speech, at 252c3–253c6, the reader is primed for the
general concept of divine patronage over types of human character;
nevertheless, the point remains valid that Socrates recalls a more
systematic classification than he actually gave. Notice that at the time
Socrates thought to name only the divine authority whose influence, in
his poetic mood, he was supposedly experiencing himself (see 237a7).
See also H. 131 n.2 and de Vr. apud 265b3 (both commentators choose
to minimise the discrepancy).

34 See 242d4–7; 243e9–244a8; and 256e4–257a2.

35 Among commentators Hackforth gives most weight to the 'serious

difficulties' here (see H. 133 n.1), difficulties which others tend to minimise (R. xliii and 71 n.1; de Vr. apud 265b2, 266a4) – although an earlier generation of scholars, as de Vries points out, were provoked to deletion. Ackrill 1953, 278–9 argues against Hackforth that there is no reason to hold that Socrates misrepresents his speeches as examples of the technique of Collection and Division, since 'there is no suggestion [in Socrates' later description of his procedure] that the analysis done *within* each speech was (or ought to have been) dichotomous'. Ackrill here properly defuses a minor item in Hackforth's list of discrepancies (to wit, that the divisions of love were not accomplished through successive dichotomies); but he leaves untouched Hackforth's most important contention: that Socrates makes it look as if an explicit assimilation of love to madness unified his two speeches from the outset, when this just isn't so. (It is therefore misleading of de Vr. apud 266a4 to suggest by omission that Ackrill has successfully disposed of Hackforth's entire case.) Yet even Hackforth opts in the end to pour oil on the waters: 'Nevertheless [Socrates' account] may be said to be substantially true: for it is true to the spirit and implication of what has happened: it describes how the two speeches might naturally be schematised . . .' Here he glosses over exactly what I take to be the point of the discrepancies: the alteration in Socrates' *spirit* between the two occasions.

36 Notice that, as the foregoing description of Socrates' progress makes clear, his 'division' of love was indeed a process of *discovery*, and not arid classification of the already known: cf. Ackrill's debate with Ryle on the issue of Platonic division, in Ackrill 1970.

37 As Burger 1980, 75–6 also notes.

38 I follow de Vr. apud 262d1 in noting that these words do not imply that we should look for actual untruths in, say, Socrates' mythic hymn; they state only that the *possibility* of being misled is put on display for us.

39 It may perhaps be thought that orators are distinguished as a class by their propensity to deceive; but, first, as we have just seen, orators do not *aim* to deceive; they aim to persuade, and telling the truth will often do the trick; and, second, we know from the *Republic* and other dialogues that Plato thought deception not incompatible with the ethos of the philosopher, where that deception would be for the best: the well-known 'noble lie'.

40 More exactly, he began his first speech in the spirit of a rhetorical exercise, responding to Phaedrus' challenge that he outdo Lysias, but is unable to maintain this pose; indeed, he becomes upset not only with the content of the speech but with the pose from which he speaks it.

41 We see now why, looking back on the *three* speeches, Socrates refers to them with a noun in dual form, 'both speeches' (*tō logō*, 262d1) – a detail which has troubled commentators (see the discussion in H. 125

n.1). Plato has Socrates treat his own two speeches as a single speech for
purposes of contrast with Lysias' effort (here I follow Hackforth's
construal), in order to set off the struggle that Socrates underwent – his
search for the many in the one and vice versa (cf. 266b5–6) – by
contrast with Lysias' slickness. So too at 265c5–6 Socrates selects as
exemplary not a feature of either of his two speeches in isolation but the
shift between the two, from blame to praise.

42 Cf. 246a4–6; and see further chapter five.
43 Notice Socrates' tell-tale reference to the 'lucky chance' (265c9) that
made his speeches paradigms of Collection and Division.

3. The Critique of Pure Rhetoric

1 We can compare here that remarkable passage of the *Politicus*, at
285c4–d9, in which the Eleatic Stranger informs Young Socrates that
the ultimate goal of their current efforts is not so much (as we might
have been forgiven for thinking) to gain understanding of the nature of
the statesman, as it is to become better dialecticians – as if the topic of
'the statesman' were simply a convenient whetstone on which to hone
their dialectical skills.
2 In the final chapter of this book I will have more to say about the
philosopher's readiness to look upon the various practices of human life
as a 'game'; for the theme underpins Socrates' critique of the written
word, which is the topic of that chapter.
3 *tekhnai*: on which see further Kennedy 1963, 54–8; Lloyd 1979, 81.
4 For example, H. 143: 'mild satire'; Burger 1980, 82: 'an almost bitter
playfulness'. It may be that Plato is playing a more particular game here
than scholars make out; for it strikes me that he makes the satirical
punishment fit the crime, moulding the presentation of each topic to its
content. Take for example Theodorus, who established the categories
of 'confirmation' (*pistōsis*) and 'additional confirmation' (*epipistōsis*);
Socrates names him only periphrastically, so that Phaedrus has to ask
for confirmation that Theodorus is the man intended, confirmation
which Socrates not only provides but to which he appends other
Theodoran *trouvailles* – additional confirmation, as it were (266e3–
267a2). Similarly, Evenus, who specialised in tropes of indirect allusion,
is introduced circuitously, and with a tentative air: 'Are we not to put
him in the limelight?' *es meson ouk agomen* (267a2–5). Readers can
amuse themselves extending the trick to other examples in the list. In
this case we are dealing with what is just a trick, and its elaboration is
only an amusement. That, indeed, would be Plato's point: to illustrate
the dangerous trivialisation to which rhetorical tropes are prone when
thematised.
5 This despite his insistence on a proper exordium when criticising

Lysias' speech; for we saw that he was not committed to the formal aspect of that point.

6 Here I follow Lloyd 1979, 81.

7 Here I develop de Vr.'s suggestion, in a note worth quoting in full (apud 268d3–5): 'Th. admired Phaedrus' "apt reply", which, in his opinion, "is evidently inconsistent with Ast's mean opinion of his understanding". Phaedrus is indeed allowed some insight; but the whole of the dialogue warns the reader not to overrate it.'

8 Thus, rather than taking Phaedrus up directly, he illustrates his mistake by appeal to a new and parallel case in the field of music, imagining a discussion between a true musician and a musical hack (268d6–e6); and similarly he draws the conclusion in the case of rhetoric by adopting the voices of Pericles and 'mellifluous Adrastus' (269a5–c5).

9 Nevertheless, all commentators that I have consulted do little more than summarise this passage.

10 There is a useful comparison to be made here with one of Socrates' earlier jibes at well-known rhetoricians. At 267b2–5, he reports Prodicus' rejoinder to Gorgias' boast of being able to speak both at great length and with extreme concision, as he pleased. Truly artistic speaking, replies Prodicus with a laugh, requires the ability to produce not long or short speeches, but speeches of suitable length (*metriōn*). Phaedrus catches Socrates' irony and chimes in: 'Oh, very wise I'm sure, Prodicus!' (*sophōtata ge, ō Prodike*, 267b6). Prodicus – a notable butt of Plato's satire in the *Protagoras* also (see *Prt.* 315d–316a), where he is portrayed as in love with the sound of his own voice – has come out with just that potentially mind-numbing truism which Phaedrus expresses on behalf of the doctors and poets (and yet, being a truism, it is *true*; and underpins such remarkable ventures as Plato's enquiry into the measurement of the appropriate in the *Politicus*, at 283b–285c and *passim*, or Aristotle's enquiry into the mean in the *Nicomachean Ethics*). Phaedrus here recognises its limitations; but that is only because he is infected, as always, by the mood of the moment, and has not missed the sardonic edge to Socrates' tongue (his 'very wise', *sophōtata ge*, seems calqued upon and designed to cap Socrates' ironic tribute to Evenus at 267a5: 'the man is wise, you see', *sophos gar hanēr*). So too he subsequently catches the disapproving tone in Socrates' presentation of the artistic hacks and weighs in with amplified invective; only to come out with a generalised version of Prodicus' dictum, soured with Prodican pomposity, and so reveal that even his earlier response was not the fruit of genuine understanding, but only an over-enthusiastic echo.

11 Hence his recourse to the example of the musician, at 268d6–e6; where he can stretch a pun on the term *mousikos*: both 'musical' and 'cultured'. It is even less apparent that doctors will tend to have any

special communicative skills (although such skills were certainly exhibited, and their advantage to the doctor acknowledged, in the medical literature: as Lloyd 1979, 86–98 has made especially clear); and Plato does not directly attribute – perhaps deliberately avoids attributing – this ability to them (cf. de Vr. apud 268e3).

12 Notice in this connection the phrasing of 271c4 and 272b2.

13 As a figure-head for rhetoric, Pericles contrasts with Socrates' rhetorical butts at 266d–267d most saliently for being an active statesman, expected to set a public example, rather than a paid teacher of private students – hence his exemplary behaviour to Socrates and Phaedrus here. However, he is only a figure-head – this, surely, is the point of pairing him with the mythical 'mellifluous Adrastus' (269a5). No substantial praise even of his rhetoric, let alone of his politics, need be assumed (*pace* de Vr. apud 269e1–2) – thus, notice how cagily Socrates qualifies his praise at that point (269e1–2); and see further Guthrie 1975, 432 and Hellwig 1973, 186. Similarly, the point of Socrates' praising him (at 270a) for having associated with the philosopher Anaxagoras is to say that Pericles had the right sort of idea in being a public speaker who welcomed philosophy, but that only with Plato is this idea bearing proper theoretical fruit (just as at *Phaedo* 97c sq. – a passage we are perhaps reminded of here at 270a5 – Anaxagoras is praised for having the right idea in putting Mind at the cosmic helm, even though it remains for Socrates to substitute more worthy flesh to put on the bones of this idea than Anaxagoras himself conceived). See further Viano 1965, 445–7.

14 For my purposes here I need not enter into the question of whether the allusion is general – to a traditional commonplace (so e.g. R. clxvi) – or more specific – to a strikingly similar passage of Isocrates (*Against the Sophists*, 16–18), generally agreed to predate the *Phaedrus* (so e.g. de Vr. apud 269d4–6, and 15–18; see further Hellwig 1973, 188 n.27).

15 See e.g. Th. apud 269d; R. xlvi; Hamilton 1973, 88; de Vr. 16.

16 In view of my theme here and throughout that Plato is giving full value to what can only be shown or recognised and not formulated or rote-learnt, it is ironic – instructively so – that Isocrates, in the passage in *Against the Sophists* (18) to which many commentators have taken 269d to allude, explicitly mentions the importance of the example that the teacher must set; while Plato does not. But this is as it should be. Isocrates enthuses about the importance of setting an example: but just look at the example he actually set (cf. 279a, at least when taken as irony). Socrates, by contrast, saves words; he just *shows* us how important it is – avoiding thereby the dangers of lip-service.

17 Hackforth, followed by de Vr. apud 270c2 and by Hamilton in his translation (Hamilton 1973, 89), interprets it differently (see H. 150). He holds that Socrates expresses a requirement not of placing the soul

within a system but of grasping its nature as a whole. But this requirement is already satisfied, surely, in the first stage alone of the method that Socrates claims to derive from medicine (270d1–3), and was adequately anticipated at 270b4–5; so that nothing would remain to which the second stage – placing the soul in a larger system (270d3–7) – could correspond. Yet Socrates clearly attributes both stages to the spirit of the medical model (270c9–10), and Phaedrus has done the same with the 'holistic' requirement: an attribution which Socrates grants (270c3–6). I submit, therefore, that my interpretation makes better sense of the run of this passage. An alternative scholarly view has it that by 'the whole' is meant 'the natural universe'; but this applies to rhetoric parameters of physical science that strike me as inappropriate. Nevertheless, in one sense the view would not be misleading; for although the relevant parameters of the system within which the soul operates can hardly be expected to be fully congruent with those of medicine, some parameters will be shared; and this interpretation does at least give proper value to the emphasis in this passage on setting the soul *within* a system in addition to considering it *as* a system. Joly 1961 can be consulted for a summary of the controversy up to that date; and among more recent work see esp. Hellwig 1973, 182–203, and Mansfeld 1980. Hellwig's arguments against construing *holon* as 'the (systematic) whole' rather than 'the universe' strike me as effective only against Hackforth's type of interpretation, not my own (see esp. her pp. 191–2).

18 In general, commentators on this passage have in fact preferred to echo Socrates' ideal rather than question it: Th. apud 271c; R. cxlvii–clii; H. 151; de Vr. apud 270b5–6; Guthrie 1975, 412–17. Burger 1980, 84–6 is again the exception; however, she stops short (to my mind) at the questioning – detecting Platonic scepticism about Socrates' programme.

19 For my purposes here I need not enter into the vexed historical question of how far Plato might be borrowing from actual Hippocratic sources. I will confine myself to noting the argument in Mansfeld 1980 that *Airs, Waters, Places* is the most likely example of the kind of Hippocratic concern for placing the body in an environmental system that Plato might have had in mind. I find this view especially interesting because of the parallel that I drew in my opening chapter between Socrates' arrival at the arbour and the arrival of the physician in a new environment as described in *Airs, Waters, Places*. Lloyd (forthcoming) counters that it is implausible to represent Plato as agreeing with the observational and empirical methodology to be found in *Airs, Waters, Places*, which is true; but we have seen that throughout the *Phaedrus* he is concerned to give the power of *recognition* its due in the application of even so theoretical a discipline as philosophy; and his nod towards Hippocrates

need imply no more than this. I shall not venture, either, into the broader question of how far Greek medical practice lived up to the ideal here attributed it – one wonders how seriously – by Plato. It seems not unfair to say that even the most theoretically-minded physicians (perhaps especially those) did not sufficiently integrate their theory with phenomena, and in practice treated symptoms, for the most part, rather than causes. See further the synoptic analysis in Lloyd 1978, 21–32, and Lloyd 1979, 49–55, 146–51. Just this may be the reservation Plato expresses by attributing his statement of method not to Hippocrates alone (as Phaedrus would, 270c3–5), but to 'Hippocrates and the true account' (270c3–5; cf. Hellwig 1973, 184–5 on this point).

20 With the inartistic procedure we should compare Plato's scorn in the *Republic* (516c8–d7) for the honours accorded those inhabitants of the Cave who have learnt to anticipate and predict the sequence of occurrence of the shadows on its walls – symptoms, not causes.

21 Compare R. xlix: 'Bref, à une théorie qui reste théorique ou formelle et qui est dépourvue d' efficacité, se substitue une théorie qui est théorie de la pratique et qui s'applique à un contenu réel.' But Robin, I feel, does not analyse in sufficient depth just how Socrates achieves this substitution. Given that this is indeed what he attempts to achieve, I will note here that the classic debate between Suess 1910 and Hamberger 1914 as to whether or not Plato is pleading the value of Gorgianic *kairos* – recognition of the particular – over Teisian *eikos* – formulaic knowledge of plausibilities – strikes me as misconceived; for Plato's achievement transcends either alternative.

22 With this emphasis, the *Phaedrus* brackets itself among such dialogues as the *Parmenides* (esp. 133b–134e) and the *Philebus* (esp. 62ab), which give due attention to recognition of the particular (see further Nussbaum 1982).

23 It is notable that Socrates aims the formal statement of his new rhetorical method explicitly at such figures as Lysias and Thrasymachus, who were primarily practising rhetoricians rather than metaphysical thinkers; for this indicates a limitation in his argument. Thus (as I mentioned also in the context of his opening sally against rhetoric, in the previous chapter) a committed relativist – of the Protagorean sort – could counter the argument with the radical response that if he can make his students *believe* his claim to teach, and to teach an art, then it is true (for them) that what he teaches is an art. Such a response is indeed attributed to Protagoras in the *Theaetetus* (at 166d), and elicits in rebuttal, as it must, full-scale metaphysical argument against relativism as such. But the arguments in the second part of the *Phaedrus* shun such deep metaphysical waters and are more pragmatic in spirit (which is why, when speaking of the 'realism' of Socrates' method, I shrouded the term in scare-quotes). It is significant

in this connection that Protagoras is cited in Socrates' list of contemporary rhetoricians only for his minor grammatical work (267c4–7).

24 Thus, when Socrates at 270b7–9 declares that, just as medicine implants health and strength in the body through the use of drugs and nourishment, so rhetoric through the use of speeches and rules of behaviour implants persuasion and *virtue* in souls, he does not beg the question (as Th. apud 270b seems to suggest); for he does not subordinate persuasion to virtue but simply coordinates them. He makes it clear where his own ideals lie; but nothing in the method that he then details would compel its user to work towards the inculcation of virtue – nor has Socrates presented it exclusively in such a light.

25 As he introduces the example he comments (at 272a10–11) that 'they say it is only fair to speak the part of the wolf' (that is, in our phrase, to play the devil's advocate). Notice the contrast: Socrates, by presenting both sides of the case, is only pretending to be that rapacious pretender, the wolf (cf. 241d1); but Teisias and his ilk, who push only one side of a case with the intention of winning at all costs, and who never attempt to give the opponent his due, do not *play* at the wolf; they *are* wolves. Compare *Sophist* 231a: the Eleatic Stranger has described a type of enquiry remarkably like Socratic elenchus, and is hesitant to call those who pursue it 'sophists', for fear of according too great an honour to claimants of this title. Theatetus protests that the procedure of elenchus does bear some resemblance to what sophists do; to which the Stranger replies: 'So does the wolf to the dog – the fiercest beast to the tamest. But cautious enquirers should above all be on their guard against resemblances; they are a very slippery sort of thing.'

26 Most commentators find here an allusion to and pun on the name of Teisias' alleged teacher, Corax, 'The Crow'.

27 This reasoning perhaps shows through the careful phrasing of 273d3–4: 'what you call "the plausible" happens to get itself into the heads of most people (*tois pollois tynkhanei engignomenon*) through resemblance to truth'; but more likely Plato simply takes for granted the general success of everyday truth-ascriptions (though not, of course, ascriptions of what is truly just and good, the 'disputable' terms; but it is not to these that Teisias' counter-example appeals). Aristotle makes the assumption explicit at *Rhet.* I 1,1355a15–18.

28 I am saying, then, that Socrates' riposte is essentially the same as the one that Aristotle makes more explicit in his treatment of the same example at *Rhet.* II 24,1402a18 sq.: namely, that of course 'it is plausible that the implausible too should occur'; but that this does not render the plausible any less plausible (that is – in view of what he says at *Rhet.* I 1,1355a15–18 – any less essentially connected with truth).

29 See chapter one, in the section 'Boreas and his interpreters'. With 273b3 compare 229c6, and with 273c7–8 compare 229d3–4.

30 To hear the echo, compare esp. 274a1–2 with 246a8 and 274d5, and Phaedrus' reaction at 274a6 with that at 257c2.

4. The Voice of Reason

1 Compare *Smp*. 182e1–183a2, in which Pausanias remarks that society praises extravagant antics in a lover that it would condemn in anyone else.

2 For this and subsequent details of the homosexual behaviour of the time I refer the reader to the discussion and synthesis in Dover 1978.

3 See esp. Dover 1978, 53 and 96–103.

4 From the outset, the non-lover does not leave the boy in any doubt that what he is asking for, no less than a lover would, is sex. No other construal, for example, could be placed on his argument that as a man in control of himself he is less likely to crow over achieving what successful lovers tend to boast about (231e3–232a6; and cf. 233a2). Thus Burger 1980, 25 is mistaken when she insists that 'only in conclusion does the speaker confirm his seductive purpose, admitting that he does not advocate granting favors to all nonlovers', and also mistaken in concluding from this that 'in revealing this purpose, the nonlover betrays the erotic particularity he had originally condemned and thus discloses his character as a concealed lover'. Rather, the originality of the non-lover's proposal lies precisely in the fact that it pushes a seductive purpose without conventional eroticism, either overt or concealed.

5 The repeated phrase may be a deliberate parody of – and certainly makes a significant contrast with – the resonant declaration with which Socrates concludes his myth of the afterlife in the *Phaedo*. Referring to the goals of a virtuous life, he asserts that 'the prize is noble, and the expectation great' (*kalon gar to athlon kai hē elpis megalē*, 114c8).

6 It is no objection to the contrast I will draw in this chapter between the ethos of Lysias' and Socrates' non-lovers that Socrates here refers back to the voice of the non-lover in a general fashion, without drawing a distinction between the two speeches; for of course the position of Socrates' non-lover is much closer to that of Lysias' man, despite significant differences, than it is to Socrates' thesis in his mythic hymn.

7 Intercrural sex seems to have been much the most acceptable method of copulation between male peers, and a boy who submitted to anal penetration was regarded as prostituting himself: see Dover 1978, 98–103.

8 What is audacious in the non-lover would be downright saucy in his alleged creator, Lysias. For consider: he would have written this

251

display-piece to attract new fee-paying customers for his service as speechwriter (perhaps from his audience at the house of Epicrates, as described at 227b); thereby risking the opprobrium that he commercialises what should have no price (on which see Guthrie 1969, 35 sq., and Kerferd 1981, 25–6). As if to thumb his nose at such a reaction, he chooses to write in the persona of one who does indeed prostitute what society attempts to shelter, and who violates social *mores* while staunchly maintaining a position of the strictest sobriety and decorum. This would be another way, in addition to that discussed in chapter two, in which Lysias is made to reveal something of himself through his fictional creation.

9 The first difference to strike us as we read, of course, is rather that Socrates casts his non-lover as a cunning deceiver, who is in reality no less passionately in love with the boy than any other of his suitors (237b3–5). This point too has its importance, which will however be better appreciated after I have examined the difference in the psychology that he so disingenuously urges.

10 This is a matter of fairly general agreement among commentators: see Th. apud 237b; R. lxx; H. 40; de Vr. 26: and *pace* Burger 1980, 34, who contends that Socrates' speech is 'nothing but the rearrangement of Lysias'... argument'. Rosen 1969 focuses only on the position of Lysias' non-lover, but appears to consider it equivalent to that of Socrates' man. Conversely, Irwin 1974, 766–70 takes Socrates' speech as representative. He detects there (a judgment he repeats in Irwin 1977, 173) the purely technical prudence which I find exemplified rather in Lysias' speech alone (as argued above).

11 Compare the discussion in Annas 1981, 109–52.

12 Burger 1980, 36 also points to this missed opportunity on the part of the non-lover, but mistakes the nature of the opportunity missed. She writes: 'Socrates' nonlover never asks whether there could be a "natural desire dragging toward pleasure in the beautiful", which would represent the motive force of the "love of wisdom"'; but it is precisely not *pleasure* in the beautiful that could constitute the goal of the philosopher's love; rather, he loves the beautiful, and pleasure follows on from this. It is just because the non-lover has equated the beautiful with the pleasure it brings that he has blinkered himself, and is unable to raise the appropriate question.

13 It is true that he mentions the possibility of agreement as well as strife between his two principles (237d9–e2); but it is significant that he has nothing whatever to say about that state of agreement. He has a name for what results when desire has come to dominate: wantonness (*hybris*, 238a2); and one for what results when judgment is on top: moderation (*sōphrosyne*, 237e3). But these are both results of strife, not agreement. Contrast the account in *Republic* IV 442c5 sq., where

moderation is described as the result not of conflict but of agreement among the parts of soul that reason should rule them. In the ethical network of the non-lover, the state of agreement is an empty slot, which he does not need or use in his moral vocabulary. But it is of course significant that he should mention it, only to neglect it; for it marks the unused space into which the mythic hymn can grow.

14 Notice, however, that a concern for definitions is not in itself distinctively philosophical, but was a common feature of rhetoric also: see e.g. Demosthenes, *Against Artistocrates* 8; *Against Boeotus* 7; Isocrates, *Nicocles* 5; and in general Kennedy 1963, 307–9.

15 This is perhaps what Plato is marking when he has Socrates correct the age of the beloved to whom the speech is addressed: 'there was once a boy (*pais*) – or rather, a young man (*meirakiskos*) ...' (237b2). The ethical stance in Socrates' speech is more suitable for one who is old enough to appreciate a principled resistance to pleasure, where Lysias' non-lover appeals only to a relatively childish scheming towards the maximum of selfish satisfaction.

16 So H. 41–2; de Vr. apud 237e2–3; and esp. Burnyeat (unpublished), from whom I take the comparison with the *Protagoras*. A different view can be found in R. lxx and esp. Nussbaum 1982: that the ethos of Socrates' non-lover recalls the earlier Platonic opposition between imperious appetites and the good judgment that resists them, as found for example in the fourth book of the *Republic*. Nussbaum, indeed, finds in Socrates' mythic hymn 'a serious recantation of something Plato has seriously endorsed' (87), namely 'the *Republic*'s simple dichotomy between good sense and madness' (88). I have attempted so far to avoid embroiling myself in the question of Plato's philosophic development across dialogues, and a full response to Nussbaum's challenging thesis would take me too far afield in dialogues other than the *Phaedrus*. It should be clear, however, from the comparison with the *Republic* that I have already adduced, as well as from the further comparison that I make in the current paragraph, that I side with the former scholarly position. The psychological analysis in the *Republic* seems to me considerably more sophisticated than that of the Socratic non-lover, and in particular to lack its odour of self-hate. This is not to claim that there is *no* development between the *Republic* and the *Phaedrus*; but I do not believe that such a position as the non-lover's here was ever 'seriously endorsed' by Plato (rather, it would represent an all too easy corruption of his philosophic ideals, and – just possibly – a psychological state into which he feared he might fall; on which see further n.31).

17 I do not claim that the parallel is perfect; for example, the timocrat of the *Republic*, though appreciative of culture (548e), seems less overtly enthusiastic about philosophy than is Socrates' non-lover (see 547e,

548b). We should not indeed expect any *exact* correspondence between the ethical hierarchy at this point in the *Republic* which has five ranks (and its own special complexity), and that represented by the development of the love-speeches in the *Phaedrus*, which has, of course, only three. This fact does not render the parallel any less illuminating, so far as it holds.

18 Notice that the white horse is described as 'a friend of true opinion' (*alēthinēs doxēs hetairos*, 253d7), and just this – 'opinion' or 'judgment' (*doxa*, 237d8) – is what Socrates' non-lover presents as the only countervailing force to desire in the soul; whereas Plato normally reserves the term, of course, for its contrast with full understanding (*epistēmē*). Notice also that at 241e5–7 Socrates claims that there is no need for him to complete the non-lover's account by detailing the positive benefit that his type of relationship would confer on the youth, since these goods are simply the opposite of the evils that he has described the lover as bringing. Here the bluntness of the non-lover's resistance emerges.

19 Pursuing the links with other dialogues a little further, I think it worthy of note that in the hierarchy of degeneration in the *Republic*, with which we have been concerned, the type into which the timocrat dissipates, namely the oligarchic man, is characterised by just that niggardly use of prudential reason for the exclusive furtherance of his desire (wealth, in his case) which we have seen in Lysias' non-lover (see *Rp.* IX 553d). Moreover, the oligarch openly seeks to satisfy this desire, which the timocrat, by contrast, refused to acknowledge (550e, 553c), just as Lysias' man made no attempt to conceal the objective that Socrates' non-lover never confessed in himself and professed to despise in others. Similarly, in the *Protagoras* (at 352e–354a) Socrates readily argues the representatives of common opinion into surrendering their 'timocratic' ideal, with its conflict of goals, and acknowledging at its root an 'oligarchic'-sounding prudential pursuit of a single aim (pleasure); as in the *Republic*, the former ideal, when espoused without the guard of reasoned conviction, easily degenerates into the latter.

20 Here, then, we witness Socrates succumbing to the temptation that later, when he comes to criticise Lysias' speech, he is able to avoid by drawing on the resources of philosophic naïveté (as shown in chapter two) – the later action being bolstered by the experience I am about to examine.

21 Compare how in discussion with Protagoras at *Prt.* 338b–e, 347c, and again with Thrasymachus at *Rp.* I 348b–349a, Socrates resorts to thematising the very difficulty of maintaining a fair discussion as a way of continuing the conversation.

22 Nevertheless, Phaedrus is not simply to be *equated* as a character with the figure of the rhetorician (nor with that of Lysias' non-lover), any

more than is Socrates with that of the philosophic lover. There are significant distinctions to be drawn between them, which I discuss in the closing pages of chapter seven.

23 The mere fact that Socrates is speaking with another's voice does not make him hypocritical, of course; indeed, he often adopts the voice of his opponent in order to present both sides of a case, notably in the second part of this dialogue (e.g. 260d4–9; 268a9–269c5). But here he takes on another's voice *in the manner of a rhetorician*, and with a rhetorical goal. It is his playing of the orator, not of the non-lover as such, that causes trouble. Notice in this connection that when he comes to embark on his mythic hymn, at 243e, Socrates now fully and willingly identifies with his fictional speaker, fusing with him in the first person: 'Where is the boy to whom I was speaking?' And Phaedrus would seem to be joining in this game of identification in his reply: 'Here he is, right beside you always, whenever you want him'. De Vries's reservation that it is impossible to imagine Phaedrus in the position of beautiful boy (de Vr. apud 243e7–8) strikes me as too fastidious. Of course there is no *actual* erotic liaison between Phaedrus and Socrates; but the point does not turn on what *we* can imagine, but, as it were, on what *they* can.

24 This ambivalence is especially clear, for example, in the final section of the *Theognidea*, which assigns the lover's voice a striking combination of the aggressive and the plaintive. The lover is a lion to the beloved's fawn (1278c West); yet he tempers threats to wound the boy (1287) with pleas for fair treatment from him (1283), and outright begging for mercy (1330); and for all his aggressiveness, he admits that the boy has 'conquered' him with love (1235, 1344). The closing lines translate the exchange of roles into the imagery of pursuit and flight: the poet–lion who has been pursuing his fawn finally confesses that no man is strong enough to 'flee' a triumphant Aphrodite (1388–9).

25 See e.g. *Theognidea* 1295–8, and cf. Sappho 31 (Lobel–Page). Socrates' non-lover also describes the lover as sick (238e4–5), but gives no hint of how the boy might take advantage of this fact; rather, he develops a different strand of the analogy; love-sickness makes the lover a cranky and imperious invalid.

26 This is the contrast between Anacreon 417 (Page) and 360.

27 To be sure, the prospect of a conjoint interest is there from the start. Socrates claims to know Phaedrus like another self (228a5–6), and both men are fanatics for intellectual talk (228b6–7). But as the dialogue develops, we see that this can mean very different things, and the prospect of pursuing a truly common interest takes on more the allure of an ideal than, as at first, of a confident projection.

28 The analogy between Socrates' and Phaedrus' exchange in this scene and the various accounts of erotic love has also been extensively

documented in Burger 1980, 16–18. However, she relates this analogy to the question of writing rather than to the ethical development of the speeches.

29 At 236b5 Socrates calls Lysias not just a friend but the 'beloved' of Phaedrus (*paidikōn*). How literally we are to take this ascription is put in doubt at 279b1–3, where Socrates correlates it ironically with his connection to his own 'beloved', Isocrates; but it certainly makes sense in terms of the analogy between erotic love and intellectual friendship, showing up the manipulative nature of Phaedrus' and Lysias' partnership. Notice that, no sooner has Socrates promised to deliver a second speech on love, than Phaedrus is relishing the prospect of using it as a lever to nudge Lysias into a return bout (243d8–e1); at which point Socrates pronounces (with a sigh? or a smile? or both?) the judgment that I have quoted already in my opening chater: '*That* I believe, so long as you are who you are' (243e2). I will elaborate on the relationship between Lysias and Phaedrus at the end of chapter seven.

30 Notice also that the inspiration for Socrates' decision to stay and deliver his hymn in the first place is unique to him: his 'daemonic sign' (242b8).

31 This is the truth that I extract from the thesis of Nussbaum 1982, discussed in n.16 above. The voice of Socrates' non-lover, I believe, is not to be heard as such in anything Plato seriously proposed in Socrates' name; but it is his (and/or Socrates') serious nightmare.

5. Myth and Understanding

1 Robin makes the same point (R. cviii), but does not develop it.

2 On which see further Linforth 1946.

3 On the hostility of Hippocratic physicians towards diviners and faith-healers, with due caution against drawing too stark an opposition between the two camps, see the opening chapter of Lloyd 1979.

4 The use of the long 'omega' in addition to the letter 'omikron', which had previously done service for both long and short 'o', was an innovation in Socrates' day (see de Vr. apud 244d1). Notice that the degeneracy of art is once again associated with a concern for writing.

5 This contrast, however, is too extreme as it stands, and we have seen Plato duly qualify it in the critique of rhetoric. Certainly the mere fact that an art has a code of explicit rules does not diminish the importance to its practitioner of the ability to recognise how the rules apply, an ability itself beyond rules. Philosophy is such an art. Moreover, this, we are about to see, is a point of contrast between philosophy and the prophetic madness of the Pythia, of whose art nothing at all can be made explicit. But Plato's point here would simply be that the modern failure to savour a distinction between the Pythia and the omen-reader is a symptom of a new tendency to place too much reliance on text-book thematisations of various arts.

6 Compare his heavily qualified praise for the results of prophecy at the close of the *Meno* (99c), where it is invoked to illustrate the type of achievement which he imputes to famous statesmen of the past who succeeded through inspired guesswork (*eudoxia*) rather than because they truly understood what they were saying and doing.

7 Compare 275b5–c2, on the 'simplicity' (*euētheia*) of the ancients who could understand prophetic oaks and rocks (a passage I shall examine in chapter seven); and recall in this connection the naïveté that Socrates displayed in his critique of Lysias' speech, as discussed in chapter two.

8 Notice, however, that the inner voice of the daemon which does prompt Socrates is actually called a sign (*sēmeion*, 242b9; cf. 244c7), as well as a voice (*phonēn*, 242c2) – whereas in the *Apology* it is called only a voice (31d3). This may in turn be a sign for the reader of how the figure of the philosopher is a combination of bird and bird-watcher; how the philosopher cannot just use poetry but must thematise its use.

9 This approach to Socrates' etymologies seems to me simply to transcend the terms of the scholarly debate over whether Plato intended them to be taken seriously or not (H. 59 gives a firm 'no', Th. apud 244b and R. cxvii a cautious 'yes').

10 This proposal can be found in H. 84 and Nussbaum 1982, 89.

11 This objection is made by Verdenius 1962, 132 and developed in Burnyeat (unpublished). Indeed, the difficulty is more acute than they make out; for not only does Socrates not specify that he is referring to uninspired practitioners alone, but in order to refer to the prophets he uses the very term that he had previously applied to *inspired* seers, in contrast to portent-readers (*mantikon bion*, 248d7, compared with the earlier contrast between *mantikē* and *oiōnistikē*, 244c5–d1). Notice also (in view of the interpretation I am about to propose) that the telestic madness of 244e2 is here conflated with the life of the prophet in the fifth rank (*telestikon*, 248e1); for with the advent of the new style of physician (in the fourth rank), healing by ritual has come to seem closer, by virtue of its religious atmosphere, to the ritual prophecy from which it was previously kept more distinct by virtue of having a different goal.

12 Compare the phrasing of 245b1–2 ('such, and more than these, are the fine achievements – *erga* – that I can recount for you of the madness that the gods send') with the previous description of the inspired poet who 'glorifies countless of our ancestors' achievements (*erga*) for the instruction of posterity' (245a4–5). Socrates too has been glorifying the ancestors; but when he arrives at what truly inspires him, and allows his mythical imagination to soar, it is not praise of the past but a new way for the future that we hear – as befits a philosophic sort of poetry.

13 Burnyeat (unpublished) reconciles the passages by concluding from the position allotted prophets and poets in the hierarchy that Plato is saying

of them, as he does elsewhere, that the fine things they have done and said are no credit to *them*, but to the god who speaks through them. While agreeing with this assessment, I believe that my appeal to the contrast between the historical and mythical perspectives of the two passages is required for a satisfactory explanation of why Plato chooses to present that view in so striking a fashion.

14 Notice that the word that Socrates applies at 274a2 to the human pursuit of dialectic, 'circuit' (*periodos*), he uses in his mythic hymn to describe the gods' vision of the Forms (*periodōi*, 247d5) – a vision he has declared beyond adequate human description (247c3–4).

15 This double perspective, as we shall learn in the next chapter, is characteristic of the way that philosophic lovers see one another.

16 It is in this sense that my general remarks here bear on Plato's caginess about whether it is possible to describe the soul as it is. Even if it were possible, we now see, this would not be our only task as philosophers.

17 I have spoken of the *potential* influence that learning about the soul as such can have on the soul of the learner, without investigating the question of whether some such influence is *necessary*. The whole thrust of my examination of the limitations of Socrates' arguments in this dialogue has been to show that Plato acknowledged that all we can reasonably expect from philosophic enquiry is a potential, not necessary effect. If Socrates actually thought that ethical benefit for the individual derived automatically and necessarily from the study of the soul as such – one of the views which we encapsulate in the slogan 'virtue is knowledge' – and if Plato ever actually subscribed to such a view, then he has certainly modified his master's teaching by the time he came to write the *Phaedrus*.

18 Most notably Barnes 1982, 114–20, to whom I owe the next point made in my text.

19 So H. 64 and Guthrie 1975, 419 n.4, who also provide a summary of the debate.

20 There is this difference, of course, between the two levels: that whereas on the cosmic level the existence of a substance which changes itself is supported by dubious principles (such as: what moves other things must itself move; on which see Barnes 1982, 118–19), when considered as an account of the character and effects of the individual soul's enquiry into itself, what is said is true and important. I am not interpreting the argument as nothing more than an enciphered description of such an enquiry. Doubtless Plato thought there was something to it as an argument, and was pleased in addition to manifest what he saw as its particular consequences in his account of how the philosophic lover changes his own soul. On the other hand, I do not think we need follow Barnes 1982, 118 in restricting the 'change' that the soul effects on itself and other things to the crude sense of

'locomotion'. To be sure, on the cosmic level locomotion (of the stars and heavenly bodies) is the dominant form of change; and perhaps this was the only form of change envisaged by Alcmeon, from whom (as is generally agreed) Plato has taken this argument either wholly or in part. My point, however, is that Plato would want us to construe locomotion as only one of the types of change that the soul can bring about, just in order that we should feel the cosmic standpoint to be lacking. Thus I agree with Guthrie 1975, 420, who understands motion here 'in the wide sense of any kind of change' (and cites in his support *Laws* 897a, in contrast to Barnes who takes his parallels only from the *Timaeus*).

21 For example, Burnyeat (unpublished) and Nussbaum 1982, 106–7.

22 So Crombie 1962, 343, and Guthrie 1975, 423–5.

23 This is Hackforth's view: H. 76.

24 For example, scholars often rather oversimplify the psychology of the *Phaedo*, especially when using it as a foil for Plato's later views, and suggest that in that dialogue reason and desire are strictly assigned to soul and body respectively; that the soul is pure reason, but its beliefs can be distorted by the desires of the body (see e.g. H. 75 and Hackforth 1955, 95–6; Gallop 1975, apud 83b5–e3). Yet in fact the division of faculties is less rigid than this (indeed, talk of 'faculties' as such is inappropriate to Plato's psychology; this I discuss in the final pages of the next chapter). A soul that is unduly influenced by the body does not simply have distorted beliefs but *feels pain and pleasure at the same objects* as the body does (83c5–6; 83d7–8). Desires originate in the body, but are not confined to it; so that Plato's account is developmental, not static. To be sure, Socrates is talking rather loosely at this point in the *Phaedo*; but his account contains the seeds of the more sophisticated theory of the developmental interaction of belief and desire that is to be found in *Phaedrus*.

25 Guthrie 1975, 423 admits that the tripartition of divine as well as human souls is a stumbling-block for those, like himself, who would interpret Plato as suggesting that souls remain tripartite only so long as they are still caught in the cycle of rebirth; and his counter-argument is to insist that Plato could not possibly have meant that the gods have a sensuous side to their nature (424). Certainly, the gods are not represented as prey to corporeal appetites; but I am about to propose a different interpretation of why Plato endows his gods with complex souls. For the stimulus towards this interpretation I gratefully acknowledge the influence of Burnyeat (unpublished).

26 This he models in the *Timaeus* by having the Demiurge simply *come across* the material realm in a state of disorder (30a), and by his appeal to the 'Receptacle' (49a sq.) – on which see further Waterlow 1982, esp. 348–50.

27 It is this recognition of the personal quality of the attempt to gain the

impersonal or cosmic view that cosmic *myth* – as opposed to cosmic argument such as the argument for the immortality of the soul – captures so well.

28 Since the gods are not prey to moral conflict, only one alternative centre of desire is needed. The divine soul is effectively bipartite – as conveyed by the information that both horses in their team are good, and act as one. That Plato sees fit to endow them with two horses nonetheless I read as stressing the importance for *human* souls of harmonising their potentially independent desires.

29 I take this point directly from Burnyeat (unpublished). But have I reintroduced a difference in kind (rather than degree) between the human and the divine soul by describing the former as not *inherently* harmonious? No; because Plato is saying that we can, as it were, overcome the disadvantage of our birthright, and turn what *seems* a difference in kind into a difference in degree.

30 In the *Symposium* he chooses rather to convey the human quality of a *failed* relationship, that between Socrates and Alcibiades – the opportunity that came too late.

31 Thus I agree with those scholars who see in this change of status only a change of emphasis relative to the different purposes of the two dialogues (e.g. H. 54–5; Guthrie 1975, 401 n.2; Burger 1980, 45–6), as against the thesis in Nussbaum 1982, 96–7 that it represents an important revision of the account in the *Symposium*; and similarly with the contrasting portraits of the gods in general.

32 Again, we are given no details as to how the two procedures might mesh; in contrast to the myth of Er in the *Republic*, in which Socrates makes it explicit that the souls draw lots for their turn at freely choosing whatever lives are left in the pool when their number is called (X 617e sq.).

33 Plato is thinking of virtue as a kind of wisdom or understanding: a state of mind which, although it will not develop without careful nurture and education, is also ultimately limited by varying degrees of natural intelligence. This he figures in the myth by the fact that the glimpses of the realm of Forms attained by some human charioteers are more adequate than those attained by others.

34 I think here of Aristotle's partiality in the *Poetics* (the partiality of a philosopher) towards the *Oedipus Tyrannus* – a tragedy in which we witness the hero not only coming to an awareness of his human ignorance, but taking on the burden of responsibility for it. There is a deep analogy between the figure of Oedipus and that of the philosophic lover, and I shall come back to it in the next chapter, when discussing the allegorised pain endured by the lover's soul (in the section, 'The love-mad philosopher: contingency and necessity').

35 Thus Socrates describes the time before the fall as a period of the

260

NOTES TO PP. 136–9

greatest happiness and fulfilment for our souls (250b6–c6), and excuses his lingering over mythical details by appealing to his 'yearning for the past' (*pothōi tōn tote*, 250c7). Those familiar with the modern philosophic literature on the topic of 'moral luck' will recognise that the feeling I describe here is what Bernard Williams has christened 'agent-regret' (in Williams 1976).

36 The *contrast* is familiar; but my direct source for the convenient labels is Annas 1981, 157 (whose discussion of the issue I have found especially useful).

37 Thus at 497a3 he declares that the philosopher will not lead the best kind of life 'unless he hits upon' (*mē tykhōn*) the appropriate kind of state; and again at 499a11–b5 that only if some 'divine inspiration' (*ek tinos theias epipnoias*) turns a current ruler towards philosophy or if some compulsion can 'by chance' (*ek tykhēs*) be laid upon philosophers to take up political power, will the ideal society be fashioned. It might be objected that at IX 592b3–4 Socrates says that 'it makes no difference' whether the ideal state will or will not ever actually exist in this world. But consider how the sentence continues: 'for he [the person who chooses to model the constitution of his soul upon that of the paradigm society] would act in a manner appropriate to this society, and no other'. Socrates is saying that such a person will so act regardless of whether he finds himself in the ideal society or not; and this is the sense in which 'it makes no difference' to him. But this is not to say that 'it makes no difference' to the *degree* of moral development to which he attains in so acting; hence there need be no contradiction here of Socrates' earlier assertion that there would indeed be such a difference of degree.

38 Of course, 'contingency' as I use it here is not synonymous with 'luck' (indeed, the term carries with it a Platonic metaphysic that I shall not and cannot fully unpack, but am attempting to clarify through use in different contexts). It is not a matter of luck that the philosophic life brings with it certain external goods; on the contrary, the philosopher can *expect* to attain them. Nevertheless, they seem contingent when regarded from the metaphysical standpoint which takes the fact of our embodiment as a contingency; and it is from this standpoint that Plato derives his conception of the proper attitude towards these goods. As a result, he sees no need to exclude from moral evaluation what seems largely the outcome of luck (as in the case of the philosopher who finds himself in the appropriate kind of society).

39 Notice that, when he describes the choice of lives subsequent to the first fall to earth, Socrates does indeed clearly distinguish the element of chance – the lottery – from the element of choice. This is presumably to point up an important role of metaphysically contingent goods: namely, as a limitation in response to which virtue can prove itself (by putting

them to proper use), and so flourish the more (on a similar issue in Aristotle's ethics see Cooper 1985). On the first occasion of the fall, by contrast, Plato is out to capture only the nature that we bring to the world (what in Williams 1976 is called the result of 'constitutive luck'), not the nature that we build by properly reacting to having been brought here.

6. Love among the Philosophers

1 No single translation of these two citations can avoid tendentiousness. De Vries and others hold that different aspects of a single person are being described (and translate *ē* as 'in other words'; see de Vr. apud 249a1–2 and 248d3–4), while Gould 1963, 117, 199 n.74 argues that at 249a1–2 two different possible lives are being envisaged (and so translates *ē* as 'or'). But are not both parties right? Aspects of a single best kind of life are at issue, yet because it is to some extent a matter of luck whether the philosophic lover encounters a truly appropriate beloved, there is a genuine possibility that he will have to practise philosophy without the special benefits of philosophic love – just as there is a far stronger possibility (which we saw from the *Republic*) that he will have to practise philosophy without the benefit of doing so in the ideal society. The *very* best human life, for Plato, would presumably need to be blessed with both of these benefits; hence my qualified statement that the life of philosophic lovers is at the very least *one* of the fullest realisations of the philosophic life.

2 Indeed, in the original description of the place beyond the heavens beauty is not explicitly mentioned; instead we hear of justice, moderation, and understanding (247d6–7). In view of beauty's power to integrate the sensible with the intelligible – as is to be established in what follows – it is a significant touch that we only learn of its presence in the place beyond the heavens after Socrates has turned his attention to goings-on in this world.

3 For documentation of this contrast see Dover 1978, 42–54.

4 *Timios* would not be a suitable epithet to describe just any object of desire or need, however casual or passing, but rather those objects of desire in which we can invest something of ourselves, with an eye to the future – objects about which we can care. For a discussion of this distinction between desiring and caring see Frankfurt 1982, esp. 260–1.

5 Plato's phrasing here strongly suggests (but does not unequivocally assert) that beauty does not just shine among the Forms but shines more brightly than the rest. This is especially indicated at 250c8–d1: 'beauty, in its place among them [the Forms], shone out' (*met' ekeinōn te elampen on*) (the Greek for the less suggestive 'beauty shone among them' would surely be *met' ekeinōn te elampen*, only); moreover, the

fact that this clause is coordinated with its successor by *te . . . te* ('both . . . and'), and that this subsequent clause appeals to the exceptional clarity of sight and of the earthly images of beauty (250d1–3), suggests that in the previous clause also an aspect of beauty's *superiority* is addressed. I examine the implications of this suggestion in n.15 below.

6 This reading is supported by the coordinating particles in the Greek at 250b1 and b5, which indicate that the unclarity of the images of justice and moderation is being adduced not as a gloss on the general inadequacy of the philosophers' discernment, but as an especial block to that discernment by comparison with beauty: 'now, on the one hand (*men oun*) justice and moderation . . . whereas (*de*) beauty . . .'.

7 Considerations drawn from dialogues other than the *Phaedrus* also tell against de Vries's interpretation. For it would lend support to the view that Plato thinks particulars can 'resemble' or 'participate' in the Forms to a greater or lesser degree (even though the difference of degree here in question is between particulars of different kinds rather than of a single kind); and I accept the arguments in Gosling 1965 and especially Nehamas 1975 which show that this 'approximation view' is not Plato's.

8 This, to be sure, is an interpretation rather than a straightforward paraphrase of what Socrates says; and I cannot here linger in defending it. However, this parallel in the *Republic* need function only to clarify the terms that I apply to my interpretation of the present passage of the *Phaedrus* – which I take to be sufficiently justified on internal grounds alone.

9 Of course, bigness and smallness can become values for us; but they are not values in themselves, but only to the extent that they are seen as good – or, it may be, beautiful.

10 In Socrates' reaction to the 'beauty' of the arbour (230b2), as considered in chapter one, we have a fine example of this saliency; for we saw how the exhorbitant loveliness of the place wrecked Phaedrus' plan, in his role of impresario, that it should remain a backdrop. But there is also a clear contrast between this case and that of the philosophic lover's encounter with the beautiful boy. Recall Socrates' insistence that fields and trees have nothing to teach him, but only people (230d4–5); and how his praise for the place was ultimately directed at Phaedrus' achievement in selecting it. Only when the physical beauty in question belongs to a human being is there a chance of fusing it satisfactorily with the person – in the manner that I shall later discuss.

11 This is not to exclude the possibility that, by an effort of the will or as a feat of abstraction, you could both be aware that what you see is a person and yet admire their beauty as if it were the beauty of an

inanimate object. But Plato is talking of the *natural* effects of human beauty on widely different types of character; that is, those effects which they feel as a direct result of the kind of person that they are, rather than through a special and localised exertion of willpower.

12 Readers will recognise the similarity here with what I have said of the interpreter's encounter with the splendours of the *Phaedrus* itself (especially in the final two sections of my opening chapter). But a written dialogue is not a person – any more than a beautiful arbour is a person (see n.10 above) – and we must beware of canting similarity towards identity. I return to this issue in chapter seven.

13 This summary analysis is to be elaborated and justified in the sections that follow. Notice an implicit consequence of this view: that the situation could not arise in which a non-philosophic type, discovering his character through meeting someone beautiful, was displeased with what he found and attempted to reform it; for such a reaction would mark him *eo ipso* as a philosophic type. It is constitutive of the non-philosophic reaction that it should not involve an ethical struggle (thus no 'shame' is felt, 251a1).

14 Something along these lines may have been in Robin's mind when he declared that the likenesses of beauty imitate their corresponding Form 'immediately'; but if so, then his chosen formulation of the thought obscures exactly what it ought to make clear. My interpretation is closer to that of Hermias apud 250b, in so far as he contrasts the difficulty of discovering what is just with the immediacy of beauty. But Hermias illustrates this 'difficulty' by referring to the elaborate argumentation required in the *Republic* (and not rather, as I think, to the elaborate course of the *life* of justice); and he does not explain what he means by the 'immediacy' with which 'the beautiful itself strikes us' (*auto de to kallos autothen prospiptei hēmin*). Hackforth endorses Hermias' account of the difficulty in apprehending justice through its likenesses (H. 94), but says nothing specific about how the likenesses of beauty are different.

15 In this feature may lie an explanation for Socrates' suggestion that not only are the likenesses of beauty brighter, but even the Form of beauty shone more brightly than the other Forms (as indicated in n.5 above). Since beauty in this world has the function of directing attention to the totality of values, its Form might well be represented as illuminating all the others; especially since the need for integration of desires does not disappear among the gods – they too, we saw, are represented as having tripartite souls.

16 Notice that, even if the soul escapes worldly incarnation in a particular cycle by virtue of an especially full vision, the best it can hope for is a continual renewal of this test (248c3–5). The soul must constantly prove that it deserves its place; there is no tenure in Plato's paradise.

17 This linked procedure I discussed in general terms in the previous chapter (in the section: 'Coping with contingency'); and we also encountered a further example of it in Socrates' recollection of his speeches in the second part of the dialogue, when he is tempted to minimise the strain of winning through to the sober perspective from which he speaks at that point (as considered in the final section of chapter two).

18 The metaphor becomes explicit at 252a7–b1, where the boy is compared to a doctor (*iatron*) who relieves the lover's pain.

19 Sappho 31 (Lobel–Page); as seen by Fortenbaugh 1966.

20 'Feathers' (as in Hamilton 1973, 58) rather than 'wings' (as in H. 96). This accords better with the fact that the *whole* surface of the soul is stated to be involved in the growth (251b7), and also with the metaphor of fledging in general (251c4); for birds are, after all, born with their wing-structure in place, and it is the feathers that need to be grown 'from the root' (251b6).

21 Socrates seems to make similar use of snatches from his other named source, Anacreon. Where the latter declares a beautiful boy to be the 'charioteer' of his soul (Anacreon 360, Page), Socrates describes the effects of the boy's beauty *within* the lover's soul in terms of an allegorical charioteer (253c7 sq.).

22 Notice that *kaulos*, the word used of the 'shoot' or 'stump' of the feather at 251b6, occurs in medical literature as a term for 'penis' (see LSJ sub voc. III).

23 Plato uses a similar trick in Diotima's speech in the *Symposium* (206d).

24 See Freud (1905) 1962, 75–6.

25 Strictly speaking, the latter passage cited is inconsistent with the former; for it describes the philosophic lovers as 'winged' (*hypopteroi*) already at the end of the first of their three lives or 'Olympian wrestling bouts', which must refer to the cycle of three lives mentioned in the former passage; yet there it was required that the soul live all three lives in order finally to regain its wings. This only goes to show that the characteristic of wing-growth with which Plato is most concerned is that it is not completed within a mortal life.

26 The Greek describing the lover's 'memory of the beautiful boy' (*mnēmēn . . . tou kalou*, 251d6–7) is nicely ambiguous on this point; for it need mean no more than 'memory of the beautiful'.

27 At 250c5–6 the embodied soul is compared to an oyster bound in its shell. Plato then applies this notion of enclosure within a bivalve to the description of the soul as such; for its budding feathers are trapped behind sealed lips (251b4–5). This adaptation of imagery is consonant with the idea that the painful growth of the feathers expresses the soul's confrontation with embodiment – as if the oyster were to batter at its shell.

28 The issue is well discussed in Annas 1981, chapter 6.

29 In this regard, notice that the phrase just cited, 'as if to a statue and a god', is a word-for-word translation of *agalmati te kai theōi*; which would seem however, to be a hendiadys for 'as if to the statue *of* a god'. But the more idiomatic translation loses the disjoint effect of the Greek. Plato chose to use hendiadys rather than the equally possible Greek equivalent of the idiomatic English: *agalmati theou* (with which Hermias in fact paraphrases ad loc.); and the effect is to point up the work that the lover must do to fashion in the beloved a single concept, as it were, from the two loosely coordinated terms; for just this is the linguistic task that any hendiadys demands of the reader's understanding.

30 It is as with the pattern of the *Phaedrus* as a whole: in its reflective second part Socrates attains a cooler and more comprehensive view of what in the first part he saw through the blinkers of enthusiasm, shaken with the pain of learning by his mistakes; yet the larger view turns out to have limitations of its own, and to require uneasy supplementation from that which it appeared to have left behind. Something is gained and something lost; and there is no easy balancing of the accounts. So too here, in assessing the lover's feelings, it is no use asking for a bottom-line – seeking to know whether, or in what amounts, the lover actually experiences pain and pleasure.

31 Notice that he sums up his account at 252c1–2 with the words: 'just this is the explanation and the experience (*hē ge aitia kai to pathos*) of being in love'.

32 We recall Socrates' praise, in his critique of rhetoric, for a Hippocratic style of medicine that looks behind symptoms for causes. But we now see that, when it comes to examining the soul rather than the body – and despite the ease with which medical metaphors link the two practices (the lover's 'fever', the boy as 'doctor') – distinguishing symptoms from causes is an immensely delicate task; and furthermore, just to identify the aetiology of the disease may in itself be the only type of *treatment* available.

33 The term *apotheton*, with which he qualified these verses at 252b5, could bear either of these meanings (as de Vr. points out ad loc.).

34 I prefer to translate *dia neotēta* (252b4) as '(you will laugh at it) because of your youth' rather than as 'because of its strangeness' (an admittedly possible alternative, which Hackforth adopts), since this seems to me to fit better with Socrates' emphasis in context on the lover's task of educating the beloved. But that the two senses are in any case not unconnected in Plato's way of thinking can be seen from Parmenides' remark to Socrates at *Prm.* 130e1–4: it is because Socrates is *young* still, and therefore too concerned about conventional propriety, that he cannot countenance that there might be a Form of such apparently

absurd or *laughable* things (*geloia*, 130c5) as hair, mud, or dirt. The idea is that in youth we are more ready to react with nervous laughter to what violates the norm.

35 Hermias saw the joke long ago: 'He shows by this [the unmetrical line] that the gods exceed all measure (*metrou*)' (Hermias apud 252b).

36 In this connection it is beguiling to hear in the word *dios* – 'Zeus-like' – an allusion to Dion and the great love of Plato's life (the suggestion goes back at least to Wilamowitz).

37 This would not be to say, of course, that only the physically beautiful can become philosophers. In the first section of this chapter we saw that there is no reason to think that Plato is even insisting on love between individuals, whether beautiful or not, as a condition of the philosophic life. But by taking as his paradigm the development of a loving couple from the moment when the lover is struck by the physical beauty of the boy, he is able to centre attention on the *particularity* of beauty, and on its place, in that aspect in the philosophic life.

38 A recent discussion of this aspect of the development from *Symposium* to *Phaedrus* can be found in Santas 1982.

39 I began to address this question in the opening section of this chapter when asking after the place of beauty. In the present section and the one that follows I develop and complete my answer.

40 Notice that the reference to a variety of inspiring gods provides a welcome qualification of the previous dichotomy between those for whom the presence of the beautiful boy does and those for whom it does not 'sharply' or 'quickly' (*oxeōs*, 250e2) recall the vision of beauty itself. Socrates here recognises that the kind of idealism represented by memory of the divine may be present also in the love of non-philosophers, although in a lesser degree (see 252c3–4: the follower of Zeus is able to support the heaviest weight of love's wings). He returns to a multiple ranking of lives, of the sort we encountered before in his cosmic law of incarnation (at 248c2–e4); suggesting, I take it, that the world does not divide neatly into the 'philosophic' and 'conventional' lovers who held our attention in the previous two sections (nor, for that matter, into the nine ranks of incarnation, or the twelve Olympian types), but that these are simplified models against which the character of real people can be judged. Notice also that there is considerable overlap between the nine ranks of incarnation and the various Olympian types. Thus the 'philosophic' follower of Zeus would correspond to the first rank; the 'kingly' (*basilikon*, 253b2) follower of Hera would find a place in the second rank with the 'law-abiding king' (*basileōs ennomou*, 248d4); the follower of Apollo belongs presumably in the fifth rank with the prophets (cf. 265b3); and so on. But the match is not precise (the follower of Ares, for example, would seem to belong, if anywhere, in the second rank with the 'warlike' king and general,

248d4; but that is where we put the follower of Hera also). This is only to be expected if, as I contend, Plato wants to contrast the fuzziness of human character with the artificial sharpness of these divisions.

41 I find this point well discussed in Griswold 1981, 488–9.

42 Notice the implication: encountering the boy need not be what first awakens the lover to the philosophic life – though this is the most striking case for Socrates' purposes – but, I take it, might rather confirm or re-confirm him in a way of life in which he is already engaged.

43 The punctuation of this stretch of text is much disputed. I am putting a colon after *agapōsi* and a comma after *arytōsin*. This is more or less how Robin punctuates (R. 48), and his translation strikes me as the best. I take it, then, that a contrast is being drawn between the exclusivity of the lover's link with Zeus and the generosity with which he spreads its effects around. Hackforth (H. 100 n.2) adopts an emendation (*kh'an* for *k'an*) which blunts this contrast, and translates: 'the draughts which they draw from Zeus they pour out, like Bacchants, into the soul of the beloved'. Yet I must admit that the unemended Greek reads a little awkwardly; and the contrast in question would emerge well enough from the passage as a whole. De Vries offers a quite different interpretation (de Vr. apud 253a6), but one which I think mistaken. He follows Verdenius in holding that at 252e5–253a6 Socrates is talking about lovers in general rather than philosophic lovers in particular, and thus at 253a6 the mention of Zeus would *recall* us to the case of the philosophic lovers (the appropriate translation would run: 'And if they draw off their inspiration from Zeus ...', i.e. 'and if they are philosophers ...'). But surely at 252e5 the words 'the practice' (*tōi epitēdeumati*) in the phrase 'and if they have not yet launched into the practice' can only refer, being definite, to the immediately preceding efforts of the *philosophic* lover to foster philosophy in his beloved? So that the description at 252e5–253a6 would not be general at all.

44 This analogy plays on the belief that ophthalmia could be contracted from visual contact alone (see de Vr. apud 255d4–5).

45 Hackforth puts this very clearly: 'This account of "counter-love" is based on the principle that the ... love of the [beloved], no less than that of the [lover], must originate in the sight of physical beauty, and on the complementary fact that the physical beauty resides wholly in the person of the [beloved]' (H. 108–9).

46 Notice that it is as a result of the emotions which the boy's physical beauty stirred up that the lover is said to 'scorn all those conventions and social graces (*nomimōn te kai euskhēmonōn*) on which he formerly prided himself' (252a4–6).

47 But curiosity is a terrible thing, and I have a further question about the 'physical' conduct of their relationship, which I will broach at this point. Why does Plato insist that the lovers not consummate their

sexual desire (as it quite clear from the contrast between philosophic lovers and lovers of the 'second-rank' that is drawn at 256b7–e2), when generally (as we have seen in the context of the *Republic*) he countenances the satisfaction of appetite provided it remain under the limits imposed by the highest part of soul? Any answer must be speculative; but it is striking that Socrates not only imagines the philosophic lover touching the boy (255b8) but goes so far as to envisage them in bed together, and having to control their desire (255e2–256a6). This suggests that what worries Plato is not so much sexual contact as orgasm – possibly as being simply too strong, too dissolving of the self, for the 'charioteer' of the philosopher's soul to allow and yet maintain overall control (which is his job, as we shall later see). There may be a parallel worth drawing with the thoughts on this topic of John Humphrey Noyes, founder in the nineteenth century of a utopian community at Oneida which resembled in many of its external social arrangements – such as multiple marriage – the community of guardians in Plato's *Republic*. In the interests of 'moral restraint' (as well as contraception) Noyes developed a method of heterosexual intercourse structured around the male's avoidance of orgasm. Like a 'skillful boatman' negotiating a stream in the 'three conditions of a fall', he was to confine 'his excursions to the region of easy rowing', or at most venture gingerly into 'the course of rapids above the fall', but not to run his boat over it, except for the purpose of conception; see Noyes (1872) 1975, 8–9 (I thank Mark Migotti for the reference).

48 Admittedly, the action of the *Phaedrus* is unusual for showing Socrates affected by inspiration of a poetic sort, coming in a spurt from which he recovers, and remarking on that fact (238c5–6 with 241e1–5; 257a3–6; 265b6–c3). But I have argued that the very vividness of the contrast between Socrates inspired and Socrates sober works to show (and here I allow slogans to recall those places where I have elaborated my case) that just as there is seriousness in his poetry, so he never ceases to be inspired even when prosaic.

49 And for Vlastos it clearly does. Thus he sees Plato's as the 'polar opposite of the ideal which has molded the image of the deity in the Hebraic and Christian traditions: that of a Being whose perfection empowers it to love the imperfect; of a Father who cares for each of his children as they are, does not proportion affection to merit, gives it no more to the righteous than to the perverse and deformed' (Vlastos (1969) 1981, 33).

50 I am thinking here of the arguments in Kosman 1976. I draw on Vlastos and Kosman for convenient and properly trenchant statements of the two sides in this debate; but see also, among many other references that could be given, Nussbaum 1979, 133–4. Burger 1980, 67 cautiously maintains the more familiar view of Platonic love: 'Socrates seems to

suggest that love is always for desire itself and not for the object of desire.'

51 Notice that I say 'commanding' rather than 'exclusive' position. In other words, this is not to deny the otherness of the partner its proper place, in a balance between commonality and divergence. It is indeed to say, however, that the point of equilibrium is canted towards the side of commonality; that its balance, in the terminology of the *Laws*, is the equality of Zeus rather than arithmetical equality (see *Lg.* 756e9–758a2). My criticism here is similar in pattern to what can be found, as it were on a macroscopic level, in two notable attempts (among others) to restore 'communitarianism' in ethics: MacIntyre 1981 and Lovibond 1983.

52 For convenience of analysis I am considering these two paths in sequence; but in the text the description of the struggle within the lover's soul is sandwiched between the general account of how lovers mould their beloved and the detail of the boy's opening up to his lover, which I discussed together in the previous two sections. In evoking the boy's reaction Socrates in fact combines both paths: the external perspective of the partners' mutual moulding of each other (through the reflected stream of desire), and the internal perspective of the growth of the boy's own psychic plumage and the tussling of his charioteer and horses. But the paths are most completely mapped through the behaviour of the lover (the behaviour of the beloved, as we might expect, evinces only an 'echo'); hence my order of interpretation.

53 The good horse does not take part in this exchange of roles: a significant fact, which I consider in the next section.

54 I use 'word of command' to translate *keleusmati monon kai logōi*, 253d7. There is a pun on *logōi*: both 'speech' and 'reason'.

55 Notice that the three uses of the word *kentrōn* occur in consecutive sentences. Hackforth found the conjunction 'awkward' (H. 104 n.1). Van Herwerden emended the goad felt by the charioteer into wings (*pterōn* for *kentrōn* at 254a1) and is rightly criticised by de Vr. apud 253e6–7.

56 After all, the phrase 'goad of itching desire' directly ascribes desire (*pothos*) to the charioteer with or without the metaphor of the goad. Several commentators remark upon it: Th. 73; R.ci n.1; Sinaiko 1965, 94.

57 Grote has a perceptive comment on this point. Speaking of the shock 'at once on the senses and the intellect' delivered by 'the visible manifestation of beauty' he explains: 'It is a passion of violent and absorbing character; which may indeed take a sensual turn, by the misconduct of the unruly horse in the team, producing in that case nothing but corruption and mischief – but which may also take a virtuous, sentimental turn, and becomes in that case the most powerful

stimulus towards mutual improvement in both the two attached friends' (Grote 1885, 14).

58 The bad horse intends an act of *hybris* (253e3; 254c3): not actual 'rape', but a completely shameless and importunate accosting (see Dover 1978, 34–9). The joint protestation of the charioteer and good horse that he is compelling them to commit a 'terrible and unlawful' act (254b1) makes it quite clear that he does not intend a legitimate seduction.

59 *homologēsante poiēsein to keleuomenon.* Admittedly, the term *keleuein* alone is sometimes to be translated as 'urge', with no implication of verbal command; and is so used of the appetitive part of soul at *Rp.* IV 439c6. But in context it becomes clear that the bad horse gives his commands verbally.

60 'He rebuked them in anger, vehemently upbraiding them ...' (*eloidorēsen orgēi, polla kakizōn*). Although both *loidorein* and *kakizein* admit the connotation of an insulting or slanderous use of language, this is certainly not always present – as is shown by an example later in the dialogue at 275e4, *ouk en dikēi loidorētheis*, 'not justifiably rebuked', where the very need to add the qualification demonstrates the neutrality of the verb. Compare *Rp.* 560a1, where *nouthetountōn te kai kakizontōn* describes father and friends in the act of 'advising and criticising' a degenerate youth.

61 Notice that the pose neatly usurps the 'commanding' (*hēgemonikos*) role that the charioteer, as representative of the philosophic and therefore naturally 'commanding' part of soul (see 252e3), ought himself to be playing.

62 Recall that the bad horse was initially described as 'barely' (*mogis*, again) yielding to the charioteer's whip (253e4–5). The parallel sets off the verbality of the laborious persuasion here all the more by contrast: a verbality stimulated by the bad horse's exhortation, not initiated by the charioteer.

63 Notice that the euphemistically titled 'proposal' (*logous*, 254d6) which the lewd horse intends to make on this second approach is mentioned in the midst of his violence and *after* we have heard his neighing, as if to accentuate the difference in this repetition; how differently the proposal sounds, as it were, on its second occurrence.

64 Given the context, there may be a pun intended on *kerkon* – the word here used for 'tail' – which can also mean 'penis' (LSJ s.v. *kerkos* I.2).

65 Later in the relationship between the lovers, when the boy has come to return the philosopher's love, Socrates imagines them going so far as to share the same bed. The lustful horse of the older man, understandably revived for the occasion, overcomes the paralysis of fear to which the charioteer had reduced him and makes bold to speak out. And again it is the language of sweet reason that we hear, in an argument based this

time on the very brutality he has endured: 'he has his piece to say to the charioteer, and claims that he deserves a little enjoyment in return for all his suffering' (255e5–256a1).

66 Most commentators content themselves with noting that the charioteer feels desire on his own account and is the agent who transfers excitement at the beautiful boy to the whole soul (253e5–254a1). Jacqueline de Romilly, however, gives due recognition to his violence: 'il s'agit là d'un dressage; mais la violence de ce dressage est sans exemple' (de Romilly 1982, 107). Ronna Burger is nearer still to the mark: 'The transformation of the charioteer in the presence of the beloved links him more closely to the natural force of desire moving the dark horse than to the conventional force of shame restraining the white one' (Burger 1980, 66). But neither de Romilly nor Burger sees that the brutishness of the bad horse is correspondingly muted – the former because she does not examine the beast's behaviour in any detail; while the latter misunderstands it. She considers the bad horse 'not even susceptible to the power of speech' (65), and with reference to his revival when the lovers are in bed together (255e4–256a1) supposes that 'having suffered and grown wise, [he] has apparently become articulate in demanding of the charioteer some enjoyment for his pains' (67); but we have seen that his articulacy is nothing new.

67 Such behaviour was for Greek culture an important aspect of the horse's power, and given cult recognition in the figure of Poseidon Hippios and what seems to have been an associated demon, Taraxippos, 'Horse-Startler' (see Detienne and Vernant 1978, 187–213, esp. 191, 208 n.28). 'Taraxippos' was also the name given to various markers on race-courses such as the red rock at Nemea described by Pausanias (VI 20.19), 'the flash from which, as strong as fire, incites terror in the horses'.

68 Notice the implication of the term 'starting-line': what the bad horse considers the end of his contest (contact with the boy) the charioteer sees as just the beginning of his.

69 LSJ s.v. *hysplēx* 2 explain it differently. They take *hysplēx* in its sense of 'wound-up spring' rather than 'starting-line' and paraphrase: 'throwing himself back as from a *hysplēx*, i.e. violently'. Yet surely the equine context makes it so much more natural to take the word in the sense of 'starting-line' (as most commentators do) that this interpretation is not a real alternative (de Vr. apud 254e1–2 is too tolerant in granting that it 'is certainly admissible'). With the riding position referred to in the phrase *anepesen hyptia* (254b8) compare Xenophon, *Eq. Mag.* 3.14; *Eq.* 8.7–8.

70 *odynais edōken*: a highly-coloured phrase ('a Homericism', says de Vr. ad loc.).

71 Alternatively: 'at the same time is compelled'. The conjunction *hama*

('at the same time') implies no purposeful link between the two actions, but merely states that they occurred *together*.

72 I am not pretending that what I have said in the previous section is somehow uncontaminated by interpretation. I simply mean that I am about to give only one among possible interpretations – obviously, the one that at present I consider strongest – of the exchange of roles just described.

73 It is in this sense that he is a 'friend to imposture' (*alazoneias hetairos*, 253e3). He will choose whichever means is the most efficient for attaining his goal. All he cares about as such is the goal. He identifies himself neither with the persuasive nor indeed with the brutal means towards it – but since the end is itself brutal, his 'imposture' shows up more readily when he adopts persuasive means. Although *alazoneia* can also mean 'boastfulness' (H. 103 offers 'vainglory'; Hamilton 1973, 62: 'boastfulness'; R.50: 'gloriole'), this is an unsuitable translation in context. The bad horse does not seem particularly boastful; but he is clearly meretricious in his methods.

74 In the terminology used by Harry Frankfurt in an article that has helped crystallise my ideas on this topic, the bad horse would to this extent be like the 'wanton', who has 'first-order desires' but no 'second-order volitions' (see Frankfurt 1971, 11).

75 I follow Hackforth's construal of this phrase (see H. 103 n.3).

76 Compare this from the account of the tripartite soul in Moline 1981, 70: the highest part of soul has 'a potential for deep psychological understanding of the other parts' that the other parts 'utterly lack'.

77 So too the sculpted model of soul described in *Rp.* IX 588b–e portrays the best part of soul (and also, be it noted, the whole person) as a human being and the two inferior parts as animals (lion and chimaera).

78 *eidon tēn opsin tēn tōn paidikōn astraptousan*, 'they saw the boy's glance flash like lightning' (254b4–5) is a considerably stronger phrase than that which describes what the charioteer first sees: *to erōtikon omma*, 'the erotic eye' (253e5). (I have translated as 'glance' and 'eye' what also permits a less specific anatomisation: 'face', 'sight', or 'vision'.)

79 Graeser 1969, 44 and Burger 1980, 66 also note this feature of the narrative. Burger draws from it the conclusion discussed in n.66 above; Graeser – over-cautiously, I feel – will assert only that 'Es darf die Funktion des *epithymētikon* nicht ausschliesslich negativ beurteilt werden.'

80 We can now also see why Plato begins his narrative by describing both horses vividly and at length (253c7–e4), but the charioteer not at all; for since only the charioteer cares intrinsically for the proper place of his partners in the soul in addition to his own, he is not to be described independently of them. His portrait is the struggle in the soul.

81 I choose this terminology, of course, in order to recall the methods of the rhetorician as analysed in chapter three.

82 Notice that this is not a once-for-all experience, but happens many times over before the dominance of the charioteer is established (see 254e5–6); and even then it may not be permanent (hence the lesser grade of lovers envisaged at 256b7 sq., who have the right ambition but succumb to sexual curiosity).

83 The difficulty of wringing out a simple answer follows, I take it, from the kind of struggle that is being portrayed: the philosopher's struggle to make his feeling for the contingent essential to himself, as discussed in my analysis of his allegorical pain.

84 I have been influenced in what follows by Harry Frankfurt's discussion of what he terms 'volitional necessity' (Frankfurt 1982, 263–6).

85 Notice the implication: that incapability of failure is simply definitive of the true philosophic type.

86 Compare this from the *Cleitophon* (407d): 'How could anyone willingly choose so confessedly bad a course [viz. injustice]? Anyone, you reply, who is mastered by his pleasures (*hettōn . . . tōn hēdonōn*). But then doesn't this very condition go against his will (*oukoun kai tout' akousion*), if to win mastery is an expression of the will (*eiper to nikain hekousion*)?'

87 Recall, however, the comparison with the charioteers of the gods' souls in the fourth section of the previous chapter ('Myth as explanation: gods and men'). The charioteer's intrinsic concern in both cases is not with the actual creatures that he finds hitched to the yoke but with *whatever* is on the other end of his reins.

88 Compare this from Frankfurt 1982, 263: 'An encounter with necessity of this sort [sc. 'volitional necessity'] characteristically affects a person less by impelling him into a certain course of action than by somehow making it apparent to him that every apparent alternative to that course is unthinkable.'

89 And the foregoing is as close as I shall come in this work to dealing with the 'extraordinary fact' which Gregory Vlastos posed as a problem and left hanging in Vlastos (1969) 1981, 27 n.80: namely that 'our ultra-rationalist, Plato' should 'not only have described, but *defined*' love as madness, and have associated it, as madness, 'in the closest terms with philosophy no less than with the mystic cults'. My treatment differs from an account such as Hackforth's in that I do not set philosophic 'madness' in direct contrast to 'the rational' (see H. 61: 'It is clear that Plato is in this dialogue quite exceptionally conscious of the value of the imaginative, as against the rational, power of the human soul'; and cf. Nussbaum 1982, 103, 107). To this extent I find myself in agreement with Griswold 1980, 538–9 and 1985, 15. However, Griswold seems to understand the 'madness' of philosophy as the vertigo induced by a

regress of justification in the matter of self-knowledge; but although I
have myself (in the opening chapter of this book) shown the connection
between philosophic madness and the attempt to walk into a
background that is always one step ahead, I would not correlate the
phenomenological quality which merits the title 'madness' with a
feeling of cognitive vertigo or uncertainty. The element of uncertainty
lies not in the experience itself but in what the lover is to build upon it
(the background has its horizon in the future); and the quality of
madness is to be sought in the fact that the experience captivates and
overwhelms the lover, shaking up his life.

90 Thus, although I basically agree with the claim in Irwin 1977, 232, 236
that since 'the rational part' is distinguished from the others by its desire
to realise the good of the whole person over the course of a whole life,
the second-order choice to realise that particular desire is the most
reasonable choice, I have been attempting to explain in addition how
Plato's philosopher, the paragon of rationality, does not just feel that he
would be *unreasonable not* to opt for this desire, but feels positively
compelled – by reverence, by love – to do so. (I consider Irwin's views
further in n.95 below.)

91 Here I fill out the parallelism first noted in chapter four.

92 Representative of this response are Irwin 1977, 191–5, 226–48;
Moline 1981, 52–78; and Annas 1981, 109–52. Penner 1971 gave a
seminal account of the cognition attributable to the 'irrational' part of
soul; Gosling 1973, 52–5 recognises that the conflict between parts of
soul described in *Rp.* IV is a conflict between different desires.
Moravcsik 1982a adapts these insights to a general classification of the
emotions. Watson 1975 takes up Penner 1971 in the context of the
modern literature on free agency. For representatives of the more
traditional approach, see the roll-call in Moline 1981, 202 n.2.

93 The noble horse, as always, occupies a transitional position. Because he
represents the sense of honour and shame, the actions that he favours
will tend to accord with those favoured by the charioteer; but the good
horse does not share the aims of the charioteer in motivating such
action, but looks only to the figure of the moment that the whole person
will cut. Indeed, it is only because the actions that he approves coincide
in this way with those that the charioteer would approve that the good
horse is distinct from the bad. Notice also that although only the
charioteer aims by nature at how best the life of the whole person
should go, this is not of course to say that a life simply could not be
organised under the guidance of the other parts of the soul; on the
contrary, the degenerate forms of life described in the eighth book of the
Republic are examples of just such lives.

94 Moline 1981, 59 rightly draws attention to the fact that these are not
the only labels used by Plato in the *Republic* – although interpreters

have gravitated towards them under the influence of 'faculty'-theory –
but that he also adopts a series of terms with the common characteristic
of being compounded with '*philo-*', 'lover of . . .', thus: *philomathes* or
philosophon, 'lover of learning', 'lover of wisdom'; *philonikon* or
philotimon, 'lover of victory', 'lover of honour'; *philokhrēmaton* or
philokerdes, 'lover of possessions', 'lover of gain.'

95 In Irwin 1977, esp. 230–48, I find too commanding an emphasis on the
capacity the reasoning part has for second-order decision. Thus,
referring to the degenerate lives described in *Rp*. VIII, he writes as if in
each case the choice to live such a life is made by the reasoning part (e.g.
of the timocrat: 'The rational decision is a second order decision to
prefer one of his first-order goals above others', 231); but this seems
untrue to the text. The oligarchic type, for example, 'installs the
appetitive and money-loving part on the throne' of his soul (553c5–6).
It is not his rational part that is kingmaker, but, so far as we are told, he,
the person; that is, we are told only that this rebellion *takes place* in his
soul (as a result of his 'fear', 553b8). So far from making the second-
order decision to prefer a first-order goal, the reasoning part is made by
King Appetite 'to sit on the ground before him like a slave' (553d1–2),
together with the spirited part; and the king then proceeds to make the
reasoning part work at nothing else but how to make the most money –
which is *not* to imply that the reasoning faculty is all on the side of the
'reasoning' part, but to say that the force of the oligarch's appetite is
such as to make him devote his *whole life* to money-making. In this
sense, the lower parts of the soul too are capable, when need arises, of
second-order desires: desires that operate upon other desires. This is not
a trick that only the charioteer can perform; but only for the charioteer
is it more than just a trick – only he *cares* about such desires.

96 These are the replies in Annas 1981, 142–6 and Moline 1981, 74–8
respectively.

97 Here it is worth remarking again that whereas Socrates paints a comic-
strip of the good and bad horses (253d3–e5) he gives us no direct
portrayal of the charioteer (see n.80 above); perhaps to suggest (in
addition) that his life would be, not a caricature, but an ideal, and so
beyond easy picturing.

98 This explanation permits configuration of the tripartite divisions of
soul in the two works but avoids the consequence, to which Julius
Moravcsik rightly objects, of ascribing to Plato 'the doctrine of original
sin – that is, the view that an essential part of human nature is basically
corrupt' (Moravcsik 1982b, 46 n.4). The lowest part of the soul is not
'basically corrupt', on my interpretation; but, to be sure, it is not to be
thought of in an entirely neutral manner. Perhaps the way to put this is
to say that it is basically *prone* to corruption. It is liable to go wrong;
but it is not consummately wrong from the first. This idea is subtly but

importantly different from the doctrine of original sin (if my understanding of that doctrine is correct).

99 Dare I suggest, then, that Plato was aware of the possibilities of what we now call 'faculty'-psychology – and found them degenerate? Notice also that on this approach to Plato's psychology there is no need to assume that in his critique of rhetoric Socrates is recommending a different type of psychological investigation than that which we find here in his palinode. It has seemed to some (e.g. H. 147 n.1 and de Vr. apud 271d1–2) that in recommending that the philosophic orator be able to enumerate the 'forms' (*eidē*, 271d2) or 'kinds' (*genē*, 271b2) of soul he envisages a catalogue of types of *person* – an enquiry different from (though not incompatible with) that into the components of an individual soul. Others cite the wavering in terminology and the fact that the 'forms' of soul at 271d3 are said to be that 'from which (*hothen*) some take on one character, others another' as evidence that Socrates' recommendation shifts between both types of enquiry – the 'forms' being components of the individual soul; the 'kinds' being types of person (see the summary in H. 147 n.1). But on my interpretation there are not two different types of enquiry but two perspectives on a single type; and there is no need for the awkward terminological distinction between 'forms' and 'kinds'(awkward because Socrates would just be using it without flagging it). For we have seen that for Plato the components of soul can always be seen both as particular agents within an individual and as the whole persons which their dominance would tend to make of the individual. Notice that the only examples Socrates gives us of the psychological distinctions with which the orator must correlate the different kinds of speech, at 277b5–c3, are those of the 'variegated' (*poikilēi*) as opposed to the 'simple' (*haplēi*) soul (or 'nature', *physei*) – for whom the appropriate kinds of talk, respectively, are talk 'that runs the whole scale' (*panarmonious*) and 'simple' talk. Hackforth can only assume that a 'new point' is being made (H. 161 n.1). But the passage is meant as a 'reminder' of what has gone before (see 277b4); and it seems to me that Plato is reminding the reader of the main contour of difference within the allegorical soul: that between the animals who simply advance their desires, and the charioteer who runs the full scale of voices within the soul. And he reminds us of this in a piece that speaks with as many voices as a variegated soul could wish.

7. Writing the Conversation

1 In the sentence after this he refers only to good speaking, but passages such as 271b7–c4 show that this is shorthand for 'speaking and writing'; for he shifts between labels without making a point of the difference.

2   Here I maintain the syntax of the Greek, which permits attribution of this 'understanding' both to the mode in which the speaker speaks and to the content of what the listener receives.

3   The passage is non-committal as to whether either Homer or Solon did have the proper attitude to their writing (although the fact that they make a trio with Lysias suggests scepticism); but since both of them can be considered to have written about their abiding preoccupations, the passage shows that treating writing as a 'game' has nothing to do with choosing unserious *topics*.

4   The interpretation in Mackenzie 1982 can be located somewhere between the 'standard' and the 'ironic'. Like the former, she takes the devaluation of writing to be meant seriously, but goes further by insisting that to repudiate writing *in writing* is to produce a 'full-blooded antinomy' (65); like the latter, she thinks Plato's own writing – at least in the *Phaedrus* – completely escaped the dangers of writing (for by the challenge of its very paradoxicality it comes 'unequivocally alive', 72), but she does not go so far as to propose that in such writing Plato thought philosophy found its highest expression. I have more to say about her position in n.32 below.

5   See Derrida (1968) 1972. A Derridean approach to the *Phaedrus* is developed by Stanley Fish in Fish 1972, 1–21.

6   The interpretation that I am about to work out through contrast with these does not lack for congeners. I find something similar in Griswold 1980 and 1983, and in Altieri 1985. Nevertheless I have some disagreements with both. Thus, with Altieri's assertion that 'we are invited' – when we assess Socrates' words here and indeed in the dialogue as a whole – 'to concentrate on what is done, not on the descriptive value of a set of assertions', I could agree only if allowed to substitute *'as well as* on the descriptive value ...'. For my point of disagreement with Griswold see n.32 below. The best general account known to me of Plato's attitude towards and use of the written word (an account I find congenial with my particular interpretation of this aspect of the *Phaedrus*) is the opening chapter of Wieland 1982.

7   Had he wished, Plato could easily have avoided the verbal link by substituting for Phaedrus' *'hypomnēson'* the synonym *'anamnēson'*. Notice – in view of the 'osmosis' that I discuss here – that in his mythical hymn Socrates describes the stirring of the philosopher's memory of his divine vision by what he encounters in this world as 'the proper use of reminders (*hypomnēmasin*)' (249c7): a rubric which could apply without verbal change to Plato's type of philosophic writing. (However, he adopts the alternative form *anamnēsis* at 249c2 and 249d6.)

8   This would also be a delicate way for Plato to imply that the use of the written word was sapping the skills of memory.

9   With the advent of the computer such internal argument need no longer

be impotent, for dubious texts can be compared with those of known authorship in terms of stylistic traits which, it is claimed, are unfakeable, because too picayune to be apparent even to the original author, and detectable only through number-crunching frequency analysis. But Plato, of course, could not have anticipated this.

10 This is not to imply that Plato was writing only for a readership of the distant future. The irony of his gesture, if not its actual effect, could have been readily apparent to a contemporary.

11 Notice the consequence if the speech is in fact a Platonic spoof: that Plato would have given himself permission to cook up his own version of a Lysianic performance – the very act that he has Socrates prevent Phaedrus from doing. The act, then, would not be dangerous or wrong in itself, but only in relation to the aim with which it is performed.

12 Notice, however, that, for exactly the reasons which have led me to mark my distance from historical curiosity, I do not assume that the historical Plato premeditated this gesture. That is to say, I am pleased to think it, but the truth of this assumption does not decide the philosophic value of my interpretation.

13 Compare the section 'Apologia pro capitulo suo' in chapter one. In practice I have confined myself up to now mostly to what the cicadas show up about the author's performance rather than the interpreter's – as it were, assigning to the interpreter the place of beloved rather than lover.

14 At 277e8–9 there is a completely explicit statement of this point. Socrates adds to his summary of the unseriousness of writing the consideration that his criticism applies equally to the kind of spoken language represented by the declamation of poetry with no aim to instruct and no opportunity for discussion. Many earlier editors deleted this passage, and I am inclined to agree with them. Not only is the language suspiciously awkward (the repetition of *lekhthēnai* ... *elekhthēsan* makes an odd jingle, given that the terms serve quite unrelated functions for the sense of the whole sentence), but it would be strange for Plato to be so flatly explicit after the elaborate subtlety of what has preceded. The lines have the heavy-handedness one might expect from a glossator. De Vr. apud 277e8–9 gives a plausible account of how they might have attached themselves to the Platonic text.

15 See her p. 101: the 'primary distinction' is not between speech and writing as such but 'between speech or writing which is merely playful and that which legitimately fulfills the claim to serious worth'.

16 Except perhaps her point that in 'its character as an address to a universal audience' writing is better suited to promote the values of 'instruction' rather than 'persuasion', and that its benefits are therefore akin to those of 'overcoming the particularity of erotic attachment';

benefits which are recognised in the course of the dialogue by the fact
that Socrates comes closest to 'the true goal of *erōs*', the universal
perspective of the place above the heavens, not in his speeches on love
but rather in his account of dialectic (Collection and Division) in the
second part of the dialogue – and with this account his speeches are in
'tension' (Burger 1980, 102–3). This argument relies on a view of the
dialogue as a whole with which, as should by now be plain, I deeply
disagree: namely, that Plato thought the true bench-mark for the
philosophic life was set by the concerns and procedures of the second
part of the dialogue rather than the first (and would advocate the use of
the written word as conforming better to such a bench-mark). I hope to
have shown that what Plato thought needed to be overcome in the
'possessive particularity of erotic attachment' was not the particularity
but only the possessiveness.

17 See e.g. p. 172 of Derrida (1968) 1972. For this reason Derrida is
explicitly ambivalent on the question of Plato's intent (which is after all
part of the very scheme of 'original' and 'trace' that he is examining). He
holds that there is no general answer to the question (108), and so
allows himself in some cases to consider it of little importance (e.g.
172), while in others weaving a definite statement of Plato's intent into
his argument (e.g. 124: 'mais ce dont *rêve* Platon, c'est d'un mémoire
sans signe'). But he clearly thinks that Plato was attempting to cope with
a problem the consequences of which he could not fully control even in
his own text.

18 Egypt for Plato is the land where the art of writing – that is, the art of
keeping written records – has attained its fullest realisation; as is clear
from Critias' story in the *Timaeus* (21a7–25d7).

19 'On commence par répéter sans savoir – par un mythe – la définition de
l'écriture: répéter sans savoir' (Derrida (1968) 1972, 84).

20 Thus he infers from Socrates' words that 'La vérité de l'écriture, c'est-à-
dire, nous allons le voir, la non-vérité, nous ne pouvons la découvrir en
nous-mêmes par nous-mêmes. Et elle n'est pas l'objet d'une science,
seulement d'une histoire récitée' (83); and later, speaking of the same
vertiginous effect under the rubric of the '*pharmakon*', he argues that
no system of philosophic terms can properly capture it: 'Le *pharmakon*,
sans rien être par lui-même, les excède toujours comme leur fonds sans
fond' (146).

21 The other arts invented by Thoth do not, indeed, range over the whole
scale but are mathematical in nature – arithmetic, geometry, astronomy
– as are the two games he also brings to Ammon: draughts and dice.
These are just the arts that most readily permit conscious formalisation,
while representing skills which we all require and use to some extent,
less formally and consciously, in our daily lives. Compare how in Book
VII of the *Republic* (522d), in the discussion of arithmetic as a

propaedeutic, Socrates points out that although Palamedes is credited with the invention of arithmetic at Troy, one can hardly imagine that before that moment Agamemnon did not even know how many feet he had. It is worth noting that the list of Thoth's inventions closely resembles that attributed to Palamedes in various tragic fragments (e.g. Aeschylus fr. 59 N; Sophocles fr. 399, 438 N) and in Gorgias' *Defence of Palamedes*, 30. Indeed, Ammon's tag for writing – 'drug for reminder' (*hypomnēseōs pharmakon*) rather than 'memory-drug' (*mnēmēs pharmakon*) – may be calqued on the phrase which Euripides has his hero apply to writing, his new invention, in the *Palamedes* (fr. 578 N): 'drug for forgetfulness' (*lēthēs pharmaka*). This would reflect the irony that Palamedes was undone by his own invention, in the shape of Odysseus' forged letter to Priam. (Perhaps too a certain wariness is expressed with regard to the formal dialectics of a Zeno: the 'Eleatic Palamedes' of 261d6.)

22 I adopt here the excellent turn of phrase in Hamilton's translation.

23 The Greek term has the semantic stretch indicated by the two translations, though the pejorative sense is the prevalent one (see LSJ sub voc.).

24 Th. apud 275b and De Vr. apud 275b8 discuss the proverbial status of the phrase, with references.

25 Accordingly, we should not imagine that Ammon is a mouthpiece for Plato – as even Derrida is prone to think: 'Or cette ambiguité [i.e. of the *pharmakon*], Platon, par la bouche du roi, veut la maîtriser' (117). This would be to ignore the fact that Ammon is a voice in a myth, and speaks for what Plato knows cannot now be had. If anything, the philosopher is a combination of Thoth, the inventor, and Ammon, the judge of arts (see 274e7–9); for by attempting to judge the good life, the philosopher brings it into being. It does not exist antecedent to his judgment, nor can the acts of judging and inventing be neatly distinguished and dated.

26 Of course, Phaedrus' sceptical remark does not have the ring of a serious request for enquiry into the sources of the myth; rather, it is just his way of suggesting that Socrates is helping himself to authority here. By taking the remark rather more seriously than it would normally be received – that is, by seeming a little naïve – Socrates is able to bring out (for the reader, at least) the real importance of his presenting the issue through a myth about a more naïve world.

27 Notice that he does not, even in mythical terms, speak directly for the people of that time. He uses the voice of their gods – who are indeed their gods just because they import the perspective of the future (Ammon is an oracular god; see 275c8) back into that distant present.

28 It should be clear that to think this true in no way commits me to the belief that the 'ironic' mode of interpretation is the genre appropriate to the reading of all Platonic dialogues (although 'ironic' interpreters cite

this point from the *Phaedrus* in their support). That Plato thought his genuine opinions might be fetishised if committed to writing is reason for him either not to write at all, or, having decided to write, to be sure to alert the reader to his worry; but it is no reason at all to commit to writing the exact opposition of his genuine opinions, as 'ironic' interpreters would have it. Indeed, such a procedure could not but encourage us to make a fetish of the text, as a repository of secrets which can be opened only by the ironic key. For a general critique of the 'ironic' method, as practised by Leo Strauss, see Burnyeat 1985a and 1985b.

29 Notice that at 258a1–b5 Socrates imagines that the politician who plays to the gallery is seeking above all a permanent place in the written legal record (a phenomenon for which contemporary analogues are ready to hand).

30 Not just any conviction is meant, of course, but – and the phrase comes to the pen with an ease ironic enough in this context – the conviction that comes from understanding. For a discussion of the contrast between the growth of this sort of conviction and a 'Cartesian' project of founding knowledge on propositions the truth of which cannot be doubted see Moravcsik 1978, and Annas 1981, 200–1, 212–15, 281–4.

31 It may be thought that I am not properly taking into account the fact that Socrates describes even the activity of writing philosophy in full awareness of its dangers as a 'game' (276d2); which would suggest a heavier devaluation than I countenance. But let us not forget that at 278b7 Socrates refers to the whole course of the day's discussion as a 'game' (*pepaisthō*), and more especially that when he came to show how his speeches exemplified the method of dialectic he was prepared to say that everything about them apart from this fact was 'really played as a game' (*paidiai pepaisthai*) (265c8–9). In discussing this passage in chapter two I pointed out that we must be wary of jumping into the deep end in Socrates' wake. The tendency to examine things not for what they happen to be but for what they exemplify – what makes them important – is indeed a mark of the philosopher; but it is in tension with the need to conduct that examination in the course of a life which, even if exemplary, must also be particular and contingent – a tension seen in the development of the philosophic lover. It is difficult, once we begin to see certain facets of life as a game, to know where to stop; and Plato's sophisticated presentation of Socrates' view of writing invites us to pause over this difficulty.

32 On this point it seems to me that several interpreters exaggerate the difficulty which Socrates' criticism poses for Plato's writing, in order then to accentuate Plato's achievement in coping with it. Thus M. M. Mackenzie (to elaborate in a new context what was said in n.4 above) finds here a 'full-blooded antinomy'; for Plato writes a book 'which

repudiates the writing of books', so that 'if he writes to convince, he writes that writing should not convince us' (Mackenzie 1982, 65); and she finds in Plato's very exploitation of this paradox the means of escaping its consequences, and making the written word 'unequivocally alive' (72). Similarly, Charles Griswold thinks that Plato has to escape a 'criticism intended by its speaker (Socrates) to prohibit all philosophical writing' (Griswold 1980, 532); while Stanley Fish finds in the final pages of the dialogue 'a condemnation . . . of anything written or formally delivered', to which Plato's own writing is immune because it 'does not exhibit the characteristics' of a written artifact (Fish 1972, 9, 14). But surely all these ways of putting it are too strong. Socrates himself, as we have seen, provides an explicit escape-clause for the philosophic writer, and delivers nothing so categorical as a prohibition, or a declaration that nothing written should carry conviction with us. On the other hand, although Plato's writing has that self-consciousness which is the antidote to false expectations, it cannot escape all the dangers of writing – certainly not, for example, the risk of his book falling into the wrong hands; nor the problem of idolatry. Plato must have thought this a risk worth taking; as I explain in the next paragraph of text.

33 Here Plato's relationship with Isocrates is relevant – a fascinating question, to which I cannot devote the space that a proper treatment would require. In the course of Socrates' critique of rhetoric Plato calques not just the ideas but the phrasing of passages from Isocrates' *Against the Sophists*, in which Isocrates inveighs against those who presume to reduce his art to a mere catalogue of rules; and at the close of the dialogue Phaedrus ribs Socrates by telling him to convey the contents of their discussion to Socrates' 'companion' (*hetairon*), the 'beautiful Isocrates' (278e5–9; cf. 279b2), to which Socrates responds by predicting that the young man (as Isocrates would have been at the dramatic date) shows promise for such talk and may go on to realise his philosophic potential (279a3–b3). My speculation is that Isocrates (as rival beloved, so to speak) represents for Plato how a worthy concern for what exceeds articulation by rules in ethical and intellectual practice can degenerate into mere conservatism and hostility to the virtues of reflection.

34 The most thorough-going statement of the central analogies can be found in Fish 1972, 17–20, who presents them in tabular form, and prefaces his tables with the following: 'It is in this implied equation of the dialectician and the good lover, on the one hand, and the rhetorician–writer and the bad lover on the other, that the unity of the *Phaedrus* – so much sought for by modern commentators – is to be found.' Especially prevalent among commentators is the inclination to identify the dialecticians of the dialogue's second half with the

philosophic lovers of the first (H. 164 offers an exemplary statement of this position).

35 In n.7 above I pointed out that the 'reminders' in both cases are strikingly linked by vocabulary.

36 In terms of the threefold classification of goods that opens the second book of the *Republic* (357bc), loving the boy is not a good desired just for its own sake (the first kind), nor a good desired only for its consequences (the third kind), but one of the second kind: desired both for its own sake and for the benefits that result from it.

37 To be more exact: even as a mere tool, I pointed out that writing has certain intrinsic capacities which render it apt for a particular set of results (bad ones) within its larger domain; so that in this case too, more than just the input of the user needs to be taken into account. But the difference remains, because the specifications of the inanimate tool, unlike those of a living boy, are fixed in advance and standard across usage; therefore they cancel out of the equation.

38 At 236b5 Socrates calls Lysias Phaedrus' 'beloved' (*paidikois*), and at 275b4 calls Phaedrus his 'lover' (*erastēs*); and again at 279b2–3 Lysias appears as Phaedrus' 'beloved' (in conjunction with the young Isocrates whom Phaedrus sees as filling an equivalent role for Socrates).

39 The 'metic' quality of the countryside beyond the walls in this dialogue is perhaps marked also by the presence there of the altar of Boreas; for his myth centres on the problem of naturalisation. Oreithyia, after all, was a native of impeccable lineage, daughter of the very first of the earth-born kings of Athens (Erechtheus), while Boreas was a savage god from the distant North. He was rejected as a suitor for that reason, and so sought by violence the entry that had been denied to persuasion (see Aeschylus fr. 281 N; Ovid, *Metamorphoses* VI 682 sq.). The Athenians came to terms and gave him his cult (Herodotus VII 189; Pausanias I 19.5); but kept his altar outside the city limits.

40 Notice that Socrates lays emphasis on Phaedrus' intention to be his own audience; for at 228c4 he asks the 'Phaedrus' before him to huddle with the 'Phaedrus' whose intentions he has just reconstructed and consider how they will jointly react to Socrates' desire to hear Lysias' speech.

41 Phaedrus vacillates in particular in his opinion of Lysias, his supposed darling (257c2–7), and only a chivvying from Socrates prevents him estranging himself from his beloved without proper thought (257c8–d3) – a comment on the value of their love.

42 This statement in no way represents a retreat on my part from the position that both parts of the dialogue offer an equally serious contribution to its message. That Socrates should retreat as he does is precisely what the philosophic lover is tempted to do, and, as we saw, is the source of his pain; so that the lover does not somehow *dispense* with the need for the perspective of the dialogue's second part. Still, Socrates

in this dialogue is no philosophic lover – in the simple but crucial sense that he and Phaedrus are not represented as being in love.

BIBLIOGRAPHY

Ackrill, J. L. 1953. Rev. R. Hackforth, *Plato's Phaedrus* (Cambridge, 1952), *Mind* N. S. LXII, 246:277–9.

Ackrill, J. L. 1970. 'In Defence of Platonic Division', in O. P. Wood and G. Pitcher, ed., *Ryle*, 373–92. London.

Altieri, C. 1985. 'Plato's Performative Sublime and the Ends of Reading', *New Literary History* XVI, 2:251–73.

Annas, J. 1981. *An Introduction to Plato's Republic*. Oxford.

Barnes, J. 1982. *The Presocratic Philosophers*. Revised Edition. London.

Burger, R. 1980. *Plato's Phaedrus: A Defense of a Philosophic Art of Writing*. Alabama.

Burnyeat, M. F. (unpublished). 'The Passion of Reason in Plato's Phaedrus'.

Burnyeat, M. F. 1980. 'Aristotle on Understanding Knowledge', in E. Berti, ed., *Aristotle on Science: 'The Posterior Analytics'*, 97–139. Padua and New York.

Burnyeat, M. F. 1985a. 'Sphinx without a Secret', *New York Review of Books* 30 May.

Burnyeat, M. F. 1985b. Reply to critics in 'The Studies of Leo Strauss: An Exchange', *New York Review of Books* 10 October.

Cooper, J. M. 1985. 'Aristotle on the Goods of Fortune', *The Philosophical Review* XCIV, 2:173–96.

Cope, E. M. 1867. *An Introduction to Aristotle's Rhetoric*. London.

Crombie, I. M. 1962. *An Examination of Plato's Doctrines*. Vol. I. London.

Derrida, J. (1968) 1972. 'La Pharmacie de Platon', in *La Dissémination*, 71–197. Paris.

Detienne, M. and Vernant, J. P. 1978. *Cunning Intelligence in Greek Culture and Society*. Sussex.

Dover, K. J. 1968. *Lysias and the Corpus Lysiacum*. Berkeley.

Dover, K. J. 1978. *Greek Homosexuality*. Cambridge, Mass.

Fish, S. 1972. *Self-Consuming Artifacts: the Experience of Seventeenth Century Literature*. Berkeley.

Fortenbaugh, W. W. 1966. 'Plato's *Phaedrus* 235c3', *Classical Philology* LXI, 2:108–9.

Frankfurt, H. 1971. 'Freedom of the Will and the Concept of a Person', *Journal of Philosophy* LXVIII, 1:5–20.

Frankfurt, H. 1982. 'The Importance of What We Care About', *Synthese* LIII:257–72.

286

Freud, S. (1905) 1962. *Three Essays on the Theory of Sexuality.* New York.

Gallop, D. 1975. *Plato, 'Phaedo'.* Oxford.

Gosling, J. 1965. 'Similarity in *Phaedo* 73b seq.', *Phronesis* X:151–61.

Gosling, J. 1973. *Plato. The Arguments of the Philosophers.* London.

Gould, T. 1963. *Platonic Love.* New York.

Graeser, A. 1969. *Probleme der platonischen Seelenteilungslehre. Zetemata* Monographien 47. Munich.

Griswold, C. 1980. 'Style and Philosophy: The Case of Plato's Dialogues', *The Monist* LXIII, 4:530–46.

Griswold, C. 1981. 'Self-knowledge and the "*Idea*" of the Soul in Plato's "Phaedrus"', *Revue de Métaphysique et de Morale* LXXXVI:477–94.

Griswold, C. 1983. Rev. R. Burger, *Plato's Phaedrus: A Defense of a Philosophic Art of Writing* (Alabama, 1980), *Independent Journal of Philosophy* IV:158–60.

Griswold, C. 1985. 'Plato's Metaphilosophy', in D. J. O'Meara, ed., *Platonic Investigations*, Studies in Philosophy and the History of Philosophy 13, 1–33. Washington, D.C.

Grote, G. 1885. *Plato and the Other Companions of Sokrates.* Vol. III. London.

Guthrie, W. K. C. 1969. *A History of Greek Philosophy.* Vol. III. Cambridge.

Guthrie, W. K. C. 1975. *A History of Greek Philosophy.* Vol. IV. Cambridge.

Hackforth, R. 1955. *Plato's Phaedo.* Cambridge.

Hamberger, P. 1914. *Die Rednerische Disposition.* Paderborn.

Hamilton, W., trans., 1973. *Plato: Phaedrus and the Seventh and Eighth Letters.* Harmondsworth.

Hellwig, A. 1973. *Untersuchungen zur Theorie der Rhetorik bei Platon und Aristoteles.* Hypomnemata 38. Göttingen.

Helmbold, W. C. and Holther, W. B. 1952. 'The Unity of the Phaedrus', *University of California Publications in Classical Philology* XIV, 9:387–417.

Irwin, T. 1974. 'Recollection and Plato's Moral Theory', *The Review of Metaphysics* XXVII, 4:752–72.

Irwin, T. 1977. *Plato's Moral Theory.* Oxford.

Joly, R. 1961. 'La Question Hippocratique et le Témoignage du *Phèdre*', *Revue des Etudes Grecques* LXXIV, 349–50: 69–92.

Kennedy, G. 1963. *The Art of Persuasion in Greece.* Princeton.

Kerferd, G. B. 1981. *The Sophistic Movement.* Cambridge.

Kosman, L. A. 1976. 'Platonic Love', in W. H. Werkmeister, ed., *Facets of Plato's Philosophy*, 53–69. Assen.

Kronman, A. T. 1981. 'Foreword: Legal Scholarship and Moral Education', *The Yale Law Journal* XC, 5:955–69.

Linforth, I. M. 1946. 'Telestic Madness in Plato, Phaedrus 244de',

University of California Publications in Classical Philology XIII, 6:163–72.

Lloyd, G. E. R., ed., 1978. *Hippocratic Writings*. Harmondsworth.

Lloyd, G. E. R. 1979. *Magic, Reason and Experience*. Cambridge.

Lloyd, G. E. R. (forthcoming). *The Revolutions of Wisdom*. Sather Lectures. Berkeley.

Lovibond, S. 1983. *Realism and Imagination in Ethics*. Minneapolis.

MacIntyre, A. 1981. *After Virtue: A Study in Moral Theory*. Notre Dame.

Mackenzie, M. M. 1982. 'Paradox in Plato's "Phaedrus"', *Proceedings of the Cambridge Philological Society* XXVIII:64–76.

Mansfeld, J. 1980. 'Plato and the Method of Hippocrates', *Greek, Roman and Byzantine Studies* XXI:341–62.

Moline, J. 1981. *Plato's Theory of Understanding*. Madison.

Moravcsik, J. M. E. 1978. 'Understanding and Knowledge in Plato's Philosophy', in R. Bubner, K. Cramer, and R. Wiehl, eds. *Aktualität der Antike*. Neue Hefte für Philosophie 15–16, 53–69.

Moravcsik, J. M. E. 1982a. 'Understanding and the Emotions', *Dialectica* XXXVI, 2–3:207–24.

Moravcsik, J. M. E. 1982b. 'Noetic Aspiration and Artistic Inspiration', in Moravcsik and Temko 1982, 29–46.

Moravcsik, J. M. E. and Temko, P. 1982. *Plato on Beauty, Wisdom and the Arts*. APQ Library of Philosophy. Totowa.

Nehamas, A. 1975. 'Plato on the Imperfection of the Sensible World', *American Philosophical Quarterly* XII, 2:105–17.

Noyes, J. H. (1872) 1975. *Male Continence*. New York.

Nussbaum, M. C. 1979. 'The Speech of Alcibiades: a Reading of Plato's *Symposium*', *Philosophy and Literature* III, 2:131–72.

Nussbaum, M. C. 1982. '"This Story Isn't True": Poetry, Goodness, and Understanding in Plato's *Phaedrus*', in Moravcsik and Temko 1982, 79–124.

Owen, G. E. L. 1973. 'Plato on the Undepictable', in E. N. Lee, A. P. D. Mourelatos, R. M. Rorty, eds. *Exegesis and Argument*, 349–61. *Phronesis* Suppl. Vol. I. Assen.

Penner, T. 1971. 'Thought and Desire in Plato', in G. Vlastos, ed., *Plato II*. Notre Dame.

Philip, A. 1981. 'Récurrences Thématiques et Topologie dans le "Phèdre" de Platon', *Revue de Métaphysique et de Morale* LXXXVI, 4:452–76.

Radermacher, L. 1951. *Artium Scriptores: Reste der voraristotelischen Rhetorik*. Oesterreichische Akademie der Wissenschaften, Sitzungsberichte Philosophisch-historische Klasse 227, 3. Vienna.

de Romilly, J. 1982. 'Les Conflits de l'Ame dans le Phèdre de Platon', *Wiener Studien* N. F. XVI:100–13.

Rosen, S. 1969. 'The Non-Lover in Plato's *Phaedrus*', *Man and World* II, 3:423–37.

Santas, G. X. 1982. 'Passionate Platonic Love in the *Phaedrus*', *Ancient Philosophy* II, 2:105–14.

Searle, J. R. 1983. *Intentionality: An Essay in the Philosophy of Mind.* Cambridge.

Sinaiko, H. L. 1965. *Love, Knowledge and Discourse in Plato.* Chicago.

Suess, W. 1910. *Ethos: Studien zur älteren griechischen Rhetorik.* Leipzig.

Verdenius, W. J. 1962. 'Der Begriff der Mania in Platons *Phaidros*', *Archiv für Geschichte der Philosophie* CLIV, 2:132–50.

Viano, C. A. 1965. 'Retorica, Magia e Natura in Platone', *Rivista di Filologia* LVI:411–53.

Vlastos, G. (1969) 1981. 'The Individual as an Object of Love in Plato', in *Platonic Studies*, 3–42. Princeton.

Waterlow, S. 1982. 'The Third Man's Contribution to Plato's Paradigmatism', *Mind* XCI:339–57.

Watson, G. 1975. 'Free Agency', *Journal of Philosophy* LXXII, 8:205–20.

Wieland, W. 1982. *Platon und die Formen des Wissens.* Göttingen.

Williams, B. A. O. 1976. 'Moral Luck', *Proceedings of the Aristotelian Society* Suppl. Vol. L: 115–35.

Williams, B. A. O. 1985. *Ethics and the Limits of Philosophy.* Cambridge, Mass.

Yeazell, S. C. 1981. 'Convention, Fiction, and Law', *New Literary History* XIII, 1:89–102.

INDEX

leisure (*skholē*), 15, 21, 27, 181
Lloyd, G. E. R., 236n.20, 246n.11, 248n.19, 256n.3
love: philosophic love, 18, 20, 66–7, 94–5, 109, 137, chapter six *passim*, 229–32; traditional conception of, 90, 92, 94–5, 107–8, 146–7, 162–3
Lovibond, S., 270n.51
Lysias: character of, 52, 226–9; criticised by Socrates, 45–59; Lysias' speech, 88–95, 98, 208–12, 225–6

MacIntyre, A., 239n.3, 270n.51
Mackenzie, M. M., 278n.4, 282n.32
madness, 18–20, 60–1, 63, 89, 103, 113–14, 118–19, 150–1, 157–8, 163, 177–8, 180–1, 195–8
Mansfeld, J., 248n.19
medicine, 5, 16–18, 76–9, 266n.32
metics, 228–9
Moline, J., 273n.76, 275n.92, 275n.94, 276n.96
moral luck, 133–9
Moravcsik, J. M. E., 275n.92, 276n.98, 282n.30
myth: and history, 118–19; of the cicadas, 26–30; of the soul-chariot, 11, 102, 125–32, 185–203; of Thoth and Ammon, 208, 214–220; philosophic uses of, 11–12, 32–4, 64–7, 84–5, 110–11, chapter five *passim*, 152–3, 158, 164–5, 217–220

Nehamas, A., 263n.7
non-lovers, speeches of, 49–51, chapter four *passim*, 224–9
Noyes, J. H., 268n.47
Nussbaum, M. C., 249n.22, 253n.16, 256n.31, 257n.10, 259n.21, 260n.31, 269n.50

orality, 204–22 *passim*
organic unity (as literary principle), 52–3

paradigms, 19–20, 24
Penner, T., 275n.92
Pericles, 72, 74
Phaedrus, character of, 5–9, 19–20, 27–9, 39, 57, 71–4, 94–5, 103–4, 108, 208–10, 227–9
philosophy: and intellectual talk, 6–9, 20, 27, 29, 39, 104–5; and

professionalism, 18–21, 55–6, 104–6, 181, 222; and prophecy, 116–17, 181; and the good life, 12, 18–21, 67, 94–5, 99–100, 121–3, 135–7, 146–8, 162–3, 195, 221, 281n.25; and truth, 9–12, 34, 45, 54, 61–2, 64, 81, 84–5, 104, 110–11, 181, 211, 216–18, 229–32; appropriate format for, 30, 32–4; philosophic love, 18, 20, 66–7, 94–5, 109, 137, chapter six *passim*, 222–4, 229–32; philosophic rhetoric, 38, 58, 74–81, 225
pleasure: and sexuality, 146–7, 150–67; attitude of Socrates' non-lover towards, 96–102, 199; of intellectual talk, 7–8, 27–9, 39, 104–5; hedonism in Lysias' speech, 93, 96, 198
professionalism, 14–21, 43–4, 55–6, 72–3, 87, 104–6, 209, 222
prophecy, 113–17
psychology: in rhetoric, 76–81; in Socrates' first speech, 96–102; in Socrates' second speech (tripartite soul), 125–6, 185–203 *passim*
Pteros, 168
puritanism, 99–100, 112, 137

reason, 91, 95, 190–203 *passim*, 225, 230–2
recognition, 4–5, 22–4, 70–81, 123–4, 129, 148
recollection (of Form of beauty), 150–167 *passim*, 183, 189, 191–4, 196, 197
reincarnation, 133–9, 157
rhetoric: and truth, 39–45, 51–2, 54, 61–2, 81, 82–5, 226; rhetorical aspect of philosophy, 38, 58; rhetorical ethos, 51–9, 81, 84–5, 87, 105, 200, 222, 225–9, 231; rhetorical manuals, 25, 70–1, 77–9, 81–5, 204; teaching *v.* practice in, 41–2, 68, 73–4; Socrates' reform of, 74–81, 225
de Romilly, J., 272n.66
Rosen, S., 252n.10

Sappho, 107, 154
Searle, J. R., 237n.28
Socrates, character of, 8, 13–15, 18–20, 54–6, 60–1, 64–7, 86–7, 103–12 *passim*, 222
sophists, 14–15, 70, 234n.12
soul: allegorised as charioteer and horses, 11, 102, 125–32, 151,